Dear Friend:
Mastering the Art of Direct Mail Fund Raising

Dear Friend:
Mastering the Art of Direct Mail Fund Raising

by
Kay Partney Lautman
and
Henry Goldstein

Foreword by David Ogilvy

Taft Corporation
Washington, D.C.
A member of The Taft Group

Taft Corporation, 5130 MacArthur Boulevard, NW, Washington, DC 20016

Printed in the United States of America

90 89 88 87 86   8 7 6 5 4 3 2

Library of Congress Cataloging in Publication Data

Lautman, Kay Partney.
    Dear friend.

    Includes index.
    1. Fund raising. 2. Advertising, Direct-mail.
    I. Goldstein, Henry. II. Title.
    HG177.L378   1984   361.7   83-5128
    ISBN 0-914756-55-9

The Taft Group provides a wide array of data and publications in fund raising, marketing, management, and communications to serve the needs of nonprofit organizations.

TAFT Profit Thinking for Nonprofit Organizations
5130 MacArthur Boulevard, N.W.
Washington, D.C. 20016
(202) 966-7086
(800) 424-3761

The book is dedicated to

HAROLD L. ORAM

mentor and friend

and

In Memoriam

to

Sanky Perlowin

who was one of us

TABLE OF CONTENTS

List of Figures

FOREWORD

Pure Gold

Americans are the most charitable people on the face of the earth. Eighty-six percent* of them (141 million individuals) give money to charity—$64.93 billion in 1983.

More than 300,000 non-profit organizations compete for this generosity. The majority of them rely on amateurs to run their fund-raising campaigns, and most of them aren't very good at it. If they hired professionals, like the authors of this book, to guide them, they would raise a lot more money at a lot less cost.

The professionals know what works and what doesn't work. They know, for example, that personal solicitation by volunteers works better than anything else, but few charities can find enough volunteers.

Next to personal solicitation, what works best in most cases is direct mail—*if you know how to use it*. Kay Lautman and Henry Goldstein, the authors of this superbly well-written book, are the preeminent experts, and they reveal their secrets with prodigal generosity.

They start by telling you how to judge whether your charity is likely to get results from direct mail; for many charities it is not cost-effective, however professionally executed.

They explain the mathematics. If you do everything right, you stand a good chance of breaking even from your first mailing. You begin to make a profit when you follow up your donors. In the first year of renewal mailings (following their formula) for every dollar you spend, you can reasonably expect up to $11.50. Thereafter, you can expect up to $20.00.

The secret of success lies in *testing*. This book explains in detail how to test mailing lists, letters, response devices, envelopes and every other component.

I have used direct mail to sell a great many products and services, but this book is full of information which has surprised me. For example:

- January is one of the most profitable months for charity mailings.
- It pays to suggest how much people should contribute. It pays even better to state what specific gifts accomplish.
- Personalizing prospect letters by computer or laser is seldom cost-effective for most organizations. Again, the key is to test.
- Telephoning to people is often more cost-effective than sending them packages through the mail. If you tell them that they are about to receive a letter from your organization, you can increase your net income by up to 50 percent.
- Long letters—up to six pages and more—almost invariably bring better results than one-page letters. This will surprise novices, but it does not surprise me; I have known it for twenty-five years.

This book is packed with specific how-to-do-it information which will be of incalculable value to fund-raisers. If you do exactly what the book says, you will get results.

Finally, gentle reader, I remind you of the "certain poor widow" who gave Jesus all she had, which was two cents. If her two cents had been invested at compound interest, it would now be worth more than the weight of the world in gold.

David Ogilvy
Château De Touffou
June 8, 1984

---

*From a 1982 Gallup poll conducted for the Independent Sector.

ACKNOWLEDGMENTS

We started *Dear Friend* reasonably convinced that we knew a lot about direct mail. What we realized in the process is how much we have learned through other people, several of whom were markedly helpful in bringing this book to fruition.

For his generous support and encouragement, a very special thank you to advertising genius DAVID OGILVY, who calls direct mail "my first love and secret weapon." His book, *Ogilvy on Advertising* (Crown, 1983), should be read by all serious practitioners of direct mail.

ROGER CRAVER, president of Craver, Matthews and Smith (Falls Church, Virginia) is an occasional (and very worthy) competitor, and a constant friend. Much of our knowledge of telemarketing is due to his generous counsel. We are grateful for his help with Chapter 11.

CAROL ENTERS, president of CELCO (New York City), and FRAN McCOWAN, senior vice president of The Coolidge Company (New York City), are two of the top list brokers for nonprofits in America. The chapter on "Lists and List Brokers" owes much to their counsel over the years.

BARBARA MARION, CFRE, was the expert we asked to review and critique the chapter on "Making Friends with the Computer." Barbara is president of FRA, Inc. (San Francisco), a fund-raising consulting, data management, and software publishing firm. She also serves as national board chair of the National Society of Fund Raising Executives (NSFRE).

BARBARA GREEN and ADRIANNA BARBIERI (Barbieri and Green, Washington, D.C.) and MARY FALCO (Graphics Options, New York City) are the talented graphic designers whose work enhances most of our direct mail packages and who taught us much of what we know about design and production.

STEVE SEATER, CFRE, Washington, D.C., helped us develop the material on Electronic Funds Transfer. Steve is a former Oram executive, and now specializes in this new area of fund-raising management.

MICHAEL McINTOSH, president of the McIntosh Foundation (New York City), and ROBERT PIERPOINT are pioneering an innovative system of *Donor Profiles*, which they shared with us so that we might introduce you to a brand new service.

Modesty forbade using only our own direct mail creations as examples, so we turned to some of our competitors (all of whom are valued friends as well). The outstanding work of five such firms and one individual appears in Chapter 7, "Successful Direct Mail Packages by the Pros."

We are grateful to the staff of Oram Group Marketing for many contributions to this book. In particular we wish to thank veteran account executives, MAURA GRANEY BLANCHARD and CORY SCOTT WHITTIER (our first readers), whose critical observations made *Dear Friend* a far more accurate book; GARY TOLCHINSKY, a superb copywriter who enjoyed developing Chapter 7 with license to comment on the work of others; LINDA BISTANY, resident computer expert, for her contribution to the chapter on computers; GARY WOHL, our own list sage, for his counsel in that critical arena; and last, but far from least, KARL YANOFSKY, account executive and resident mathematics genius, for verifying (and, in some instances, creating) the numbers, charts, and financial data throughout the book and especially for the thankless job of helping—under tremendous pressure—to review and correct the final galleys.

At the Taft Corporation we would like to thank our publisher, DICK TAFT, for his enthusiasm, which kept us going and SHELLEY RUDICK, not only for her talent as a publicist, but also for her never-failing support. JEAN BERNARD was our superb editor and ANN WILLIAMS the talented and patient artist who designed the book and its cover.

ROBERT C. LAUTMAN survived a year of virtually solitary weekends with customary patience and good humor; LINDA BROESSEL read the first draft with good counsel and a sharp eye.

Finally, we thank our clients, past, present, and future, without whom. . .

KPL
HG

HOW TO USE THIS BOOK. . .
A NOTE FROM THE AUTHORS

The track system—the key to the organization of this book—respects the varying interests and sophistication of the reader.

If you are a novice, you should begin with Track I. If you are experienced, you may wish to skip Tracks I and II and proceed to Tracks III and IV. Before you decide to do this, however, read the following brief description of Track I.

TRACK I: "Getting Started" is a beginner's guide to costs, budgets, schedules, planning, and lists. It includes *basic* advice on creating the package, and working with list brokers, printers, and lettershops. To help you see the big picture, Track I details a hypothetical campaign from pilot mailing to roll-out.

TRACK II: "Getting Results" contains but a single chapter. Titled, "Renewals: Making Your Investment Pay Dividends," it discusses writing the renewal appeal, scheduling renewals for maximum return, upgrading the gift, gift acknowledgments, and more. For continuity, the pilot and roll-out mailings conducted in Track I are used as the basis of a hypothetical renewal campaign.

TRACK III: "Getting Creative" begins with a comprehensive chapter on "Creating the Direct Mail Package." This chapter expands on the basic information presented in Track I, and through the use of samples and examples, shows how to create great letters, response devices, envelopes, and special enclosures. Another chapter, "Successful Direct Mail Packages by the Pros," is a collection of some all-time great fund-raising appeals contributed by our colleagues.

There is also a chapter on failed campaigns (to show you our fallible side and to help you avoid the same mistakes). The final chapter in Track III deals with the vitally important subjects of production and postal regulations.

TRACK IV: "Getting Sophisticated" includes chapters on sophisticated techniques to test, using the computer to maximum advantage, and telemarketing in conjunction with direct mail. There's even a chapter showing how direct mail, properly used, can enhance other fund-raising activity, including major gift acquisitions, capital campaigns, and planned giving (i.e., bequests, trusts, gifts of insurance or other property.)

TRACK V: "Getting on the Inside Track," addresses other important issues. When we were writing *Dear Friend* numerous colleagues suggested that we include information on (1) how to hire and work with a consultant and (2) how to break into the direct mail fund-raising profession. Thus in the final two chapters, we present our personal views, developed from more than 20 years of experience. For some readers, Track V may be the ideal starting point in reading this book.

At the end of the book, we have included a glossary of direct mail fund-raising terms and an index to assist you in locating all references to a single subject.

This is not a book for those who think they already know everything there is to know about direct mail fund raising. It is a book for direct mail professionals who continually seek to improve their skills, learn new ideas and, refresh their memories about things learned long ago. (This certainly happened to us in the course of writing this book.) It is also for young hopefuls who would like to make a career of direct mail fund raising and for development directors (and even executive directors and organization presidents) who, in order to run a department or an organization, need to become more knowledgeable about a specialty which they do not practice themselves.

—Kay Partney Lautman
—Henry Goldstein

INTRODUCTION

DIRECT MAIL—MORE THAN A FUND-RAISING TOOL

It is axiomatic that the primary purpose of direct mail fund raising is to raise funds. Yet there are other objectives that you will want to consider. These include its role in educating the people to whom you mail, presenting them with a positive image of your organization and your cause, and sometimes encouraging them to take action in the political arena. In a prospect mailing of 150,000 pieces, you may locate only 1,500 contributors. Of course, a high portion of the remaining 148,500 will be received by people who trash your appeal right off. But there are also a significant number who will at least look at your material and a significant minority who will read it thoroughly. Even though these people may not send money just yet, they represent a broader potential constituency which supports your organization. That's where the other objectives come in.

Education

Direct mail serves an important educational function. Once again, while only 1 percent of the "cold" prospects you mail to may contribute, you nevertheless have an opportunity to reach thousands of others and tell them about your program to combat a disease or to help the elderly or to preserve our environment. A case in point:

Today, everyone is aware of endangered animal and plant species. In fact, today's children, when visiting a local zoo, are apt to be the ones to tell their parents which animals are endangered. This was not always the case.

In the early 1960s when the World Wildlife Fund was founded internationally, few Americans knew or cared that this country's own national symbol—the bald eagle—was in imminent danger of extinction. Certainly environmental awareness did not come about solely as the result of direct mail. But direct mail did play a major role in educating the public about wildlife conservation.

The prospect letter on the following page is representative of the educational fund-raising appeals The Oram Group mailed on behalf of the Fund from 1962 to 1966.

As was the style then, it was a one-page letter. (Later letters produced for the Fund were longer.) But while we are critiquing our own work, other things date the letter.

- The board of directors listing, while important, is overwhelming.
- The appeal asks for a contribution, but does not specify the amount of the desired gift or explain what it will do.
- The letter states the problem, but does not explain how the Fund planned to accomplish its mission. (This information, incidentally, was relegated to an attractive accompanying brochure—a technique rarely used today.)
  On the other hand, the letter had some important things going for it including:
- It used a one-line, hand-typed salutation (the forerunner of computer-fill).
- The closed-faced envelope was also hand-typed.
- It was mailed first class. (In 1962, first class, at 8¢, was affordable when mailing to the best prospect lists.)

World Wildlife Fund

709 Wire Building, Washington 5, D. C., DIstrict 7-1774

June 19, 1962

Dear Miss Palmer:

Too few people realize that hundreds of species of living creatures are in danger of extermination. Modern processes are destroying the natural habitat of many birds and mammals. Wildlife is menaced through the development of towns and cities which cover the land, through the multiplication of roads and industrial installations, through the pollution of streams due to industrial and human wastes, and through the destruction of wetlands. Whatever the reasons -- and they are complex -- hundreds of wildlife species face extinction.

The wondrous American whooping crane, the grizzly bear, the rhinoceros of Africa and Asia, the noble Arabian oryx, and some 250 others are known to be among the wildlife species whose survival is threatened. They are on the "Danger List". More than 200 species of birds and mammals have been exterminated directly or indirectly by man. They can never be recreated.

More men and women must realize the facts of this worldwide tragedy. Let us not stand by until even the great American bald eagle, our national symbol, is exterminated.

Together we can stop this sacrifice of living creatures. We can work through the World Wildlife Fund whose aims are outlined in the accompanying brochure. We can provide sanctuaries for wild birds and protected areas for endangered wild animals. We can bring to people the knowledge that wildlife has its place in God's plan. That the world will be much the poorer if the day comes when a child says, "Father, what <u>was</u> a wild animal?"

I hope that you will join in this effort to save for your children's grandchildren some of the most beautiful creatures the hand of God has fashioned. Please send me your tax deductible contribution today -- together we can do much to save the severely threatened birds and mammals. More than that, we will save humanity from the guilt of having stood by, doing nothing, while much of our great treasure of wildlife which enriches every human being is facing extinction.

Sincerely,

Kermit Roosevelt

Kermit Roosevelt

HELP SAVE THE WORLD'S WILDLIFE AND WILD PLACES

Despite the letter's shortcomings, however, it and others like it pulled an overall 3 percent return, an enviable achievement then and now. And in just five years of what would now be considered small mailings, the Fund's list grew to more than 25,000 names. The average gift, very healthy for those times, was over $20.

The letter is unquestionably dated—not just because of changes in direct mail style, but because more than 20 years later, Americans are knowledgeable about the threats to wildlife and wild places. What is more, by supporting various wildlife organizations, people are doing something about the problem.

Today, there is a proliferation of environmental organizations not only raising money through the mail for their various specialities, but simultaneously educating their readers about the dangers of acid rain, the giveaway of public lands, the poisoning of our air and water, and much more. (And because an increasingly sophisticated public wants to learn even more about such problems, the letters have become not just longer, but more educational.)

Public Relations

An example which shows how direct mail can be valuable in creating the right public image is the impact of a package our firm wrote for the Boy Scouts of New York. The stereotype, of course, is a good looking kid, in uniform, helping a sweet old lady cross the street.

But our appeals (see Figures 4-2 and 4-3) describe what the Scouts are doing to help kids adjust to the harsh realities of life in the inner city, including one in which New York's "latch-key" kids are instructed on how to take care of themselves, and another designed to help them find a satisfying career. We know that if we can raise money *and* change old fashioned perceptions about the Boy Scouts along the way, the campaign will have served an important dual purpose.

Encouraging Political Action

Closely related to education and public relations is the role of direct mail in the political arena. Candidates for office may solicit funds through the mail, but even if a prospect doesn't contribute, the overall purpose of the political campaign is served if the direct mail encourages more voters to lend their support to the candidate. Similarly, a group fighting for lower taxes may not do exceptionally well in the mail. But if it can reach enough voters, perhaps a referendum supporting lower taxes will be passed.

In the case of our client, the American Israel Public Affairs Committee (AIPAC), education and political action have been at the core of most appeals. In one particularly successful appeal (September, 1981) AIPAC educated potential supporters to the danger of the potential AWACS sale to Saudi Arabia. But they did not stop at education or even fund raising.

The appeal (see Figure 5-8) asked readers to send the message to Congress that the sale was not in the best interest of the United States. In an unprecedented response, the prospect mailing produced a 6 percent return and the average gift was almost double the amount requested. True to its word, AIPAC covered the desks of the members of Congress with the petitions just days before the final vote. There is an interesting postscript to this example: AIPAC *lost* on this issue; the AWACS sale was approved by Congress. But AIPAC's expanded membership base was maintained and enhanced through renewal and additional prospect mailings.

TRACK I
Getting Started

CHAPTER 1

The Successful Pilot Mailing:
More Than Beginner's Luck

IS DIRECT MAIL FOR YOU?

When a nonprofit organization explores the possibility of raising funds by mail, our first task as consultants is to determine whether it can do so successfully by virtue of its name, reputation, or the cause it represents.

In ascertaining your own organization's direct mail potential, you may wish to apply our firm's formula. We ask ten basic questions of any potential client seeking our help.

1. Does your organization or cause have broad name recognition?
   (a) in the local community?
   (b) in the state?
   (c) nationally?
2. Does it deal with specific issues rather than broad or abstract ideas?
3. Does it serve or help specific constituencies—for example, minorities, the ill, the elderly, children, handicapped, the poor or disadvantaged, or animals?
4. Are there other organizations performing the same or similar services? If so, how is your organization unique?
5. Does your organization have a demonstrable track record?
6. If your organization is new, does it expect to respond to a critical issue in a dynamic way?
7. Is there a threat to the organization, those it serves, or to traditional funding sources? In other words, is there an issue, a crisis, or an emergency to be dramatized?
8. If yours is a membership organization, are tangible membership benefits offered? If yours is a cause-oriented organization, can you show the donor how his or her gift will make a difference?
9. Will your organization survive three years without a successful direct mail campaign?
10. Would your organization be financially able to survive a loss of 40 percent or more of its investment should the test mailing fail to recoup costs?

If you have answered "yes" to half these questions, yours may be a mail-viable cause and a test mailing can be made at low risk. If you answered "no" to questions (9) and (10), however, think twice. To proceed under these conditions, it is imperative that you answered "yes" to *all* other questions.

HOW MUCH WILL IT COST?

If your organization scored well on the questions, your next question is: "How much will it cost to test direct mail?" Most organizations should estimate their direct costs at $200 per thousand names mailed.

Direct cost components include printing, postage, lettershop, and list rentals, which in the spring of 1984 looked like this:

Printed materials—4 pieces (four-page letter, response card, carrier envelope, and business reply envelope, not including one-time investment of art & typeset)	$80/M
Nonprofit Postage	$52/M
Lettershop	$15/M
Lists (average)	$60/M
	$207/M

Oops! You are already over your budget by $7 per thousand names. Why? Because never having done direct mail, you don't have a donor list of your own to exchange with other organizations. Exchanges bring costs way down from an average rental fee of $60 per thousand to between $6 and $7.50 per thousand for brokerage fees (free if you arrange the exchanges yourself).

But wait! Maybe you do have a list of names which you can exchange. If you have even a small file of donors—ideally 5,000 or more—who have contributed to your organization within the past two years, those names are considered "active" in the trade. Also check your files to see whether you have any of the following lists (they will vary depending on the type of organization): inquiry lists, guest registers, gift shop customers, ticket buyers, etc.

In addition, you often can persuade other organizations to allow you to use 5,000 of their names now, with promise of a payback in the future. Why? Because good new lists are not easy to come by, and most mailers are anxious that you develop a larger list which they can then exchange on behalf of their organization.

Thus, on a mailing of 75,000, if you could exchange even one-third of the needed lists, you would save $1,350 and be *under* budget at a per thousand cost of $189. Note: This savings of $1,350 will cover the cost of art and typeset for your entire package.

Despite the savings, some organizations tenaciously resist exchanging their own donor list. For more on this subject, see Chapter 2.

HOW LARGE SHOULD THE FIRST MAILING BE?

Following are three possible schedules for a *national* test or pilot mailing. Which do you think would be the ideal size in a first effort?

Test #1 75,000 names from 15 lists of 5,000 each.

Test #2 75,000 names from three lists of 20,000 each and one list of 15,000.

Test #3 30,000 names from six lists of 5,000 names each.

If you chose Test #1, your intuition is right on the money. Here's why: In Tests #1 and #2, the cost per thousand names mailed (on a prospect mailing) can be kept to an average of $200, including list rentals, printing, postage, and lettershop. And while the overall cost is lower in Test #3, the per thousand cost goes up to about $250. However, in figuring profitability on each of the three tests, cost per thousand is not the only variable. In the chart below, we assume that each mailing receives the same percent return (1 percent, which is very good) and average gift ($20, which is good for most organizations).

	TEST #1	TEST #2	TEST #3
# of Names:	75,000	75,000	30,000
# of Lists:	15	4	6
Cost per M:	$200	$200	$250
Total Cost	$15,000	$15,000	$7,500
% Return:	1%	1%	1%
# of Gifts:	750	750	300
Average Gift:	$20	$20	$20
Income:	$15,000	$15,000	$6,000
Income/Cost	Break Even	Break Even	($1,500 loss)

Note: Costs are good approximations, but will vary slightly depending on locale, elaborateness of package, and whether lists are rented or exchanged.

To look at the test results another way:

Test #1: Percent return based on half the lists—35,000—producing 1 percent return, one-fourth producing 1.5 percent return, and the last one-fourth producing .5 percent.

Test #2: Percent return based on two lists producing 1 percent; one list producing 1.5 percent, and one list producing .5 percent.

Test #3: Percent return based on one-half of the list (15,000) producing 1 percent, one-fourth producing 1.5 percent, and one-fourth producing .5 percent.

At first glance, Tests #1 and #2 appear to have produced the same results. But have they?

In Test #1, you not only recoup all costs, but you also add 750 new names to your donor base. You also learn the profitability of 15 lists; that 11 of the lists worked and four did not—valuable marketing information to be used as a guideline in selecting future test lists.

In Test #2, you recoup costs and add the same number of new donors to the file. But as you have tested only four lists (three of which worked), you have learned very little about potential markets. *A larger roll-out based on such a limited list test would be at high risk.*

In Test #3, you suffer a loss of $1,500 for two reasons. First, the proportional expense was greater, and second, *the quantity mailed was insufficient to cover the costs.* In order for the mailing to have paid for itself at a $20 average gift, the return would have to have been at least 1.25 percent.

Or, at a return of 1 percent, the average gift would have to have been at least $25. Such results are unlikely in most pilot mailings.

At this point, some may ask—if Test #1 is the best test—why not mail 100,000 or 150,000 or more?

Well, some mailers do. Certainly larger quantities enable you to reduce the printing costs and test even more lists. On larger mailings you also can test letters or envelopes or other variables economically. But unless you have the experience that comes with many years of mailing for many causes—and thus have developed an intuition for projecting the likelihood of success on an initial 150,000 piece mailing—why risk $30,000 instead of $15,000?

For most organizations new to direct mail, 75,000 is a sufficient test quantity to gain maximum knowledge at minimum risk on a national mailing. If yours is a local mailing, you will want to test 30,000 pieces initially and no more than 50,000.

ESTABLISHING A SCHEDULE

The next priority is to establish a schedule for mailing.

We tell our clients that it takes a *minimum* of two months to produce an initial direct mail package. Some think it should take less time; others don't see how it can be done in only eight weeks. We have included a chart (see Figure 1-1) adapted from a training manual for our own Oram Group Marketing staff. It is arranged in two sections—List Ordering/Mechanics and Copy/Graphics—because you are going to be doing two different things simultaneously.

WHEN TO MAIL—AND WHY

When do you want to mail? Have you always heard that summer is a poor time? That December is the best? That January is to be avoided because of the bills from Christmas? That you should avoid mid-April because of the income tax deadline?

For every rule, there's one that can be broken by a particular organization. However, in sending acquisition mailings, it is wise to avoid the three weeks before Christmas during which time donors will be receiving numerous renewal appeals from the organizations they regularly support. This is clearly not the time to test your cause on a new prospect.

We have found that some organizations can mail successfully in June and July. In general we avoid those months and urge you to avoid them too until you know more about the general viability of your mailings.

There is an exceptional summer month, however. August is a good mailing month for many causes, although no one really knows why. One of our colleagues espouses the novel theory that June and July are not good because people are experiencing the joys of warm weather and don't take time to read their mail. In August, however, as the hot weather becomes oppressive, they retreat into air conditioning and begin reading their mail again. As a theory this is as good as any but not very helpful to you, your cause, or your particular circumstances. Hence caution.

Like August, January is a month that (for some reason) is also excellent for almost all mailers despite the competition. Here is why *we* think it is good. January is a let-down month following the festivities that start with Thanksgiving. Thus, people are more inclined to read their mail then than they would have been in December. This theory is about as good as the one that explains why August is a good month. In general, the best months for mailing are January, February, March, April, September, October, and November. This is not a theory. Results prove it.

In establishing a timetable, try to avoid the month of May for your first test. This is because it takes almost three weeks of returns before you will have enough results to make an interim analysis of your mailing, and another three weeks to verify success or failure. By this time it is early

June which, as we have explained, is not an optimum time for mailing. You will now have to wait until September for your roll-out (or continuation mailing), and will have lost momentum.

The ideal test months in the first half of the year are January and February (for a March or April roll-out) and August and September (for an October or November roll-out).

If you *must* test at a less than ideal time, be cautious in the continuation mailing until you have more experience. Better to postpone your test mailing until the next season than to risk a financial loss.

Figure 1-1. The Ideal Schedule*

	List Ordering/Mechanics	Copy/Graphics
WEEKS 1&2	Discuss list schedule with broker. Contract with mail house.	Write first copy draft. Throw it away. Write second and third drafts. Discuss concept with artist.
WEEK 3	Broker orders lists and sends confirmations. (Minimum of 2½ weeks from list order to delivery.) Obtain postal permits (first class for reply envelope and nonprofit for mailing envelope.)	Present revised copy draft and rough art to signer or whomever must approve package. (Allow a minimum of 3 days to revise or approve.) Get bids from printers.
WEEK 4	Send written order to mail house.	Revise copy (2 days) and return to signer for final approval (3 days). Artist prepares camera-ready mechanicals (6 days).
WEEK 5	Request postage check (to arrive at mail house one week prior to mail date). Check in lists as they arrive. Allow one week for late list arrivals; alert broker.	Camera-ready art to printer. Bluelines due at week's end.
WEEK 6	Send labels to mail house.	Return corrected bluelines to printer. Most printers want 7 working days to print (*can* be done in 4-5).
WEEK 7	Mail drops at the end of the week. Most mail houses require 5 working days unless special arrangements are made.	Deliver materials to mail house on Monday or earlier if possible.
WEEK 8	Set up a system for receiving returns and acknowledging gifts.	
WEEK 9	Begin tabulating first returns.	

*In reality this schedule will assume a life of its own—but it is a guide for planning.

HOW TO IDENTIFY YOUR MARKET

Assuming that you don't have professional counsel, we recommend that you work with a good list broker. There are hundreds of list brokers, but few specialize in fund-raising lists. Those who do are listed at the end of Chapter 2.

Brokers have the advantage of working with many organizations. They cannot tell you the actual results of other mailers by name, but they can help you select lists that work for others and avoid those that don't. Brokers won't be right in their recommendations 100 percent of the time, but unless you have a genuine crystal ball, their knowledge will be better than your guesswork.

Don't expect your broker to do a good job for you without your help. The broker needs to understand your organization and the nature of your appeal. He or she will ask for literature and a sample of the appeal letter you plan to send. Share this information generously if you want to be successful.

A good broker will continue to be invaluable long after you have ceased being a novice. As consultants, we rely on brokers for at least half of our list ideas, and most of our paperwork.

Because the subject of lists and list brokers is complex, we have devoted all of Chapter 2 to the subject.

WRITING THE FUND–RAISING LETTER (the basics)

Many books on direct mail begin with lessons on how to write the letter. However, we believe it is more important for you to first understand the mathematics of direct mail, the inherent risks and the planning that undergirds the effort.

As you just learned, your list broker will want to know something about your appeal (the direct mail package) before he or she can intelligently help schedule your lists. So while you are budgeting and planning, you also should be writing the first draft of your appeal letter.

Or have you already written it?

And you say it's not like all those other fund-raising letters that break sentences in the middle and use too many dashes and "buts" and "ands"? It isn't one of those four- or six-page letters. (Who reads them anyhow?) Yours has—if you do say so yourself—class! It's a letter the president of your board won't be embarrassed to sign because it's grammatical, it's less than two pages, and while it does imply that you need money, it isn't—well—pushy.

We won't argue every point. Some two-page letters are masterpieces. Some organizations can condense the essential information onto one page. Some highly productive letters have a dignified tone, unless by "dignified" you mean long words, stilted phrases, and jargon only insiders understand. As for being pushy, we don't consider it pushy to come to the point. Nothing is more frustrating than a veiled request for help.

Most causes cannot be described adequately in one page. People want more information on subjects in which they have even a small interest. They want to learn about the problem and the program that will help solve the problem. To provide such information, a two-page letter—printed on one piece of paper for economy—is usually required. Often it means a four-page letter (two pieces of paper) and sometimes—yes—a six-page letter!

Many of the best letters we have written for clients were four pages!

"I don't care what you say," you protest. "I wouldn't read a four-page letter and no one else will either."

Don't be so sure. If you were interested in a subject, would you read a four-page magazine article? A six-page one? Would you read more than one article? Would you read a pamphlet? A book?

Of course, you would—*if* the information was presented in a lively, interesting manner that aroused your curiosity, convinced you the author knew his or her subject, and taught you something.

And that is exactly what a good appeal letter should do—arouse curiosity, stimulate interest, instill conviction, and one more thing: inspire action: *a contribution to your cause!*

MAKE YOUR LETTER INTO A "BEST SELLER"

How did you select *Dear Friend*? Have you noticed how you choose books? You pick up one after another, looking for those which catch the eye. The jacket appeal, the title, the author's name are key. You open the crisp new pages and read the first paragraph, then perhaps the second. If the author doesn't hold your interest through the second paragraph, the book goes back on the shelf. No sale! But if page one is satisfying, you begin leafing through the book, reading bits and pieces, convincing yourself that the book will sustain your interest. That is exactly what you must achieve with the *first* paragraph of your letter! (And with your envelope too, but we'll discuss that later.) In the opening, you must grab enough reader interest so that even if he or she doesn't read your entire letter instantly, at least it will be saved for perusal later, and not go into the trash with all the competitive fund-raising appeals and commercial offers of the day.

The Rules of Letter Writing

There are 13 basic rules for effective direct mail copy.

1. Don't typeset the letter. Reproduce it from perfectly typewritten copy. (When was the last time you sent a typeset personal letter?)
2. Don't have the copy photographically reduced to cram a long letter into a short format. Remember, most of your donors are likely to be over 40 and may have difficulty reading small type. (We do!)
3. Don't omit the ("Dear Friend") salutation, and do try to include a date line if possible. They are part of the real letter look.
4. Long paragraphs are admittedly hard to read, but don't over-react with a letter composed of a series of short paragraphs of identical length. They are equally difficult to read.
5. Don't overdo the underlining. Call attention to pertinent phrases or paragraphs through indented copy blocks, check marks, bullets, giant quotation marks, color, and photographs. The longer the letter, the more important this is.
6. Pretend you are writing to one person. Indeed, you are.
7. Re-work the opening and closing paragraphs until they "sing."
8. Don't wait until the last page to mention money. It's okay to ask on page one.
9. Don't try to be funny. Your cause is serious and so is charitable giving. We've tried humor. It doesn't work.
10. Don't bore the reader with the merits of your organization. Rather, write about the people it serves. Give the people names—real people and real names if possible.
11. Write with emotion and back it up with facts, not vice versa. People don't give because your organization needs the money. They give because they are touched or angry or saddened and want to do something to help!
12. Use your P.S. wisely because it will be read. Too many postscripts just take up space.
13. Don't use big words or jargon.

The fund-raising letter is the most important part of the direct mail package. Still, it's only one *part* of the package.

While direct mail packages vary, most have four items in common: (a) the letter, (b) the outside (or carrier) envelope, (c) the reply envelope (or BRE), and (d) the response device.

Now that your letter is written, it's time to turn your attention to the copy and design of these other elements.

The Outside Envelope—Plain or Fancy?

The envelope is the subject of great debate among professionals, but basically the controversy should not be about whether photos or "teaser copy" are good or bad. Rather, the debate should be confined to two questions: "Will something extra call attention to my envelope and get it opened?" and "Is the envelope message appropriate to the enclosed letter?"

It is hard to go wrong with a simple envelope carrying only your organization's name and address in the upper left hand corner. But it is very easy to go wrong with art and teaser copy *if* it promises something it doesn't deliver inside, and *if* it is inappropriate to the image of your organization.

Our advice to beginners is to leave the testing of "fancy" envelopes until later. However, if you are intent on pursuing this subject you can read more about it in Chapter 5.

The Response Device—Making it Work Overtime

The first purpose of the response device is to provide a record of the donor's name and address. It has other functions as well:

1. When the outside (carrier) envelope has a window, the pre-addressed response device gets your letter delivered.
2. When the card is returned by the donor with his contribution, it eliminates the need for him to write out his name and address, and saves *you* the agony of deciphering his handwriting.

If these were the only purposes of the response card, they would be adequate. However, you will do yourself a service by making it serve another purpose: stimulating a larger contribution.

In Chapter 5 we will discuss a variety of response card techniques. But the basics remain the same: make sure your response card includes the following:

1. Name and address of your organization. Should the letter or envelope become separated from the card, the card has all essential information.
2. Sufficient space for the mail label, corresponding to the opening on the outside envelope.
3. A very brief statement of what the contribution will do. Example: "YES! I want to help send a kid to camp this summer!"
4. Suggested gift amounts. Example: "Enclosed is my gift of $25 to send a kid to camp for a week; Enclosed is my gift of $50 to send a kid to camp for two weeks."
5. Either the mail label or the card itself coded to identify the list from which the donor came.
6. A reminder that the gift is tax-deductible.

The Reply Envelope

It is absolutely imperative that you include an envelope pre-addressed to your organization or to your bank's lock box. Normally, a nonprofit organization will guarantee payment of return postage by printing a first class return indicia on the reply envelope. You may have heard that it is *not* essential to pay for return postage. In some cases this may be so, but do not even consider putting your first mailing at risk by not paying the return postage.

TABULATING RESPONSES

If this is your first mailing, the task of tabulating responses will be the most exciting part of the entire program. Slitting envelopes and watching checks fall out is extremely satisfying.

Don't be alarmed that the first responses you receive contain only "hate" mail, complaints, requests to "take me off your list," and envelopes stuffed with junk including appeals from other organizations. People feeling the need to vent their frustrations in this manner react faster than those who take your appeal seriously. Unfortunately, you do have to pay the postage due on these returns, but generally it does not add up to a large sum.

Most such "mail" is not worth responding to and can safely be trashed. Be on guard, however, for legitimate complaints. If properly answered, they sometimes can be turned into contributions—often sizable. We recall one instance where an almost indecipherable note was scrawled across a conservation organization's business reply envelope stating that the writer had read that a board member had been on safari killing endangered species. A letter was sent to the writer explaining that the news account had been totally inaccurate. Several weeks later, the complainer responded with a check for $1,000!

Responses usually begin with a disappointing trickle. On the first Monday following your mailing (provided your mail dropped the previous Monday), you will receive perhaps one response; then on Tuesday, three; on Wednesday, six; on Thursday, five; and on Friday . . . nothing.

Could the money have dried up already? You have received only 15 contributions and you need 750 to break even.

Don't panic! During the first week of returns, most people are still receiving your mail. That's the way it is with third class mail—get used to it. And Fridays are often barren. We suspect that the post office saves a lot of Friday mail for Monday delivery. (Much of what goes on in the post office is mysterious.)

In the second week, returns will pick up. *And by the middle of the third week of responses, you should have received one-half of the expected total income.**

This means that three weeks after your first response, you can prepare not only an interim analysis, but a projection for the entire mailing. But before you can do this, you are going to need a system to record the gifts.

There are several systems that might work effectively for you. We are going to share one that has worked effectively for the majority of our clients.

The List Tracking Form (see Figure 1-2) may be photocopied and used in your own campaigns. Each sheet represents the use of one list over a period of days (or approximately eight weeks of returns). If, after eight weeks, income from your mailing is still coming in at a healthy rate, you may wish to continue tabulating results on another page. However, if the response rate has slowed down to a trickle, you may wish to combine results from all lists. This way you include income from the campaign in your final report, but not necessarily on a list-by-list basis.

---

*This formula is derived from the most frequent patterns experienced by our clients. It does vary from organization to organization, however, and after several mailings you will learn your particular pattern.

Figure 1-2. List Tracking Form

ACCOUNT: _____ LIST: _____ PACKAGE: _____

CODE: _____ DATE MAILED: _____ QUANTITY MAILED: _____

MAILING COST PER M: _____

DATE	# RET	CUM RET	$'s TODAY	$100+ GIFTS # / $ AMT.	TOTAL $'s	DATE	# RET	CUM RET	$'s TODAY	$100+ GIFTS # / $ AMT.	TOTAL $'s

Figure 1-3 shows you how to use the five columns. In the sample, we stopped tabulating after two and one-half weeks of returns to analyze the potential success of the mailing in relation to the performance of this particular list to date.

Here is what we found. After 13 business days, the list had attained a .82 percent return and an average gift of $18.33. Using the rule of thumb mentioned earlier, we projected that the list eventually would produce twice the number of returns and that the eventual return would be 1.6 percent at an average gift of $18 for a total income of $1,480.

The cost of the mailing—noted at the top of the form—was $210 per thousand names mailed or $1,050 for one list of 5,000. Thus, this particular list did better than break-even—earning a net profit of $430. Naturally, not all lists will do as well.

ANALYZING YOUR MAILING

After 60 days of returns, each of your List Tracking Forms will be complete and you will want to translate the totals into a List Report that looks like the one portrayed in Figure 1-4.

If you already peeked, you know that congratulations are in order! As the 60-Day Analysis of Test Mailing proves, your pilot mailing was an unqualified success!

From a mailing of just under 75,000 pieces, 809 new donors were added to your organization's file. What is more, you spent less money than you made. Thus, you have a profit of $935 when a break-even would have been acceptable. Especially encouraging is the fact that your appeal generated a healthy average gift of more than $20 and you discovered six highly profitable lists for use in future mailings.

Incidentally, list "A" on the 60-Day Analysis of Test Mailing represents the list of 5,000 which we used as the sample on the preceding List Tracking Form.

The next step, working with your list broker, is to analyze what those lists that worked—and those that didn't—have in common. Often there is no clear answer in the beginning. But after several successive mailings in which you eliminate test lists that perform poorly and add new tests to the schedule, you and your broker will gain greater insights.

All this is discussed in Chapter 3, "The Roll-Out: Reinvesting Your Money."

Figure 1-3. Sample List Tracking Form

ACCOUNT: _____ LIST: *Generous Givers* PACKAGE: *Prospect*

CODE: *A-1* _____ DATE MAILED: *April 6* QUANTITY MAILED: *5,000* _____

MAILING COST PER M: *$210.* _____

DATE	# RET	CUM RET	$'s TODAY	$100+ GIFTS # / $ AMT.	TOTAL $'s	DATE	# RET	CUM RET	$'s TODAY	$100+ GIFTS # / $ AMT.	TOTAL $'s
4/13	1	1	25⁰⁰		25⁰⁰						
4/14	1	2	25⁰⁰		50⁰⁰						
4/15	6	8	54⁰⁰		104⁰⁰						
4/16	4	12	128⁰⁰		232⁰⁰						
4/17	7	19	107⁰⁰		339⁰⁰						
4/20	7	26	130⁰⁰		469⁰⁰						
4/21	1	27	5⁰⁰		474⁰⁰						
4/22	4	31	43⁰⁰		517⁰⁰						
4/23	3	34	90⁰⁰		607⁰⁰						
4/24	1	35	10⁰⁰		617⁰⁰						
4/27	2	37	23⁰⁰		640⁰⁰						
4/28	2	39	76⁰⁰		716⁰⁰						
4/29	2	41	35⁰⁰		751⁰⁰						

Figure 1-4. List Report:
60-Day Analysis of Test Mailing

June 12, 1983

List Name	Code	Number Mailed	Number Returns	% Response	Gross Income	Average Gift	Dollars/ Thousand	Cost/ Thousand	% Cost Recovered
List "A"	A1	5,000	81	1.62%	$1,485	$8.33	$297	$210	152%
List "B"	A2	5,000	103	2.06%	$1,563	$15.18	$312	$210	149%
List "C"	A3	5,000	33	.66%	$633	$19.18	$127	$210	60%
List "D"	A4	5,068	65	1.28%	$1,558	$23.97	$307	$210	146%
List "E"	A5	4,863	20	.41%	$370	$18.50	$ 76	$210	36%
List "F"	A6	5,000	41	.82%	$719	$17.53	$144	$210	69%
List "G"	A7	4,725	71	1.50%	$1,357	$19.11	$287	$210	137%
List "H"	A8	5,000	47	.94%	$884	$18.81	$177	$210	84%
List "I"	A9	5,000	48	.96%	$1,035	$21.56	$207	$210	99%
List "J"	A10	5,000	23	.46%	$845	$36.74	$169	$210	80%
List "K"	A11	4,834	83	1.96%	$1,789	$21.56	$423	$210	210%
List "L"	A12	4,999	34	.68%	$629	$18.49	$126	$210	60%
List "M"	A13	5,000	38	.76%	$828	$21.80	$166	$210	79%
List "N"	A14	4,689	58	1.24%	$1,362	$23.49	$290	$210	138%
List "O"	A15	5,000	43	.86%	$1,033	$24.02	$207	$210	99%
Miscellane- ous Returns	—	—	21	—	$595	$28.33	—	—	—
Total Returns		74,178	809	1.09%	$16,685	$20.62	$225	$210	107%
				Cost:	15,750				
				Net:	$935				

Note: The best lists (circled) recouped 90 percent of costs or better.

21

CHAPTER **2**

Lists and List Brokers

A brilliant appeal to the wrong market will produce poor or even disastrous results. But an ordinary appeal directed at the right market can—and often does—produce respectable results.

This is not to say that a poor appeal to good lists will produce top results. But if you spend all your time producing an award-winning package and are uncertain who your market is, you are going to be very disappointed come judgment day.

Following are five laments of those who have made typical marketing errors:

1. "But I mailed to lists my board members recommended. They were certain those people would be interested in contributing. Besides, they were free!"

MORAL: Doubtless board members are well meaning and we know how hard it is to turn them down. But if you want your board's praise in the final analysis, be brave enough to ask how the lists were compiled, how clean they are, and most important—whether the people on them actually are *donors* to other organizations.

2. "But it was a bipartisan cause. I was *sure* that liberal lists would work as well as conservative lists."

MORAL: This mailer *wanted* to believe in solidarity. But had he examined the issue in more depth, he would have realized that it was a cause supported primarily by liberals. Instead, clinging to his idealism, he split tested the lists 50-50. The results? The liberal lists made a net profit. The conservative lists recouped only 35 percent of costs. (Note: Even in our initial appeal for the Vietnam Veterans Memorial Fund, which was truly a bipartisan effort, conservatives accounted for some 70 percent of direct mail gifts. You can guess the direction of our list selection from then on.)

3. "But they *should* have been interested in our conservation cause. After all, they're the people who *use* the out-of-doors, buying all that fancy hiking and camping equipment. Maybe they don't have any money left over for clean air."

MORAL: One would indeed think so, but it's a hard-earned lesson that buyers are not necessarily donors, even if similarity of interest appears to exist. This is not to say that all buyer lists should be avoided. Some work. But let your broker guide you cautiously through the wilderness.

23

4. "We weren't sure who our constituency might be, so we covered all bases taking health lists, conservation lists, youth lists, political lists, and so on. We didn't think they would all be winners but we sure didn't think we would lose almost 80 percent of our costs!"

MORAL: If yours is an organization in search of an identity, you would do well to conduct a survey first to get a profile of your present donors or members. This can be done by mail or telephone. (You can even conduct a pre-call campaign to *prospects* to identify which aspect of your work interests which market; see Chapter 11.)

5. "But a lot of local organizations mail nationally with great success. Just look at New York's ASPCA and Berea College in Kentucky. Why didn't it work for us? We lost our shirt!"

MORAL: The organization asking this question had not come to terms with the fact that: a) it was not well known nationally as are ASPCA and Berea College, and, b) its program, while worthy, was strictly helping the local community. What is more, it had counterparts all over the country. (True, there are numerous SPCAs nationwide, but the ASPCA—the most famous of them all—has been able to demonstrate that its national legislative and educational programs help animals all over the country. Berea College is local in the sense that it serves the poor students of Appalachia. It has national appeal, however, because the situation with which it deals is unique to the area. In addition, it is not a school that competes with the donor's alma mater.) We call this last example "The case of the package that strayed too far from home." Still, if you must test a local appeal in the national marketplace, do so only if you can afford a financial loss. Then mail a limited test to the very best lists your broker can identify.

LOCATING YOUR MARKET

Your market of potential donors is represented initially on thousands of lists that either can be rented at a cost of X dollars per thousand names or exchanged on a name-for-name basis. (In either case it is for one-time use only.) To the untrained, however, the descriptions on the list cards provided by list brokers seem sketchy, and many of them even sound alike.

How, then, do you know which lists are right for you? Following are capsule descriptions of the three types of lists available to you through a broker.

1. **Donor lists** (likely to be the most responsive you can use)

    a. Organizations similar in purpose to your own, whose constituencies make annual donations or pay annual membership dues.
    b. Organizations not similar, but made up of donors or members whose profiles (interests, politics, life styles, etc.) seem compatible to your cause.

2. **Commercial lists** (the most productive will have *mail responsive* selections)

    Magazine, catalogue buyers, etc., whose tastes, hobbies, and interests are indicative of a potential interest in your cause.

3. **Compiled lists** (probably cannot be successful unless income, age, etc., overlays are used)

    Names and addresses derived from directories, newspapers, public records, voting lists, retail sales books, etc., to identify groups of people with something in common.

For almost all nonprofit organizations, the types of lists that work best are other donor/member lists, followed by well-chosen commercial lists. The least profitable (although a category not to be overlooked) is compiled lists.

But even if you confined yourself to the first category (donor/member lists), you'd find yourself overwhelmed by stacks of list data cards briefly describing the merits of the list. For example, a typical data card, accompanied by a guide of what to look for in addition to the description of the list appears on the card shown in Figure 2-1.

With literally thousands of cards like this from which to choose (some of which have far less information), how do you know which ones are appropriate for testing? Especially when so many of them sound the same.

As we advised in Chapter 1, we suggest that you work with a good list broker.

WHY YOU NEED A LIST BROKER

"A list broker can give you more arms than an octopus—with a telephone in each one of them."

Most direct mail campaigns are not put together under the guidance of a professional consultant. Rather the majority are done in-house, and many manage to do fairly well. Often, the packages produced scarcely change from one year to the next. Nonetheless, many of these "do-it-yourself" organizations manage to keep their heads above water in the process of constituency building.

What is their secret?

To begin, a successful organization working without counsel will inevitably have the following two things going for it:

- A well established and/or irresistible and timely cause.
- An exceptional list broker.

What Is a List Broker?

There are three common misconceptions about lists and brokers.

1. A list broker does not own lists. Rather, he or she is essentially a middleman who brings mailers together with list owners. Not only is it uncommon for a broker to own lists, he or she will rarely, if ever, tell you who actually owns those lists.
2. Lists are not "bought" by either you or your broker. Rather, they are leased or rented for one-time use on a specified date for a specified fee based on the number of names you use.
3. The price of a list rental is not more expensive when you use a broker. Like travel agents, who are paid by the airlines or resorts, the broker's 20 percent commission comes from the list owner. You pay only the standard rental fee. In arranging exchanges, however, your broker will charge a fee of between $6 and $8 per M to handle all the paperwork and phone calls. It's worth it!

What the List Broker Does

To earn the 20 percent commission, a list broker does the following:
1. Recommends lists for a specific mailing that will have the highest probability of success.
2. Gets your package approved by the list owners.

25

Figure 2-1. Sample List Card

80,662 Donors ①   ②$60/M

    Protecting our environment is the motivation which compels these donors to give. Our natural resources are important to these contributors, who have given anywhere from $5 to very large sums to express their concern for our planet.

    This list has been quite successful for other appeals besides conservation, and could bring a high response rate and large average gift for your organization, too.

    Mail dates must be requested well in advance.

    Sample mailing piece required.

DATE: ③
11/83

SOURCE: ④
100% Direct Mail

AVERAGE GIFT: ⑤
$17.50

MINIMUM ORDER: ⑥
5,000

SELECTION: ⑦
state/scf/zip $3/M

KEY CODING: ⑧
$1.50/M - 5 digits

⑨
ADDRESSING FORMAT:

4-up Cheshire
Mag tape -
   $25 charge if
   not returned
   in 60 days.
Pressure sensitive
  labels

ORAM GROUP MARKETING
275 MADISON AVENUE
NEW YORK, N.Y. 10016
(212) 889-2244

1. *Quantity:* After taking a 5M sample for a test, is the list large enough to roll out to? (If it is three times the size of the original test, you can roll out only once in the next six months. If it is ten times the test size, you can roll out between two and three times depending on the size of your roll-out.)

2. *Cost per Thousand Names:* The best fund-raising lists cost between $45 and $70, with a typical cost being $55 per M.

3. *Date List Card Was Produced:* Indicates how recent the information is.

4. *Source:* 100 percent direct mail is the best you can hope for. If the source is other than mail, discuss with your broker those mailers for whom the list has worked.

5. *Average Gift:* If it is far below the average you are seeking, test cautiously.

6. *Minimum Order:* A 5,000 minimum order is the industry standard. A few lists require a 10,000 sampling and a few will allow 3,000.

7. *Selection (sometimes called arrangement):* This describes special selects possible and the per M charge for each. (In other words, on the list shown, you could order "Conservation Donors" in the state of New York only for an additional charge of $3 per M names.)

8. *Key Coding:* This is the per M charge to imprint *your* mailing key on the label. (Note number of digits allowed.)

9. *Addressing Format:* This describes the various formats in which the list can be delivered to you and notes special charges, if any.

Some list cards also describe the sex breakout of the list (i.e., 60 percent women) and whether EXCHANGES (rather than rentals) can be arranged. In addition, if a list has been cleaned recently, this usually is stated.

3. Clears a date when you are entitled to mail.
4. Issues written orders to list owners, sending confirmation copies to you.
5. Follows up with owners if lists do not arrive as scheduled.
6. Sends invoices.
7. Helps you evaluate list results and makes recommendations for new lists to use in your continuation mailing.

Most list brokers can do the above—and do it fairly well. But the really good broker does far, far more—truly earning his or her 20 percent commission—and then some!

Of the hundreds of list brokers in the country, very few specialize in fund-raising lists and the rest have limited, if any, fund-raising experience at all. So to begin, you need a broker who specializes—or at least one with some experience—in fund-raising lists. A list of fund-raising brokers may be found at the end of this chapter.

Even within the specialty of fund raising, many brokers have carved out categories of expertise in particular fields, such as:

Civil Rights
Jewish Causes
Conservation and the Environment
Health and Welfare
Social Action
Membership Organizations
Educational Organizations

and so on.

Thus, if yours is a membership organization in the education field, you will do well to ask your new broker whether he or she has other clients with similar profiles.

Why the List Broker is Indispensable

To begin with, the broker knows far, far more about lists than you *ever* will. Your knowledge of a list is usually limited to the brief description printed on the list data cards. In addition to providing a brief profile of what the list represents, the list card tells you the size (universe) of the list, the cost per M (thousand) names to rent, whether the list can be exchanged, the range of memberships or contributions included (i.e., whether $100 and over donors or donors giving less than $5 are included, etc.), and the source of the list (direct mail or otherwise).

When you think about it, that's not an awful lot of information. But it's all the information the list owner wants you to have because, in most cases, the owner has an investment in protecting the *real* name or source of the list, as well as other pertinent information.

On the other hand, the broker knows the following:

- The other organizations for whom the list works.
- The other organizations for whom it does not work.
- The type of appeal and special offers which make the list work.
- The time of the year when the list works best.
- Whether the list is truly clean (all undeliverable addresses removed), all new names added, or whether it is a dying list.

You also benefit from the broker's knowledge (which he will not reveal to you) of the following:

- Whether the list owner stacks first-time rentals with the best names.
- If the list owner over-rents the list—i.e., does not allow a window between mailings.
- If the list owner is a prompt shipper, or whether your list is more than likely to arrive late.
- What the actual name is of the organization (existing or defunct) behind the improbable-sounding name printed on the list card.

Last but not least, the broker's entire business is set up to:

- Check the very latest results of organizations who used the lists you are scheduling.
- Get immediate clearance dates and confirmations.
- Follow up on late list arrivals and do *something* to expedite their prompt dispatch.
- Placate the idiosyncracies of the list owners.
- Keep track, where names are exchanged between organizations, of who owes whom what.

Questions a List Broker Needs Answered

The list broker will ask you many of the same questions a direct mail consultant would ask:

- What does your organization do and for whom does it do it?
- Who, other than direct beneficiaries, does your program help?
- How many people now support your organization and how was that list built?
- Is your list computerized and are you willing to exchange your active names?
- Are you offering memberships or asking for charitable contributions? If a membership, what are the basic dues and what are the benefits of membership? If a charity, what is the average gift to your organization?
- If direct mail has been used in the past, what lists were used and what were the results?

For those new to the mail and for those who have been mailing since the invention of the envelope, we cannot over-stress the importance of sharing results with your consultant and/or broker. Show these professionals samples of the packages that were used. Tell them about the tests that were conducted, the mail date(s), the type of postage used, and so on.

Finally, give your list broker a copy of the list and package analysis which shows, in terms of percent return, average gift and percent of cost recovered, which lists and packages worked, and which did not. The more information the broker has to construct the "crystal ball," the more successful your campaign will be.

HOW MANY BROKERS DOES IT TAKE TO . . . ?

We advise novices to work with two or three list brokers until it becomes clear which is providing the best service, the most productive recommendations, and, last but not least, in whom they have the greatest degree of trust.

In the long run, we usually recommend that an organization settle on one broker. Here's why:

1. The exclusive broker will be able to become thoroughly familiar with your organization's strengths and weaknesses, strategies, offers, marketing plans, past successes and failures, etc. Thus he or she will be able to make recommendations that go beyond the obvious.
2. The exclusive broker naturally is going to work harder for you, and that dedication will pay off in the long run.

3. The more the broker has at stake in making recommendations, the more he or she will research and follow up on those recommendations.
4. The exclusive broker—by virtue of being able to deliver volume orders to a list owner — is in a stronger bargaining position to negotiate the best possible terms and concessions for you.
5. The exclusive broker makes your work easier because you will not have to keep track of "who placed what and through whom." (This can get to be a real killer.)

Frequently, when an organization with previous direct mail experience goes to a fund-raising consultant or to a new list broker, it is because the organization has hired a new development director or membership director.

The new employee, anxious to improve on his or her predecessor's record, consults with a firm or a broker prior to plunging into a campaign. But too often, these new employees—in misguided haste to prove themselves—wave aside as unimportant any past records and insist that the consultant start from scratch.

Let us tell you a true story of one such client.

John A. became development director of a small health organization with 4,000 individual supporters on file. His job had been held previously by a woman who (regardless of what John thought) was a good practitioner of direct mail. When we asked John for package samples and list reports of his predecessor, he insisted that she had taken everything with her. All he could produce was an incomplete report showing that the last mailing had lost 15¢ on the dollar and one complete (although undated) sample package. John wasn't even certain whether the report and the sample went together. Under our prodding, John did come up with a file of list orders placed through a reputable broker, but could not find an analysis of how these lists performed.

As we resigned ourselves to starting from scratch, the director's secretary happened to come upon a file cabinet stuffed with coded response devices from earlier mailings. The key codes matched up with the list orders that had been located and the design of the response card clearly showed that it had been part of the package we had seen.

The director protested our request to re-tabulate the hundreds and hundreds of response cards on a list by list basis, but we felt it so important that we assigned one of our own clerical workers to the task. The results provided valuable insights into which lists had worked and which had not. What was even more exciting was the discovery that a package test had been conducted and that the theme of one had brought in 20 percent more gifts!

Now we were no longer in the position of gambling with the organization's money, but were able to write a fresh package based on established guidelines. Moreover, we were able to schedule proven lists, while recommending new lists for testing. (Knowing past results can save money by preventing re-use of nonproductive lists, thereby allowing the use of new and perhaps more successful lists.)

The mailing was a success. But was the director pleased? Sorry to relate, he was not. He insisted that we should have been able to create a successful campaign without "stealing" past information. But what was really bothering him, it turned out, was that he wanted all the credit for himself—to show his superiors that he had pulled off a campaign with no help from his predecessor.

At the conclusion of our campaign, we presented a comprehensive campaign analysis to John A. He did not re-hire us. Later we heard through the grapevine that he had approached a new consultant whom he told that we had not turned in any list reports. The consultant, knowing our firm's reputation for professionalism, declined to take on the organization's work.

Moral of the story: don't assume that your consultant or broker isn't earning his or her fee simply because they are building on past successes. Withholding of information will hurt you far more than it will hurt them.

TESTING LISTS

Assume that you wish to test 50,000 names, followed by a roll-out if the test is successful.

Most lists are available on minimum orders of 5,000 names. This figure is a compromise between the smallest number of names which is statistically valid—3,000—and a greater number—more than 6,000—which is an unnecessary financial risk.

Thus, in a test of 50,000 pieces, you will likely use ten lists of 5,000 names each. But when you plan your continuation mailing, in which you will want to double, triple, or even quadruple the total number of names, you can use larger quantities of each original test list that worked.

Do not be lured into fantasies of great riches simply because several of your lists performed in excess of expectations. And do not be too quick to discard lists that worked only marginally.

Let us examine the results of a hypothetical pilot mailing where all average gifts were identical at $20 and where all of the test lists used had universes of between 100,000 and 300,000.

PILOT LIST PERFORMANCE

Lists A, B, C	.50-.65% return
Lists D, E	.85% return
Lists F, G	.90%-1.00% return
List H	1.20% return
List I	1.50% return
List J	2.10% return

The most common mistake made by the inexperienced is to put together a roll-out by scheduling only the top performing lists. Thus a novice might schedule a roll-out that looks like this:

List H	50M names
List I	50M names
List J	100M names
TOTAL	200M names

Here is the roll-out schedule we would have put together. We call this plan "pyramiding on success." It is also called not putting all your eggs in one basket.

Best	List H	25M	(5 times original test)
Lists	List I	25M	(5 times original test)
	List J	50M	(10 times original test)
Good	List F	15M	(3 times original test)
Lists	List G	15M	(3 times original test)
Marginal	List D	5M	(re-test same amount)
Lists	List E	5M	(re-test same amount)
Total Re-Uses		140,000	

Approximately 25 percent of the roll-out should be reserved for testing new lists. On the following chart we are testing seven new lists—only one less than on the original pilot test.

New Test Lists

List K	5M names
List L	5M names
List M	5M names
List N	5M names
List O	5M names
List P	5M names
List Q	5M names
Total New Test Lists	35,000
Grand Total	175,000

Strategy for the List Schedule

The schedule put together by the inexperienced fund raiser has a good chance of earning a handsome net profit provided that the three lists that earned well over a 1 percent return on the test hold up in the large continuation quantities ordered. But what if they don't?

We have had numerous experiences where a 5,000 test worked beautifully and the roll-out bombed. Even on the most promising lists, roll out no more than five to ten times the original test. (Ten is the maximum!) If, after the first roll-out, results still hold or are only slightly diminished, one can make the second roll-out up to ten times the size of the test (or twice the size of the first roll-out). Higher than that, we do not gamble.

Why, everyone always wants to know, do such good test results go sour? Does the list owner "salt" the first order to get you to come back for more names? We would like to say that never happens, but we know that, very occasionally, it does. Therefore it is always best to be cautious. When the first 5,000 names are given to you exactly as ordered—a pure and random "nth select" across all categories of giving and across the entire nation—a roll-out still can be disappointing because:

- Timing of the roll-out is wrong; the situation has changed or other causes have grabbed the spotlight.
- Competing mailers did not stick to their assigned mail dates. As a result the arrival of their appeals coincided with yours.
- You changed your package or eliminated a key ingredient responsible for its past success.
- The list owner's computer bureau did not keep a record of the names used in the test and included them in your roll-out order.

There are other reasons to re-use and re-test lists other than those that performed at the very top level. To be sure, the hypothetical mailing just cited made a handsome profit on three of the lists tested. And they may continue to work. But what are you going to do when those three sources of new names dry up—after you have mailed to them again and again?

Surely you don't want to wait until then to start testing other lists. If you are serious about finding out who your potential constituents are, never stop the process of re-testing marginal lists and testing promising new lists.

IMPORTANT THINGS TO KNOW WHEN ORDERING LISTS

Order Lists in Advance

Too often, a new mailer will concentrate all of his energies on developing the package and leave the selection of the lists until the last moment—only to find that the best lists are unavailable on the scheduled mail date, and often for several months thereafter.

Good lists are in heavy demand, thus it is wise to place your orders as far in advance as possible. This is especially true of exchange only lists because often these list owners allow only limited use (sometimes as few as ten exchanges a year). Because of such use limitations, the wise mailer will order exchange lists up to six months in advance, although lead time of two months is sufficient to obtain most lists. Commercial lists have an altogether different usage policy and it is often possible to get mail dates for such lists only weeks in advance.

But until you are a highly experienced mailer with an encyclopedic knowledge of list timetables, it's best to order all lists as far in advance as possible.

Keep Your Mail Date

Mail dates are scheduled by list owners not for their benefit, but for yours. When you contract for a mail date, you have the list owner's assurance that the names you are renting or exchanging are not being used by another mailer at the same time. Failure to keep your mail date jeopardizes the success of your mailing—especially if the mailer next in line is a competitor.

If, for reasons out of your control, you cannot mail within the week allotted to you, contact your broker to see whether the following week is available. If it is, you are in luck. If not, the broker will have to clear a new mail date for you. The bad thing about this is that the next available date may be during a period when you do not wish to mail for a variety of reasons. You may be planning a house mailing or the next available date may be in mid-summer or it may go into your next fiscal year.

Missing mail dates happens to the best of us, but of all the things that can go wrong on the technical end, it is the one to be avoided most carefully. This means advance planning and diligent follow-up.

Bear in mind that if you cancel your mailing after labels are run, you have deprived the list owner of an opportunity to derive income from his lists during the exclusive period (or window) you reserved. In such an instance, you will be obligated to pay for running charges of between $6 and $9 per thousand names, and you may also be charged a cancellation fee.

This is a good time for you to reproduce the planning chart provided in Figure 1-1 and place it in a conspicuous location.

Check the List Before Mailing

As each list arrives, make certain it is checked for the following:

- *Correct quantity.* Regardless of the number of names you ordered, chances are you will receive just under or over that amount. Should you receive a quantity more than 5 percent fewer than the ordered amount, ask your broker for a credit. (Proof can be verified by submitting the count that is supplied at the end of each label or tape run.)
- *Correct ZIP selection.* If you have ordered the list on a random across-the-board select (called an "nth select") be sure the zip codes you obtain correspond to the order. Similarly, if you have requested that certain zips be omitted or have ordered selected zips, be sure that is what you receive. An error here can be fatal to a targeted geographic/demographic campaign.
- *Neatness and legibility of printing.* Even if the post office can make out the smudged addresses, you don't want to ruin the look of your beautiful package with a sloppy looking mail label. If there's time, ask for a rerun.

- *Correct type of label.* Labels are almost always "four-up Cheshire" unless otherwise represented (or requested) in advance. Your mail house may not have the necessary equipment to affix one-up Cheshire labels and it will cost more to hand-affix pressure-sensitive labels. If you have been specific in your order, mistakes are unlikely. However, should you receive the wrong type of label and there is no time to re-run and still make your mail date, ask the broker whether the list owner will pay your cost to apply the labels (assuming there is a greater cost involved). Of course, if the owner originally stated that he could *only* provide one-up Cheshire or self-adhesive labels, you must bear the extra cost.
- *Damaged labels.* It doesn't matter whether the labels were damaged before they were shipped or in transit. Your mail house cannot affix badly bent or warped labels. Ask for an immediate re-run and rush shipment.

Ordering Lists on Magnetic Tape

If you are doing a "merge/purge"—the process of combining many lists and removing duplicate names—your broker will not be ordering Cheshire labels direct from the list owner. Rather, magnetic tapes will be ordered and shipped directly to your computer service bureau.

Merge/purge is also discussed in Chapter 10, but it is important to note the list ordering aspect here.

CONDUCTING A MERGE/PURGE

Before placing a list order with your broker for a magnetic tape, you will have selected a computer house with merge/purge capability. The broker will arrange to have the list owner ship to your computer bureau a magnetic tape, a "dump" and a "layout" (see Glossary). When all the tapes have arrived—and only then—can the merge/purge begin. When the merge/purge is completed, Cheshire labels are generated 95 percent free of duplications and shipped to your mailing house, from which point you proceed as usual. If you are doing a computer letter, no labels will be generated following the merge/purge. Computer and laser letters are discussed in Chapter 10.

Merge/purge mailings take longer for the following reasons:

- The process cannot begin until all tapes have arrived. Many will be late, so allow for lost time.
- The merge/purge itself takes three days to three weeks, depending on the service bureau. Ask in advance.
- Unless the computer bureau is also a lettershop, you lose another day or two shipping the labels to your mail house.

EXCHANGING YOUR LIST

Many nonprofit organizations will not be persuaded that it is safe and profitable to exchange their own list with those of other organizations.

Even the most sophisticated fund raiser may have a difficult time convincing a board of directors to alter its "no exchange" policy. As consultants, we frequently are called in to explain why an organization should exchange its names. Here is what we tell our clients.

First, and most important, many of the best lists are available *only* through exchange; the owners will not rent their names commercially. Thus if you refuse to exchange, a great source of new support is forever cut off to you.

The second argument in favor of exchange is cost. List rentals average $45-$75 per M names, often representing the single largest item in your direct mail budget.

List exchanges are free and, when arranged by a broker, cost only $6 to $8 per M names as a service fee for handling the paperwork. In a mailing of 250,000 names, where exchanges could amount to one-third of the total, this could represent a savings of as much as $4,500 to an organization. But this savings is only part of the financial picture.

If you had exchanged your list with eight other organizations, giving each of the eight 10,000 names in exchange for like names from their list, you now would have 80,000 excellent prospect names to mail to. Let us now assume that these 80,000 names brought in a 1 percent return and a $20 average gift (a modest estimate as freshly exchanged names often do much better). Even with our modest estimates, you would have gained 800 new supporters and earned $16,000 *in addition to your savings of $4,500.*

Now, $20,500 in the bank is a sum large enough to make most boards reconsider a "no exchange" policy. Even so, some remain reluctant, and for the following reasons:

1. Our donors will be bothered by other appeals.
2. Our donors will be bothered by other appeals and will be angry at us for giving out their names.
3. Our donors will be bothered by other appeals and will be angry at us for giving out their names . . . and will write us nasty letters.
4. Our donors will be bothered by other appeals and will be angry at us for giving our their names and will write us nasty letters . . . *and will stop giving to us.*
5. They will stop giving because they are mad at us and will give to the other mailers *instead* of to us.

Here is our thinking on these issues. Perhaps your donors *will* receive appeals from organizations with whom you exchange names. Whether these appeals "bother" your donors is a matter of debate.

Most *direct mail donors* enjoy receiving mail. And if 1 percent or so of your donors contribute to Organization X, that would indicate that they not only weren't annoyed, but that many were actually interested in the other organization.

"Ah ha!" we hear some of you saying now. "That's exactly what we were worried about. They'll be giving to the others instead of to us!"

But, think about it for a moment. If you had been a long-time supporter of your local hospital, would an appeal from your volunteer fire department (whether or not you contribute) cause you to abandon your interest in the hospital? Of course not! The primary way an organization loses a long-time donor other than to death or disinterest—is by not mailing frequently enough. That's right! You endanger your own list far more by infrequent mailings than by exchanging your list. You've got to keep reminding your constituents that you're there—doing a job for them!

"But what about the annoyance factor?" you persist. "Once we exchanged our list as an experiment and we received a whole slew of complaints from our members."

Almost always, when we are able to review such a "slew of complaints," we find that the number is quite small compared to the size of the exchange (usually less than .03 percent, or six on a list of 25,000).

We advise clients to respond to all complaints with a simple, straightforward letter of explanation, a prototype of which appears below.

Dear Supporter:

We are sorry you were troubled by an appeal from the (name of organization). In exchanging our list of supporters with (Organization X), it certainly was not our intent to alienate you or to break any confidences.

The reason we exchanged names is because, frankly, our donor list is suffering from normal—but nonetheless potentially devastating—attrition.

As you can imagine, in order to continue in the black—to continue to provide the services in which you believe so deeply as evidenced by your past generous support—we must locate new donors to replace the old.

I feel sure that you will be excited to learn that as a result of exchanging lists with (Organization X), we enlisted 340 *new members*. And because it was an exchange (and not an expensive list rental) the mailing was very economical.

I also hope that you are as pleased as we are that the members of Organization X regard our work as worthy of support, just as you and I do.

Now I realize that you may have another concern—and that is whether (Organization X) will keep you on its list and continue mailing to you. The answer is no. The only names they keep are the names of those who responded to their mailings with a contribution. (By the same token, the only names of theirs we keep are those who sent *us* a contribution.)

When you think about it, it makes sense that many who are interested in the work of (Organization X) would also be interested in us (and vice versa). Because of this, we probably will arrange an exchange again later this year.

If you still want your name withheld from this exchange, let us know. I have enclosed an envelope addressed directly to me. If you use it to ask that your name not be exchanged, we will program our computer to take care of this for you at a cost of approximately $5, which we will absorb.

On the other hand, as you now have a better understanding of the importance of exchanging names, you have several other options:

(1) You can ignore the enclosed envelope, and when you receive an appeal from (Organization X) or any other organization with whom we exchange, you can simply throw it away.

(2) You can read the appeals from these other groups to learn whether they interest you—and it might just be fun to judge whether our own appeals are as good. We welcome the opinions of our supporters.

(3) You can use the enclosed envelope to make a special contribution to (name of your organization).

As I mentioned earlier, we are suffering from a loss of supporters through death, relocation, and general attrition. This is greatly offset by the generosity of our friends who make more than one tax-deductible gift during a calendar year. I hope that you will be one of these special friends.

Regardless of your decision, thank you for your concern and interest. I look forward to hearing from you.

Sincerely yours,

This letter puts some pressure on the member (or donor) to go to the trouble of writing to you again, thus enabling you to "weed out the grumblers from the serious complainers." Many will not respond at all and you will be surprised how many will send additional contributions—often more generous than in the past. Do not fail to thank the donor promptly for this extra gift. In fact, a telephone call in this instance might be just the ticket!

Now if the "serious complainer" replies that he still wants his name protected from exchange, immediately comply by flagging his name on your computer with a no-exchange code. And don't forget to send a note saying you have responded to his request.

Still Unconvinced about Exchanging?

If after these persuasions, you are still reluctant to exchange, consider this fact. We estimate (and most list brokers concur) that some 90 percent of nonprofit organizations whose member or donor lists number between 10,000 and 500,000 names have been exchanging their names with each other for ten years or more with no ill effects. In fact, the lists of most of these organizations were built through the practice of exchange. And so it remains today.

One final thought. If you aren't exchanging your list based on the belief that you are protecting your donors from other appeals, think it through.

For most groups about 5 percent of their list is really unique, i.e., their names alone. Perhaps less than that.

If 5 percent of your list is unique, 95 percent are members of or contribute to one or more other organizations and are therefore already on many other lists that are continually being rented *and* exchanged. Your own list was built, in part, through use of these names.

There is just no such thing as protecting your donors. What's more, most of them are perfectly able to protect themselves. They have wastebaskets of their own.

GUARDING AGAINST LIST THEFT

Until recently, most list owners would not ship lists directly to the organization using them. Rather, all mail labels or magnetic tapes were shipped to a third party—in most cases, the mail house or lettershop employed by the intended user.

This precaution against list theft has relaxed considerably over the past several years as methods for "salting" or "seeding" lists have become more sophisticated.

In our 20 + years of arranging rentals and exchanges on behalf of a multitude of clients, and in renting and exchanging Oram-owned fund-raising lists, we have not discovered a single case of list theft due to shipping labels or tapes directly to the mailer.

The isolated instances of list theft that do occur almost always are perpetrated by an organization's own employee(s), and even that is rare.

Even beginners know that all professionally maintained lists are decoyed. The chances of getting caught and prosecuted are extremely high.

List theft is low on your list of things to worry about in direct mail fund raising. However, if you have not done so already, we do caution you to take steps to protect your list.

We have mentioned salting or seeding your list. It is not sufficient simply to insert the names of your staff and/or board members at home addresses. Should a thief be intent on stealing your list, these names are precisely what he would look for and remove. Instead, place bogus names at the addresses of trusted associates, friends, and relatives. Or spell real names incorrectly. For example, if your name is Mary Hendler, the postal carrier will almost certainly realize that a letter addressed to M.W. Wendler at the same address is intended for you. But how would a list thief know to look it up under "W"? If you still don't feel secure using your home address on the chance that the thief would look it up (remember, he or she would have to look up the home addresses of all of your board and staff members), we suggest you subscribe to a special service.

One of these is the U.S. Monitor Service. The way a monitor service operates is through dummy names and addresses scattered through the country. Regardless of the segment of your list which is exchanged or rented, decoys will be included in your list order. These decoys are mailed to the appropriate address, collected, and mailed back to the service's home office, then forwarded to the list owner (you).

The list owner should then check two things: (1) that the organization mailing the package was authorized to do so, and (2) that the mailer abided by the mail date that was cleared.

The charge for this service is approximately $1 for every ounce of mail received and forwarded to the list owner.

KEEPING YOUR LIST CLEAN

The highest accolade that can be given to a list (other than that it works) is that it is clean. Virtually all lists that work really well are clean. The two go hand-in-hand.

When you mail first class to your house list, you routinely receive bad addresses from the post office. But mailing at the nonprofit rate does not entitle you to receive this information. (And while we grant you that a few such returns do slip by, they are insufficient in number to be of value to you in cleaning your list).

Thus what you must do at least once, and perhaps twice a year, is to make one of your house mailings do double-duty to clean the file.

On the face of the carrier envelope, have the following words printed:

ADDRESS CORRECTION REQUESTED
RETURN POSTAGE GUARANTEED

It's as simple as that. Insofar as is possible, the post office will return the forwarding address to you at a cost of 25¢ each piece. If your file of 20,000 has a 5 percent bad address rate, you will pay $250—a moderate sum to be able to reach those 1,000 donors with future appeals.

What is more, those addresses that are not found by the post office will also be returned to you, thus you will save even more money by not sending repeated appeals that never reach their intended destination.

"A one time solicitation *only* with no guilt attached. No mailing lists to get on... No heart-breaking renewal letters... No bequest mailings... No trading your name."

37

LIST BROKERS SPECIALIZING IN FUND RAISING

- A.B. Data Corp., 8050 N. Port Washington Road, Milwaukee, WI 53217 (specializing in Jewish donor/membership lists)
- Accredited Mailing Lists, 3 Park Avenue, New York, NY 10016; 7316 Wisconsin Avenue, Bethesda, MD 20814
- American Mailing List Corp., 7777 Leesburg Pike, Falls Church, VA 22043
- Atlantic List Co., 1101 30th Street, NW, Washington, DC 20007
- Barbara Bancroft Lists, 10505 Adel Road, Oakton, VA 22124
- Briggs Associates, RD #2, Carversville Road, Doylestown, PA 18901
- George Bryant & Staff, P.O. Box 190, 71 Grand Avenue, Englewood, NJ 07136
- Bernice S. Bush Co., 15052 Springdale Street, Huntington Beach, CA 92649
- Catholic Lists, 10 Fiske Place, Mt. Vernon, NY 10550
- Charles Crane Assoc. Corp., One Executive Drive, Ft. Lee, NJ 07024
- Carol Enters List Co. (CELCO), 381 Park Avenue South, New York, NY 10016
- The Coolidge Co., 25 West 43rd Street, New York, NY 10036
- Dependable Mailing Lists, 120 E. 16th Street, New York, NY 10003; 1825 K Street, NW, Washington, DC 20006; 333 North Michigan Avenue, Chicago, IL 60601
- Direct Media Group, Inc., 220 Grace Church Street, Port Chester, NY 10573
- Guild Company, P.O. Box 160, Engle Street, Englewood, NJ 07631
- Walter Karl, P.O. Drawer J, 20 Maple Avenue, Armonk, NY 10504
- The Kleid Company, 200 Park Avenue, New York, NY 10017
- E. J. Krane, 20 Nassau Street, Princeton, NJ 08540
- List America, 1202 Potomac Street, NW, Washington, DC 20007
- Master List, 1625 I Street, NW, Washington, DC 20006
- MEGA, P.O. Box 16836, Baltimore, MD 21206
- Name Exchange, 7015 Old Keene Mill Road, Springfield, VA 22150
- Names in the News, 530 Bush Street, San Francisco, CA 94108; One Penn Plaza, New York, NY 10001
- Names Unlimited, 183 Madison Avenue, New York, NY 10016
- National Fund Raising Lists, 9418 Annapolis Road, Lanham, MD 20706
- Old Dominion Lists, 809 Brook Hill Circle, Richmond, VA 23227
- Omega List Co., 8330 Old Courthouse Road, Vienna, VA 22180
- Parrish Assoc., 721 Olive Street, St. Louis, MO 63101
- Preferred Lists, Inc., 499 South Capitol Street, SW, Washington, DC 20003
- Prescott Lists, 17 East 26th Street, New York, NY 10010
- Religious Lists, 86 Maple Avenue, New York, NY 10956
- Uni-Mail List Co., 1 Lincoln Plaza, New York, NY 10023

CHAPTER 3

The Roll-Out: Reinvesting Your Money

If your pilot mailing recouped between 90 and 100 percent of cost, it was a success. If it made even a small profit, it was extraordinarily successful. If it recouped 75-85 percent of costs, you are in a grey area, and require a thorough analysis of your appeal and marketing strategy.

The primary reason most campaigns fail is not because the letter wasn't good or the lists weren't well chosen. Rather, most campaigns fail because the organization was not completely objective in assessing whether its cause had real potential for success in the mail. Many organizations able to raise funds successfully from corporations, foundations, the government, and even from select individuals have learned the hard way that they cannot raise money through direct mail.

This chapter, however, assumes that your first effort—like the hypothetical test in Chapter 1—broke even. Now you should be eager to maintain the program by a continuation—or roll-out—mailing.

EVALUATING THE PILOT CAMPAIGN: CAN YOU IMPROVE ON SUCCESS?

To improve upon the success of your test, you should reassess your package. It is a rare package that cannot benefit from hard scrutiny and perhaps a change. But not change for its own sake. After all, your package worked well in the test, didn't it?

But perhaps you had wanted to try an envelope teaser, but didn't come up with a really good idea until after the envelopes were printed. Or perhaps, since your package was mailed, a leading newspaper has published a favorable story on your organization. Would its inclusion in your package have improved results?

There is only one way to find out. Incorporate the envelope teaser or newspaper reprint into your next mailing. Be sure to test the revised package against the "control" (the original, *totally unchanged* package). And above all, *never* test more than one thing at a time. If you do—be warned—the test results will be absolutely meaningless. Let us give you several examples of what can go wrong.

One organization decided to test first class postage against nonprofit postage. This is an expensive test and the results must be analyzed carefully. Though first class postage *usually* improves results, the increased income often does not offset the increased postage cost.

In this case, the membership director decided also to include a re-designed response card. However, there was a sufficient supply of the *old* response cards in stock to fulfill half of the total mailing and the director felt it would be wasteful not to use them. Thus in segmenting the mailing, the old response cards were sent with the third class part of the mailing and the new response cards were sent with the first class part.

The results of the test? The half of the mailing sent first class outpulled the other half by 25 percent. Thus the membership director decided to mail the entire roll-out at the first class postal rate. Would you have made the same decision? If your answer is no, you made a wise decision.

When the mail program was later analyzed (and new tests conducted) it was learned that the primary factor accounting for the improved results was not the first class postage at all, but the exciting new response device!

Not incidentally, the first class postage at 20¢ per letter versus the nonprofit rate of 5.2¢ per piece had cost an additional 14.8¢ per piece, while the cost of artwork for the new response device added only a fraction of a cent to the cost of each piece.

Testing New Markets and Old

You will want to look carefully at lists before scheduling your roll-out. Not only must you thoughtfully evaluate the lists that worked, but you must also evaluate those that were disappointing—and why.

In Chapter 2 we discussed lists in greater detail, but the point we want to make here has to do with building on initial successes and failures—list by list. For example: If, of 15 lists tested in the pilot described in Chapter 1, seven were successful, you can roll out increased quantities to these lists. The total goal for your roll-out schedule should be to mail approximately twice the quantity of the test, or 150,000.

Given this goal, which of the following options would you pursue?

(a) Schedule all seven good lists (good meaning those recovering at least 90 percent of cost) at a quantity of 20,000 each? Your total here would be 140,000.
(b) Mail 5,000 from each of the seven proven lists for a quantity of 35,000 and test 20 new lists at 5,000 each for an additional 100,000? The total here would be 135,000.

If you chose (a) as your answer, you are partly correct. An increase from 5,000 to 20,000 names is not unreasonable on lists that performed at 90 percent cost recovered or better.

However, if you re-schedule only proven lists, you will not learn very much more about the potential market for your cause. Continually testing new markets is one of the key factors in a successful prospect campaign.

If you chose (b) as your answer, you are simultaneously overly conservative and far too daring. By rolling out in the same quantities as the test (5,000 each list) you cripple your campaign. But by testing 20 new lists—two-thirds of your schedule—you put the entire campaign at unnecessary risk.

Our advice: Roll out to 15,000 names on six of the seven lists that worked best in the pilot, and 20,000 names on list K which performed exceptionally well. Also, retest 5,000 names from list H because it *almost* qualified as a winner, producing a .94 percent return and recovering 84 percent of costs.

You now have a schedule of 115,000 names, but you still haven't included any new test lists, which in general should comprise one-quarter of the schedule of each roll-out mailing (or in this case 35,000 names).

Now you and your list broker can research new lists whose profiles most closely match those of the lists that worked on the pilot mailing. Here is where the broker becomes indispensable. Not only does he have your list performance report as a guide, but he can compare it to reports from similar organizations in helping you put together the best possible schedule (seven new test lists of 5,000 names each).

You now have a total schedule of 150,000 names for your roll-out mailing—exactly twice the size of the original test.

It may be argued that this increase is on the conservative side. Several of our colleagues said that given *such* a successful pilot, they would mail up to 30,000 to each of the good lists, re-test all lists that earned at least 75 percent of costs, and test at least ten new lists at 5,000 names each list for a total roll-out over 250,000!

Sound risky? In fact this is not an unwise decision, but it *is* one requiring experience and in-depth familiarity with the past performance of many lists for many campaigns—not a decision for a neophyte.

Also, the *first* roll-out is only one of a series of many in a successful ongoing campaign. You can take risks later when you are more experienced and can better afford them.

Now take a look at the roll-out schedule for the rest of the year (Figure 3-1).

Reaching the Saturation Point

In studying the mailing schedules for Years One, Two, and Three, you immediately notice that the quantities do not increase dramatically. You have stayed at 1 million pieces the first two years, and increased to 1.5 million in the third year. Why didn't you mail 2 million pieces in the second year and 3 million in the third?

The hypothetical campaign outlined here is based on a composite of several successful national campaigns for causes with a medium/high universe of good prospects. For some causes, a 1,500,000 annual prospect mailing is the ceiling. Others—causes with unusual strength of appeal and larger markets—may mail many times this amount. Still others will find that their marketing universe stops at a million or a half-million. Most local causes will saturate their markets at even lower levels.

This does not mean that the organization with the smaller market should cease to send prospect mail. Nor does it mean that no new list will ever be discovered (although they will turn up less often). It means only that at some point (usually within three to five years) every organization will reach its zenith in the marketplace. And at about the same time, those organizations will have pretty much reached their optimum size. Thereafter, prospect mailings will be done to offset natural attrition—usually between 20 and 35 percent annually.

Frequency of Prospect Mailing

In studying the preceding mail schedules you may also have noticed that in Year One, five prospect mailings were made (the pilot test, followed by four roll-outs). In Years Two and Three, while the total quantity increased each year, the number or frequency of mailings decreased to three per year.

This is because in Year Two you should have gained sufficient experience and judgment to plan larger single mailings which will take less of your time. You also will save money because it is less expensive to order printed materials in larger quantities.

For some organizations lacking the clerical staff to open, post, and acknowledge numerous contributions within a restricted time period, there is a drawback to larger, less frequent mailings. Often, such organizations prefer to stagger the mailings to spread the clerical work load and even

Figure 3-1. From Pilot Test To Roll-Out Success

Year One

January
(1st week)   Pilot test 75,000.

February
(2nd week)   Prepare interim analysis and projection.
(3rd week)   Schedule lists for 150,000-piece roll-out.

March
(1st week)   Verify projections and re-order printed materials.
(3rd week)   First roll-out mailing of 150,000 drops.

April   Repeat analysis, scheduling.

May
(2nd week)   Second roll-out mailing of 200,000 drops.

June   Repeat analysis, scheduling.

July   Develop a new package (or components) for testing against control package.

August
(2nd week)   Third roll-out mailing of 250,000 drops (175,000 control package/75,000 test package).

September   Repeat analysis, scheduling. Plan to mail winning package.

October
(last week)   Fourth roll-out mailing of 300,000 drops.

November   Repeat analysis, begin scheduling for next year.

December   Do final report.

Total prospect mailings in Year One: 975,000 pieces

Year Two	Pieces Mailed	Year Three	Pieces Mailed
January/February	300,000	**January/February**	500,000
April/May	300,000	**April/May**	500,000
September/October	400,000	**September/October**	500,000
Total for Year Two:	1,000,000	**Total for Year Three:**	1,500,000

out the cash flow. If your organization's structure restricts you in this way, or if you have other compelling reasons for mailing monthly, there is nothing inherently wrong with such a solution. In fact, in certain cases, it is the right way to do things.

COMPUTERIZING THE DONOR LIST (the basics)

Now you need to know what to do with the 9,750 donors you have added to your file.

The answer, of course, is to computerize. Any organization with a list of 2,000 or more that is not on computer in some way, shape, or form should be.

Our advice to almost all clients who do not *already* have a computer in-house is that they hire a service bureau—at least in the beginning. Here is our reasoning.

1. Service bureaus already have the expensive hardware in place. To be competitive with other bureaus, they must maintain the most up-to-date equipment which few nonprofit organizations can afford.
2. Service bureaus have already devised numerous programs, one of which may be exactly right for your organization, saving you the costs of recreating a program which already exists.
3. Service bureaus have trained, experienced personnel who probably know more than you ever will about how to maintain your file.
4. If you hire the wrong service bureau, you can always change. It's far more difficult to get rid of an in-house computer operation.
5. Most service bureaus prefer to take on larger files and many will not consider a file of fewer than 20,000 to be profitable. Therefore, you may have to do some searching—possibly going outside your own community—to locate a good bureau willing to service your smaller file. The search is worth the trouble.

If you follow our advice and go to an outside service bureau for your maintenance and fulfillment needs, it is important that you know what you need in order to match your organization with an existing program or to create a new program. To help you select the right service bureau and further understand the many ways the computer can help you organize to raise more money, we refer you to Chapter 10, "Making Friends With The Computer."

TRACK II
Getting Results

CHAPTER 4

Renewals: Making Your Investment Pay Dividends

In Track I you learned how to market your organization in order to build a list. While you haven't lost any money, you haven't made any either.

In this chapter, you will learn how to capitalize on your investment. The purpose of all your hard work in building a donor base is to enable you to return to those interested people year after year to raise spendable net income.

PROJECTING RENEWAL COSTS AND INCOME

Having now identified people interested in your cause, you should expect them to renew at a rate of between 8 and 20 percent each time you appeal to them. This high renewal rate, coupled with lower costs (because you no longer pay for lists for one thing) makes renewal mailings profitable indeed.

If you have followed our program thus far, you have presumably mailed 975,000 prospect pieces during the first year of acquisition and you have 9,750 donors on your file.

What will it cost to renew them and what net income can you expect to earn?

To arrive at the answer, let's backtrack for a moment and figure out what obtaining each donor cost in the first place. Your cost to mail just under one million pieces was roughly $200,000 and your gross income was about the same. Thus, each donor cost you nothing—correct?

Well, not quite. In fact, you spent approximately $1 per donor, on average, in postage due mail, in putting the donor's record on a computer system, and in acknowledging the contribution. Thus, you expended roughly $9,750 above and beyond the direct costs of acquisition. Now store that figure away for a moment while we figure how much it will cost to renew your donors and earn a surplus.

Most organizations find that in year one of their renewal campaign they are able to retain between 50 and 60 percent of their donors. Thereafter, renewal rates *can* increase to 75 and even 80 percent. However, you never wait an entire year to begin your renewal campaign. In fact, as Figure 4-1 shows, you begin renewing first-time donors in the fourth month after the pilot mailing.

IT PAYS TO PLAN AHEAD

To mail that first renewal three to four months after the initial contribution, you must begin planning your renewal campaign soon after you learn that your pilot was a success. This means that if your pilot was conducted in January, your first renewal should be sent in April or early May, the second renewal in August, the third in November, the fourth the following February, and so on. (Note: this is a mildly aggressive formula. Some would advocate a second appeal in March, a third in May, a fourth in August, a fifth in October, and a sixth in late November.)

And, because your list is growing continually as a result of continued prospect mailings, the size of the list you can renew grows also.

To help you plan your renewal campaign *in conjunction with* your prospect campaign, we have devised a chart: *Combining Quarterly Renewals with Appeals for Special Gifts* (see Figure 4-1). Note that it is based on the campaign outlined in Track I where we mailed 975,000 prospect pieces in the first year of acquisition.

Even though your file totals 9,750 donors at the end of the first year, you do not mail renewals to all these donors during that first year. The following chart illustrates how this works:

Month	File Activity	Notes
Jan.	750 New Donors	From pilot mailing.
March	1,500 New Donors	From first roll-out mailing.
April	750 Renewals	Donors from the pilot have been on the file for 3-4 months and are now ready to be renewed. A 12.5 percent response brings 94 responses.
May	2,000 New Donors	Second roll-out mailing attracts additional support for your group.
August	2,156 Renewals	Donors from the first roll-out, who have been on the file for 4-5 months are now renewed. In addition, you mail to the 656 donors who did not respond to your first renewal in April. Twelve and one-half percent equals 270.
Late August	2,500 New Donors	Larger roll-outs increase the speed at which your file grows.
Oct.	3,000 New Donors	Final roll-out for the year increases file by almost one-third.
Early Nov.	3,980 Renewals	Donors from the second roll-out have been on the file for 5-6 months and can now be renewed. Donors from the first renewal who did not respond to the second renewal can be mailed to. Finally, since the first renewal was more than six months ago, *all* of the donors to the pilot can be mailed to. At 12.5 percent, you receive 498 contributions.

End of year

Total File	Total Renewals Mailed	Total Number of Renewal Gifts
9,750	6,886	862

Recap: Each renewal mailing is sent to donors who have been on the file at least three to four months *less* those donors who have responded to the most recent renewal. This prevents donors who have just contributed from receiving an additional appeal in the same three-month period.

Now we can take a look at renewal income. Since all renewal contributions are received from people who have demonstrated an interest in your organization previously they will renew with gifts of increased size—if they are asked. In the case of our example this increases the average gift by $3, from $20 to $23.

The gross income from the first year of 862 renewals at $23 raises $19,826. From this income, subtract all costs including printing, postage, and mailing. At 25¢ per piece from three mailings totalling 6,886, the cost is $1,722. This is a realistic cost for renewal mailings of this size, if you work to keep package costs low.

To be absolutely thorough in these calculations, however, it is important to add the cost to receive, computerize, and acknowledge the donors in the first instance—roughly $1 per donor or $9,750, and another $1 per donor for repeat gifts ($1,022).

RECAP

Renewal Income	$19,826
Less	
Cost to Renew	$1,722
Original Processing Costs	9,750
This Year's Processing Costs	862
Net Income	$7,492

Thus, at the end of the first year, renewal income covers *all* expenses of mailing, file maintenance, and acknowledgments while still earning a net profit of over $7,400. To learn how renewal profits will increase in the future years, refer to Figure 4-1 which illustrates continuing growth of renewal returns in Years Two and Three. (This growth naturally depends on continued prospect mailings.)

WHEN AND HOW OFTEN TO RENEW

Too many organizations wait six to nine months or more before appealing to donors again, lest they offend donors by "bothering" them. Tests have proven, however, that when an organization waits too long to renew a gift, income from the renewal mailing actually diminishes.

On the other hand, new donors who receive an early renewal request, three to four months after the first gift, tend to respond far more generously.

To find out why, let's examine one donor case history for an entire year. For purposes of illustration, let us assume yours is a conservation organization.

In January, you send a "cold" letter to someone who had never contributed to your organization previously and who, in fact, had never before heard of your cause. That person not only opened and read your appeal, but was sufficiently motivated to make a contribution.

In late February, you acknowledged the first gift with a brief but warm letter from your chief executive officer. (Acknowledgments will be discussed later in this chapter.) It is now September and you plan a late October mailing to this group of late January donors. To those who do not respond, you plan a follow-up in December.

At first glance this seems a reasonable plan. But let us look for a moment at what has happened in the donor's life between January and October.

49

February	The same day your thank you letter arrives, the donor receives an appeal from an organization not unlike your own. He might have contributed to the competitor, but your acknowledgment letter reminds him of his gift to you.
March	Your donor receives no less than 17 appeals, including six from organizations having to do with conservation, the environment, or animal welfare. He sends a gift to his local humane society and to his local Public Broadcasting System station.
April	This month brings another dozen appeals including one from his alma mater, which gets priority.
May	Of all this month's requests, two stand out! Both are appeals from competitive organizations and both are urgent. He might have contributed $50 to one, but decides to divide his gift between them. (Note: This—the fourth month after your donor's original gift—should have brought a letter from *you*.)
June	Your donor makes his annual gift to his local hospital. He also succumbs to an appeal to send a kid to camp.
July	Back from vacation in late July, your donor finds nine appeals in his mail box and discards them all.
August	There are fewer appeals this month and they receive your donor's undivided attention. (Note: This is the month your *second* appeal should have been mailed. Had it been, he might be contributing to you instead of—*or in addition to*—your arch competitor.)
September	After Labor Day the donor receives an average of two appeals a day, including renewal appeals from the two conservation organizations to which he had contributed $25 each in May. Your donor renews both gifts. *Any why not? He didn't hear from you, did he?*
October	At last, your renewal letter finally arrives. Does the donor appreciate the fact that you haven't "bothered" him for nine months? Hardly. During this period he has received more than 150 appeal letters and has made a dozen contributions. In fact, he hardly remembers you at all. And despite the fact that your letter salutes him as "Dear Supporter," your appeal is put aside in favor of a very compelling renewal letter from his local PBS station causing him to upgrade his gift from $50 to $100. Then, having given more than he intended, he vows to make no additional gifts until next year.
November	True to his word, your donor does not respond to a single direct mail solicitation.
December	On December 3, the donor cannot resist an appeal from a children's hospital "to give a sick child a merrier Christmas." Your second renewal letter arrives on December 15, and along with 37 other *late* appeals, ends up in the trash. (Merry Christmas!)

Figure 4-1. Combining Quarterly Renewals with Appeals for Special Gifts

PROSPECT CAMPAIGN YEAR ONE   RENEWAL CAMPAIGN

Month	Mailing	# New Donors	Cumulative Donors	Mailing*	Projected Returns	List Balance*
Jan.	Pilot 75M					
Feb.		750				
March	Rollout #1 150M					
April		1,500	2,250			
May	Rollout #2 200M			Renewal #1 to 750	12.5% = 94 Gifts	656
June		2,000	4,250			
July						
August	Rollout#3 250M			Renewal #2 to 2,156	12.5% = 270 Gifts	1,980
Sept.		2,500	6,750			
Oct.	Rollout #4 300M					
Nov.		3,000	9,750	Renewal #3 to 3,980	12.5% = 498 Gifts	3,752
Dec.						
Total	975M	9,750	9,750	6,886	862	6,252

PROSPECT CAMPAIGN YEAR TWO   RENEWAL CAMPAIGN

Month	Mailing	# New Donors	Cumulative Donors	Mailing*	Projected Returns	List Balance*
Jan.	Prospect #1 300M					
Feb.		3,000	12,750	Renewal #1 to 6,252	12.5% = 782	5,968
March						
April	Prospect #2 300M					
May		3,000	15,750	Renewal #2 to 8,968	12.5% = 1,121	8,629
June						
July						
August				Renewal #3 to 11,629	12.5% = 1,454	11,296
Sept.	Prospect #3 400M					
Oct.		4,000	19,750			
Nov.				Renewal #4 to 14,296	12.5% = 1,787	13,963
Dec.						
Total	1,000M	10,000	19,750	41,145	5,144	17,963

*Note: Each renewal mailing omits those new donors who came in on the previous prospect mailing as well as those donors who responded to the preceding renewal mailing.

Figure 4–1. Combining Quarterly Renewals with Appeals for Special Gifts (Continued)

PROSPECT CAMPAIGN   YEAR THREE   **RENEWAL CAMPAIGN**

Month	Mailing	# New Donors	Cumulative Donors	Mailing*	Projected Returns	List Balance*
Jan.	Prospect #1 500M					
Feb.		5,000	24,750	Renewal #1 to 17,963	12.5% = 2,245	17,505
March						
April	Prospect #2 500M					
May		5,000	29,750	Renewal #2 to 22,505	12.5% = 2,813	21,937
June						
July						
August				Renewal #3 to 26,937	12.5% = 3,367	26,383
Sept.	Prospect #3 500M					
Oct.		5,000	34,750			
Nov.				Renewal #4 to 26,383	12.5% = 3,298	26,452
Dec.						
Total	1,500M	15,000	34,750	93,788	11,723	31,452

*Note: Each renewal mailing omits those new donors who came in on the previous prospect mailing as well as those donors who responded to the preceding renewal mailing.

The point of this depressing story is to show how easily a donor's attention can wander unless you make your presence continually felt. It *is* possible, of course, to appeal too often, and we do not recommend that you bombard your donors with monthly appeals. But we generally recommend that new donors receive appeals three to four months following their original gift, and again four to five months after making a second gift, and so on. If you follow this plan, you will find that not only will you renew up to 70 percent annually, but also that a large segment of your donor file—perhaps as large as 20 percent—will contribute *more* than once a year!

To emphasize this point, we borrow a lesson from David Ogilvy, founder of Ogilvy and Mather, and unquestionably one of the five or six advertising men who ever wrote great copy. In his book, *Ogilvy on Advertising*, Ogilvy relates the following story:

> "On a train journey to California, a friend asked Mr. Wrigley why, with the lion's share of the market, he continued to advertise his chewing gum. 'How fast do you think this train is going?' asked Wrigley. 'I would say about ninety miles an hour.' 'Well,' said Wrigley, *'do you suggest we unhitch the engine?'"*

Ogilvy then goes on to establish that consumers do not buy one brand of soap, coffee, or detergent, but that they have a repertoire of four or five brands (just as donors have a repertoire of charitable organizations that they support). The main purpose of advertising as Ogilvy sees it is not only to make new sales, but to reinforce and assure current buyers. He points out that a company can increase sales not by converting new consumers to its brand, but by inducing its *existing users to use it more often.*

Our point exactly!

WRITING THE RENEWAL LETTER

A letter written to someone who has already made a contribution should be different from a letter written to a prospect. This is not to say that the letter to the donor should be a better letter, or that it should be shorter or longer. And it certainly is not to say that it doesn't have to be as compelling—on the theory that the donor is *already* interested in your case and won't take too much convincing.

What we mean by "different" is that the renewal letter must, first and foremost, let recipients know immediately that you *recognize* their past interest, generosity, and better than average understanding of your organization. And that, because of this, the recipient is very special indeed.

And the recipient is indeed special for you already have invested $20 to add this donor to your rolls and you want to keep him or her as a long-time friend. This is your opportunity to make the most of that friendship, so don't blow your chance of success by beginning your renewal letter with the salutation, "Dear Friend."

In Chapter 10, we will discuss sending personalized letters to your donor file. But for now, let's concentrate not on special techniques, but on how to personalize a renewal letter without spending additional money.

The five simplest personalization techniques are as follows:

1. Date the renewal letter.
2. Use the salutation, Dear Member or Dear Supporter—adding, of _____ (the name of your organization).
3. Thank the donor for his *recent* past support somewhere in the opening two paragraphs.
4. In asking for a gift, refer to it as *renewed support* or a *renewed gift.*
5. Make the overall tone of your letter more personal. (Use phrases such as "as you know," "because of you," etc.)
6. In the closing, simultaneously thank the donor and ask for renewed (and increased) support.

As an example of a renewal and donor upgrade appeal, we refer you to the sample package portrayed in Figures 4-2 and 4-3.

This appeal from the Greater New York Councils/Boy Scouts of America is the most successful renewal out of a series of six mailed annually. The 1983 appeal pulled one-third of the entire gross renewal income and had a profitability ratio (income over cost) of 1,089 percent.

Although the letter is obviously preprinted, it sounds very personal by focusing on the donor and all that he or she has helped make possible. (Note illustrated case histories.) In addition, the following techniques were used:

1. Monarch-sized envelope and letter for the personal look, enhanced by the use of a live stamp.
2. Reply card designed to look official.
3. Computer fill-in on reply card stated total giving for previous year and suggested a gift amount for the current drive.

Figure 4-2. Boy Scouts of America Renewal Appeal

GREATER NEW YORK COUNCILS
345 Hudson Street, New York, N.Y. 10014

Dear Friend of Scouting,

Thanks to you, the Greater New York Councils has become the
largest Boy Scout Council in America!

No other council in this country can come close to equaling
New York's youth membership enrollment or depth and scope of
programming. And that's because New York has something about
which no other council can boast ...

... loyal friends like you!

And it's generous, selfless, caring people like you and
other supporters of Boy Scouting that deserve the credit for so
much of the tremendous growth and development we've been able
to accomplish over the years on behalf of the kids in this city.

In fact, I wrote to you last year about 4,000 New York City
boys who needed Scouting programs desperately. Our goal for
1983, with your help, was to reach as many of those youngsters
as possible with a way to put hope, pride and self-respect into
their often troubled lives.

A lot of people thought we were aiming too high, pursuing
an impossible dream. After all, very seldom does a council
increase their youth enrollment by so much in any single year....

But we did -- thanks to our real friends like you.

You and other "believers" in Boy Scouting rallied to meet
the challenge. Together, you gave us the strength we needed to
find those 4,000 deserving kids and give them their chance to be
part of the New York Scouting experience.

          By the end of 1983, our enrollment had risen
          to an unprecedented 75,000 youths!

I've got to admit it -- I'm really proud of the team spirit
we enjoy with our supporters. We don't ever want to let any of
you down. After all, when you give to the Greater New York
Councils, you're making an investment in the principles and
decent values of Scouting as well as in our young people.
You're investing in the sound traditions of hard work, good
citizenship, self-reliance and leadership. But most of all,
you're investing in teamwork -- people helping people ... kids
helping themselves and their city.

And isn't that what Scouting is really all about? Isn't that what we're all working for ... why we're investing our time, energy and our money in New York City youngsters? Together we're helping them grow into the kind of adults we'd all be proud of — brave, generous and true.

Let me tell you about a few of the special Scouts your dollars have already helped ... boys whose actions truly embody what Scouting in this City really means.

Scouting is Troop 75 in Queens taking matters into their own hands...

No one else in the community cared enough to clean up Brookville Park, but they did! And they didn't just spend one Sunday afternoon picking up pieces of litter, tin cans and broken bottles. They put their backs into it and labored for months. They carted away literally <u>tons</u> of debris. And in the end, they turned an 80-acre neighborhood disaster into a recreational jewel for everyone to enjoy.

Scouting is Anthony Chiusano of Staten Island ...

... who comes from a long line of Scouting enthusiasts — his twin brother is a Boy Scout and his father is a Scoutmaster. In order to win his Eagle Award, the highest honor to which a Scout can aspire, Anthony had to undertake an elaborate service project which, by definition, would be of significant value to his community. Anthony worked long and hard, and finally won his Eagle Badge last year by building a three-ton footbridge so visitors could enjoy strolling through their neighborhood park.

You probably remember our letter to you about Eric Sorenson ...

... the Tenderfoot Scout who awoke
one morning to the sound of a car
crash outside his Brooklyn home,
raced out the door in his pajamas,
ran barefoot over broken glass and
gasoline puddles to save the lives
of two people trapped inside in the
smouldering wreck ... a wreck that
could have ignited at any moment
like a time bomb .... all while a
handful of adults watched and
refused to help. Eric won the
coveted Heroism Award for his
bravery. But more importantly, he
won the hearts and the respect of
all New York.

And which of us could forget the poignant story of Scout John Huneke ...

... a courageous young man who,
losing a long and valiant
battle with cancer, put aside
his own personal agonies to
devote the last few weeks of
his life to helping other
people. To earn his Eagle
badge -- his ultimate life's
ambition -- he organized and
managed a major blood drive
from his hospital bed ... and
successfully recruited 100 new
donors to Lenox Hill Hospital.
"It'll pay back a little of all
that the hospital has done for me,"
John said.

    You know, there are lots of good kids in New York City who
want to be Scouts but can't ... because nobody's shown them the
way ... or given them the financial means. They are good kids
who, alone or in groups, would make us all proud.

    Because Scouting gives youngsters something to believe in ...
a standard to live up to ... a sense of belonging to something
noble and clean and powerful. And that's important to a lonely
boy growing up restless in a big, seemingly anonymous city.

We want to reach these boys. We know they won't all
rebuild community parks or perform breathtaking feats of heroics
-- although a lot of them will. But they will become people
we'd want to have as our friends and neighbors, and that's just
as important.

I'm writing you today to ask you to give us the means to
find these youngsters by renewing your commitment to the Greater
New York Councils. Now is the time to reaffirm the values we
hold in common -- and your belief in the thousands of children,
teenagers and young adults we serve together.

This year, we're setting a new goal for ourselves: 80,000
Scouts served by December 31, 1984. I think we can do it. For
all the youngsters who want to belong, I know we have to do it.
But it will take that special brand of teamwork that's made this
Council so unique. It will take a greater pledge of your
financial support than we've ever asked before.

Don't let us down. Please mark your increased gift on the
enclosed personalized renewal card, and mail it with your tax-
deductible contribution today. Don't put it off for another
time -- it's too important to risk forgetting. Do it now -- for
all the Scouts and future Scouts of New York City. Thank you.

Sincerely,

Ralph Darian

P.S. It takes only $53 to bring Scouting to a boy in New York
     City. The reason for this low cost is the efficient way
     in which the Greater New York Councils is organized. Of
     our 25,000 adult leaders, only about 100 professionals are
     salaried workers. This means that more than 90% of our
     annual operating budget goes directly into our programs and
     services for the kids.

     And that also means that every donation of $53 or more
     directly assists us in reaching one or more deserving boys
     with a valuable Scouting experience. How many youngsters
     will you help today? Please give $53, $106, $159, or
     whatever you can afford now. On behalf of all our boys,
     thank you.

Figure 4-3. Boy Scouts of America
Personalized Response Card

GREATER NEW YORK COUNCILS 345 Hudson Street, New York, N.Y. 10014
(212) 242-1100

IT'S TIME TO RENEW

THANKS TO YOUR GENEROSITY IN 1982 TOTALLING $15,
75,000 YOUTHS ARE NOW INVOLVED IN SCOUTING PROGRAMS.
HELP US REACH 80,000 SCOUTS IN 1984 BY GIVING $25.

AMOUNT ENCLOSED ....

07452PINCU001946   C84A

MR P SEYMOUR
94 MARDEL AVE
GLEN, NJ 07452

The Boy Scouts depends entirely upon your generous support. The Greater New York Councils does not receive funds from the Tri-State United Way. Please help us reach the many young people who need us by sending in your contribution today!

Warmest Thanks,

Ralph Darian, Scout Executive

Return this card with your tax-deductible gift today!

RENEWING MEMBERS

If yours is a true membership organization in which members receive benefits such as membership cards, discounts on products, regular magazines, or other publications, and if memberships have expiration dates at given points in the year—renewal methods will differ from those used to renew donors.

Naturally, you cannot ask members to renew four months after they have joined. However, you can start writing to them several months *prior* to expiration asking for early renewal.

One traditional renewal plan uses the following format:

First Appeal:	Two months prior to expiration
Second Appeal:	One month prior to expiration
Third Appeal:	Month *of* expiration
Fourth Appeal:	Month after expiration
Fifth Appeal:	Two months after expiration
Recapture Mailing:	Five months after expiration

For renewal mailings to be most effective, it is important to vary the way the letter looks and reads. There is no set rule for achieving the best results, and we encourage you to experiment with various copy approaches and with mailing schedules as well. Following is one technique that has been successful for several of our clients.

First Appeal:	Renewal notice (in bill form) accompanied by a short note from the Membership Director asking the member to renew early.
Second Appeal:	Renewal notice with no other enclosure. But the envelope is over-printed with a line similar to "Your Membership Expires Next Month."

Third Appeal:	Renewal notice accompanied by an interim membership card and a note from the Executive Director stating that membership expires *this* month, and that the real membership card will be sent as soon as the member's dues are received.
Fourth Appeal:	No renewal notice this time; just a note with the message, "Did you forget to send your dues last month, or did your check cross this follow-up in the mail?"
Fifth Appeal:	A full letter reminding the member of how much you valued his support and stating that if he renews now, you will send him all the benefits (magazines, etc.) that he may have missed.
Recapture Mailing:	This letter asks the donor whether he misses belonging and the benefits of membership, and goes on to describe some of the aspects that might have compelled him to join in the first place. You might wish to leave room at the bottom of your letter (with ruled lines) for the member to let you know why he hasn't renewed until now, or why he is not going to renew.

This is not the end. Each and every time you send a renewal mailing to your dwindling file, you will reenlist new members. And while each successive mailing will enlist fewer members, rarely will a mailing not make a profit.

After the Recapture Mailing, wait five months and send your former members a prospect letter. We will wager that the returns on this lapsed list will do as well, if not better, than returns on any of your best cold prospect lists. Continue using the lapsed list every six months until it is no longer profitable.

ASKING MEMBERS FOR SPECIAL GIFTS

Even more important—in terms of fund raising—you *can* ask members *at any time* to make a special contribution, above and beyond membership dues.

Why, you may ask, should donors who have already paid their dues and who are already receiving all the benefits of membership want to make an additional contribution to your organization?

The answer is that if your members do not care enough about your organization to provide extra support, no one else will either. The fact is, if people are interested enough in your organization to join in the first place, and if they are not disappointed in membership services, they become prime prospects for giving even more. That is, if your appeals are timely and compelling.

You cannot expect members to respond to an appeal that simply says, "We need more money than we raise from membership dues." To motivate your donors to send a gift equal to or even larger than the amount they paid to join in the first place, you must be creative. But then, you must also be creative to compel a new *donor* to give an additional gift during the course of the year. It's the same thing, except that the timing of the mailings is a little different.

When writing a letter requesting a gift above and beyond membership dues or a special gift, do not ask for a *general* contribution. Rather, ask for money for a *specific project* or, if you find that too restrictive, at least describe a specific project for which your organization needs help.

For example, if yours is an educational institution, describe your need for a bus to take students on special tours, or the need for scholarship funds for especially needy students. If you represent a youth organization, describe your project to take city kids to the country, or a special neighborhood beautification program. If you work for a conservation organization, talk about specific problems you are helping to solve, such as acid rain, or your project to save a particular animal species.

Focusing on a special project to generate renewed gifts is of particular importance because you are going to be writing to most donors at least four times a year. And if you want them to pay attention you'd best vary your appeals as you proceed. Even if you find that one particular appeal meets with unusually high success, it is probably best to alter that renewal at some point by changing the envelope or the opening paragraph, so that when the donor receives it the immediate response is not "Oh, I've seen this one before."

Many people tell us that their organization simply doesn't have a variety of compelling projects for which to raise funds—that all the monies raised are used for one purpose and one purpose only. If that is the case in your institution, then the challenge becomes one of finding new ways of presenting the same old story.

Some new ways might include different letter signers, different colors, different stationery, or different envelope teasers. But aside from format, there are possibilities to make each appeal unique.

For example, if your organization *only* raises funds to send needy children to camp, then tell your story in the words of one child who yearns to go to camp. Then the next time, tell the story through a child who recently returned from camp. And the next time, have a parent of a child tell the story and so on.

We have never encountered an organization that could not vary its appeals if it tried hard enough.

RENEWAL AND UPGRADING STRATEGIES

Offering Premiums

Another technique that often prompts renewal—especially renewal at a higher category—is the offer of a special bonus for a gift of a specified amount.

In choosing your premium, be certain that it is appropriate to your organization. For example, T-shirts and backpacks are appropriate to a conservation or recreation organization but might not be appropriate to another group. On the other hand, the *right* books, posters, calendars, bumper stickers, etc.—if relevant to the cause—are welcomed by almost everyone.

You need not feel confined to offering the usual type of premium. Certain organizations whose constituencies are more active and personally committed to the cause often welcome special benefits such as being invited to staff or board meetings, receiving "in-house" briefing papers, and even (for major donors) personal updates by the Executive Director or another member of the senior staff. (Let your imagination wander through what your organization might have to offer.)

Finally, almost everyone who has made a substantial contribution (especially if it is larger than that which has been customary) appreciates receiving attractive certificates of appreciation. In the final analysis, *recognition* of the donor is key.

Matching Gifts

One highly effective method for motivating renewed gifts (and new gifts as well) is that of a matching gift. Were this a simple matter, every appeal in the mail would employ the technique. But the matching gift first has to be secured from a donor who understands how his gift may be parlayed into a greater amount.

Matching gifts can be done on a two-to-one, four-to-one, or any other basis. The point is, you are able to state in your letter, that for every $1 the donor contributes, the X Foundation (or an anonymous benefactor) will contribute $3 (or whatever the amount might be).

To maximize the effectiveness of this approach, do not fail to illustrate what this figure means to the donor. In other words, if Mr. Smith will contribute $25, his gift will actually be worth three times that amount—or $75.

For many people, it's an offer they can't refuse.

Other Techniques

For some organizations, premiums are not suitable and matching gifts not possible. How else then do you get a $15 donor to consider giving $25 or a $50 donor to consider a gift of $75 to $100?

There's one sure way *not* to achieve the desired response: don't ask for more money. This seems obvious, but too many organizations are *embarrassed* to ask a donor to upgrade his gift. So instead of writing a compelling letter asking in a straightforward way for a larger gift, they write archly: "Won't you consider increasing last year's contribution?"

What the letter should have said is: "Last year you contributed $50, which helped us send a child to camp. But did you know that for only a little more—$75—you can *personally* send one child to camp for an entire week?"

In a large file, to mention a specific donor's previous gift requires personalized or computer-generated letters. If you can't afford this, you can always segment your donor list and ask each segment to give at the next category. Here is how it works.

First, you segment your file by gift size: donors giving between $10 and $24.99, donors giving between $25 and $49.99, donors giving between $50 and $75.

After the list is segmented, send the same basic *printed* letter without reference to a specific donor's past gift. However, one element changes from letter to letter: the requested gift amount. Ask the first category to contribute $25, the second category to contribute $75, and the third category to contribute $100. And tell what each increased gift will do.

Suppose that you have figured out that it costs $26.10 to send one child to camp for a week, or $51.90 to purchase a month's food supply. Do you round off the dollar amount and ask for gifts of $25 or $50? We suggest that you do not. This is especially true when the *actual* amount needed is slightly larger than the standard gift requests of $25, $50, $75, and $100. In the case of a gift of $51.90 it doesn't take too many additional $1.90 contributions to pay for the cost of postage for the entire mailing.

But the fact that this technique brings in additional income is only one reason for using it. Odd dollar amounts are meaningful. They show that you've done your homework carefully and not just guessed a figure. What is more, the use of this technique often increases not only the average gift but the percent return as well.

TWO SPECIAL SYSTEMS WORTH LOOKING AT

In addition to our traditional advice on renewing and upgrading your members and donors, we call to your attention two unique systems which—if right for your organization—may help to maximize the potential of many of your donors.

The first, Electronic Funds Transfer (EFT) was unknown in charitable giving just five years ago, but is gaining acceptance. The second, an innovative system called "Profiles" is brand new, and might be likened to a *Foundation Directory* of individuals.

ELECTRONIC FUNDS TRANSFER FOR AUTOMATIC MONTHLY GIVING PROGRAMS

Nonprofits constantly are being told that they must contain costs and increase their income to stay ahead of inflation. One way to increase revenue is to explore monthly giving programs.

Monthly giving is, of course, not new. Many religious organizations and some political and cause groups have used it with great success for many years. However, administering such programs can be a real headache and quite costly if the monthly amounts collected are small. This is one reason many nonprofits avoid monthly giving programs.

An efficient alternative is automatic monthly giving programs that work via EFT—electronic funds transfer.

EFT was legalized for interstate banking in 1979. Since then, it has spread rapidly and has many applications, such as direct deposit of payroll, social security, and pension checks; point-of-sale terminals; billpaying by phone; home banking; and pre-authorized transfers.

The last of these is of interest to development officers who wish to institute automatic monthly giving programs. A person may now pre-authorize automatic payment of mortgages, insurance premiums, utility bills, membership dues, and pledges to charitable groups. For pre-authorized charitable giving, the donor signs a special form and returns it to the charity along with a check for the first month's payment. The check provides the bank the checking account numbers necessary to facilitate the electronic transfer of the monthly debits. It also provides the charity with immediate money while the paperwork is being completed to place the donor on the EFT system.

We have found EFT programs particularly effective on renewal appeals directed to the lower end of the giving spectrum. It should be coordinated carefully with telemarketing of direct mail schedules to maximize effectiveness. EFT programs can increase per capita giving significantly because total gifts are spread over many months.

EFT is really akin to payroll deduction for United Way—i.e., it allows a gift to fit conveniently into the small contributor's budget. For instance, it's not unusual for a $25 a year donor to authorize a $5 per month or $60 annual gift. Nor is it unusual for $50 a year donors to authorize $10 to $15 a month, which means $120 to $180 annual gifts.

Increased contributor retention is another major benefit of pre-authorized gifts. Because a donor's gift is made automatically each month, it requires a decision to stop support. This means that a letter or phone call from the donor to the organization receiving his support is required to terminate the payments. This "negative option" feature is troublesome to some nonprofits, but the simplest and most honest solution is for the institution to let their EFT donors know that they can stop at any time.

The steady and predictable cash flow provided by an automatic monthly contribution plan is helpful to many nonprofits in their budgeting and financial planning. And as EFT gains increased acceptance, it is sure to play an increasing role in fund raising in years to come.

For additional information, contact EFT at 1010 Turquoise Street, Suite 315, San Diego, CA 92109.

PROFILES: IDENTIFYING DONORS CAPABLE OF INCREASED GIVING

Nearly every charitable organization with a donor list of decent size suffers the frustration of knowing that there are unidentified people among their large group of donors who have the capacity to increase their giving substantially if only they were given special attention. Most organizations conduct some research to identify these people but, because of the enormous cost involved, that research usually is limited to donors of $100 or more—only a tiny fraction of most organizations' donor lists. On a list as small as 10,000 donors, the job of researching more than that tiny fraction is far too costly and practically impossible.

A new service has been founded recently—Profiles, Inc.—which seeks to solve this problem. Profiles, Inc., has created a huge data base made up of donor information on hundreds of thousands of the largest charitable donors in the United States. The information is current and detailed. Profiles, Inc., sells subscriptions to its service which allows subscribing organizations to overlay their own donor list against the Profiles data base. In this way they can identify those of their donors whose actual charitable giving to other groups indicates a capacity to increase their support to the subscriber.

In addition, Profiles is developing biographical material, all from public sources, on most of the donors in their data base. By the end of 1985, they will be in a position not only to tell a subscriber that, for example, Mr. John Smith, who is giving them $30, gives substantially more to other charities, but also to provide the kind of key biographical material needed to plan a successful solicitation. Finally, Profiles can identify a subscriber's donors who are trustees.

Profiles subscribers pay fees starting at $600 per month, for organizations with donor lists of 10,000 or fewer names. Fees increase based on the size of the organization's list. The subscription fee entitles them to identify potential large gift donors at the beginning of the year by comparing their files to Profiles' and to continue to use the service to identify large donor prospects from among new donors throughout the year.

The benefits to subscribers are obvious. The Profiles system will identify who among their entire list of donors has the potential to become a larger contributor thus helping to set priorities for their annual special gift campaigns, deferred and other planned giving, capital campaigns, and the like. The system also will help to identify the smaller donors who, although they may not have the capacity to be considered large gift prospects, are prospects for increased giving at a smaller level. The subscribing organization can adjust its renewal system to take advantage of this information.

There are also benefits for the donor. As organizations learn more about a donor's charitable interests, they will be able to eliminate much of the annoying "shotgun" solicitation of donors for support of programs and projects in which the donor has no interest. Further, by centralizing this research in one place, Profiles is able to provide information to charitable organizations at a cost significantly below what the organization would have to spend if it tried to undertake the research alone. This can mean more efficient fund raising and, thus, a larger portion of the donor's dollar being spent to further the organization's charitable program.

For additional information, contact Profiles at 300 Lexington Avenue, Suite 1901, New York, NY 10168.

THE CARE AND FEEDING OF MAJOR DONORS

A major donor to one organization is a small or medium size donor to another. If half of your donors give $40 or more, then you probably consider donors of more than $100 to be major. On the other hand, if the majority of your list is made up of gifts under $20, then a $50 contributor is a major resource.

Regardless of the dollar amount, it is important to maintain a special relationship with your major donors. We advocate treating *all* donors as though they were special through thank you letters, annual reports, and responses to letters of complaint as well as to letters of praise. If you already are doing these things, how do you go a step further with your major donors?

Here are ten ideas to consider:
1. Use a first class "live" stamp in soliciting their gift.
2. Send a personalized letter.
3. Acknowledge the gift within three days.
4. Acknowledge the gift with a telephone call. (The donor will never forget this!)
5. Acknowledge the gift with a letter from the person who benefited from the donor's gift (i.e., recipient of a scholarship, etc.).
6. Visit the donor. (Provide members of your executive staff, board, and other volunteers with lists of major donors in their area, or match a list to someone's travel schedule.)
7. List the donor's gift in your magazine or newsletter (with permission, of course).

8. Hold an annual special event at which you honor major donors and volunteers.
9. Invite the donor to join a special committee or even the board. Involve the donor in your fund-raising campaign.
10. Establish a Special Gifts Club for donors whose present level of giving indicates that they can afford more if properly motivated. For an excellent example of how this technique can work, read the appeal (see Figure 4-4) from Leontyne Price in behalf of WETA's "26/91 Club" in Washington, D.C.

In sum, keep your donors involved. An involved donor who feels he is important to you will maintain his friendship and therefore his support for many years to come.

Figure 4-4. WETA Special Gifts Club Appeal

Leontyne Price

January 27, 1984

Mr. Chris Cunning
14 S Joy St
Arlington, VA 22202

Dear Mr. Cunning:

There is nothing like the thrill of opening
night at the opera. Except, perhaps, opening at The
White House!

You will know what I mean if you watched "In
Performance at The White House" this past September
on WETA.

On that occasion, I had the pleasure of intro-
ducing six exceptionally talented young opera singers,
and was honored to perform myself.

That evening was very special to me, and I was
grateful to share it with thousands of others (perhaps
you were among them) through WETA's simulcast of the
program on TV 26 and FM Radio 91.

As one who has a special appreciation of WETA,
I'm sure this is just one of the many exciting presen-
tations you have experienced as a viewer and listener.
Whether it's been the drama of a "Masterpiece Theatre,"
"Tinker, Tailor," or "Brideshead Revisited,"... the
fascinating and awe-inspiring "Cosmos" or "Nova"...
or the in-depth reporting and commentary of "The
Macneil/Lehrer News Hour" and "All Things Considered,"
you know you've been able to count on WETA for a rich
diversity of cultural and educational experiences each
day of the year.

That is why I'm sure you share my sentiments
about the tremendous importance of public broadcast-
ing to the people of this community. For that reason,
and because you are in the vanguard of those supporting WETA, I want to extend to you a special invitation
to join WETA's "2691 Club."

Members of the "2691 Club" (named after WETA's television and radio call numbers -- 26 and 91 respectively) contribute $1,000 or more to WETA annually. There are some exciting benefits to members which WETA's Chairman, Aaron Goldman, describes in his accompanying letter. These benefits could be reason enough for joining, but it's what your membership will do to help the Washington community that compels me to invite you to join.

You see, WETA is available to virtually everyone. Many who cannot afford to attend a play or concert or opera are able to attend these cultural events through WETA. Moreover, subjects ranging from art to science to history enlighten and enrich all those who discover these fields through public television and radio.

Your past generous support has helped WETA to sustain itself as a non-commercial station; one which can freely present such superb shows without worrying about the so-called "ratings game." This means a college student can learn about foreign affairs by watching "Vietnam: A Television History." A business person can keep informed about the stock market through "Wall Street Week." A child can learn everything from arithmetic to life on "Sesame Street" and "Mister Rogers." And I wouldn't want to forget about all the opera lovers in Washington either!

The list could go on, and if you have ever had to miss your own favorite WETA program due to unavoidable circumstances, you realize even more how it enhances our lives. Those times when you are unable to enjoy public television and radio remind you how much you really do appreciate all it offers. Perhaps that is why there are over 125,000 supporters of WETA who contribute to maintain its tradition of quality programming.

Yet in this endeavor, there is a need for a special group of people to step forward and make the extra pledge to excellence. Currently, more than 140 people have made such a pledge by joining the "2691 Club." (They are listed on the enclosed invitation.) Through their efforts, we are building for the future with the security that these concerned members are behind us.

I recall discussing my life in the opera with a correspondent from The Washington Post. I told him that I was never relaxed or complacent, and believed that it was dangerous for anyone to rest on past laurels. Then I mentioned the most wonderful thing about being an artist -- the constant creating.

When I think about what WETA gives to the Washington area community, and what you yourself have given to support it, I find these comments relevant to WETA's "career" as well. After all, in twenty-two short years it has brought countless hours of pleasure to countless numbers of people. Its innovation and creativity make us all proud.

But if we should ever become complacent, something very dear to this area will be threatened. Indeed, like the young opera singers I told you about at the beginning of this letter, WETA needs the nourishment and encouragement of its friends to reach its full potential.

Please accept my invitation to join the "2691 Club" so that we can do just that.

Thank you most sincerely,

Leontyne Price

Leontyne Price

P.S. I hope you were able to watch my performance of gospel music with the Howard University Choir under musical director Howard Roberts last month. It was simulcast on Channel 26 and FM 91. I believe it typifies the excellent programming you can always count on from WETA.

Also, please remember to read Aaron Goldman's letter explaining the membership benefits in the "2691 Club."

ACKNOWLEDGING GIFTS

We have just emphasized the importance of thanking a major donor by mail within a few days, or even telephoning him. What about acknowledgments in general? Is it sufficient to note in your letter or on your response card that "To help us save money, gifts will not be acknowledged unless specifically requested"?

We believe that most donors would like to know that you received their gift and that it meant something to you. Not only would they like to know, they are *entitled* to know. In an ideal world, you would send a *personal* thank you letter for every gift your organization receives regardless of the amount. But this is not a practical or affordable undertaking for most organizations. What, then, are your alternatives?

You can send a *form* thank you. At least, you can send a form thank you to your smaller donors. We still believe that major donors should receive a personalized acknowledgment.

But even with form letters there are certain techniques that can be employed to make the donor feel good. For example, a postcard might read as follows:

Dear Supporter:

While this post card is inexpensive, we do not stint on the heartfelt thanks that it conveys. Your contribution is deeply appreciated by our staff, our board, and most of all by the children we serve. And although the money we have saved by acknowledging your gift in this manner does not amount to much by itself, it adds up to a lot when you consider that quite a number of other wonderful people were moved to contribute as you did.

And I know that you and the others who wanted their gifts to be used to send a child to camp will be thrilled to know that, because you are understanding of this simple "thank you," another boy and another girl are experiencing the joy of camp this very summer.

On their behalf, I thank you doubly.

Sincerely,

If you had sent a $10 contribution, would you be offended by this charming card? Of course not! In fact, it might motivate you to send another, perhaps larger, contribution. And that is precisely why the post card is a weaker format than a form letter carrying the same message. *Because a form letter is mailed in an envelope in which you can include another, specially coded, business reply envelope.* And believe it or not, many of your donors will use it to send an additional gift!

LAPSED DONORS: DON'T LET THEM GET AWAY

At this point, many people ask: "What can I do about donors who don't renew after three or four appeals?"

The answer is that you continue writing to them at periodic intervals until the mailings no longer prove profitable. By profitable, we mean that you continue mailing until your lapsed house list stops being *as effective as* pure prospect lists. Most mailers find that their own lapsed donors are their *most* lucrative prospect list—almost always earning *net* income.

68

TRACK III
Getting Creative

CHAPTER 5

Creating the Direct Mail Package

Since its founding in 1940, the Oram firm has created thousands of direct mail appeals for education, health, welfare, social action, civil rights, the environment, and the visual and performing arts.

In the 1940s and 1950s direct mail was not as widespread as now and competition was not as keen. The great concerns of that time for which our firm worked—the nearly fatal wounds of the great Depression, the mass movement for social justice, and the needs produced by World War II—produced issues of such dramatic consequence that they rarely required much in the way of cosmetics or gimmicks to produce remarkably successful results.

TEN RULES FROM THE PAST

The firm's founder, Harold L. Oram, was a brilliant copywriter who taught the authors of this book his own ten rules, which he never read in *any* book.

1. Hand-type all envelopes.
2. Use first class postage whenever possible.
3. Use one-line salutations on otherwise printed letters. People won't be fooled, but they like to see their names anyhow.
4. Write the opening paragraph as if describing a matter of life or death. *It often is.*
5. Make the letter urgent and keep it brief. People are busy.
6. Ask straightforwardly—even forcefully—for the gift and explain what it will do.
7. List the board of directors without fail.
8. Endeavor to get the most distinguished, most credible signer possible.
9. Make the letter look like a real letter. Don't typeset it.
10. *Believe* in what you write—or else you will lose part of your soul and soon become a hack.

Retired in 1979, Harold L. Oram has witnessed many changes over time. But he also has seen many of his basic tenets verified and even lauded.

Of his ten basic rules, there is only one with which we would quarrel today. That is, of course, the length of the letter. Other seemingly arcane rules such as hand-typing envelopes, using one-line salutations on printed letters, and using first class postage on prospect letters may seem anachronistic. They are not.

First class postage has been abandoned largely because soaring costs make its use prohibitive. If it still cost between six and ten cents to mail first class, as it did in the beginning of our careers, we still would be doing it. As for hand-typed envelopes and one-line salutations, the computer has taken over these functions of personalization. But the theory remains valid.

The industry has changed, however. In fact, until ten years ago, it couldn't even be called an industry. Competition for the philanthropic dollar grows ever stronger as thousands of new nonprofits come onto the scene each year. As a result, all of us are forced to experiment with new techniques, new ideas, new incentives, all the while struggling to keep within hard-line budgets as inflation mocks our efforts.

Not all of what you are about to read on creating the direct mail package will be new to you. Moreover, you may not always agree with us. Still, it is important for you to know that we have not included here any ideas, suggestions, or techniques which we have not thoroughly tested on behalf of one or more of our own clients over long periods of time. What is more, we will show you not only those ideas that worked, but also (in Chapter 6) some that did not.

This chapter covers seven topics:

Part I: The Letter
Part II: The Response Device
Part III: The Envelope
Part IV: Other Enclosures
Part V: The Package as a Whole
Part VI: The Integrity of the Appeal

PART I. THE LETTER

Almost everyone agrees that the letter is the most important component of the direct mail package. We therefore have chosen to begin here—focusing on four critical lessons of letter writing:

Lesson Number 1: STYLE
Memorize these words: tone, flow, suspense, personality, language.
Lesson Number 2: FORMAT
Your letter should follow a pattern: create interest . . . state the problem . . . arouse emotion . . . offer hope . . . offer participation . . . induce response . . . offer thanks.
Lesson Number 3: CREDIBILITY
Your credibility is established by your board or other committee, the letter signer, the length of the letter, the address from which the letter comes, the address to which your contributions are to be mailed.
Lesson Number 4: APPEARANCE
You have to pay attention to such details as layout, letterhead, paper stock, typeface, margins, subheads, underlining, marginal notations, color, and art.

LESSON NUMBER 1: STYLE

Most experienced direct mail letter writers have developed a style of their own. And although they may not realize it, they pay careful attention to the following five elements of style:

- Tone
- Flow
- Suspense
- Personality
- Language

Tone

Before you begin, give careful thought to the tone your letter will take. Is your letter going to be gloom and doom? Is it going to be upbeat? Is it going to play on guilt? (This is a step beyond tugging on heartstrings.) Will you describe, in detail, the process of a child starving to death? Or will you alter the tone by being less graphic?

Flow

Flow is critical in a fund-raising letter if you want your reader to read all—or at least most—of what you have to say. Flow is construction and order and logic—but it is much more than any of these things. To achieve good flow, you will have to do a lot of cutting and pasting on your draft letter, and when you have finished, you will probably have to do it again to get it exactly right. (Remember—your best lead is probably buried in the copy.) The same is often true with the P.S. and the punch line. Pretend you are writing a suspense novel when you work to achieve flow in your letter.

Suspense

Suspense is that aspect of style which pulls you into the letter and won't let you put it down until you have reached the end. Books that have suspense are called page turners. Fund-raising letters that have suspense are called money makers.

Personality

Each letter has, or should have, a personality. The first draft cannot help but take on the personality of the writer. But the second and third drafts should begin to assume the personality of the signer to give the letter credibility. A letter signed by a woman should not sound like a letter from a man. The differences are subtle, but they are there. Similarly, a letter from the president of a college should sound altogether different from the accompanying endorsement letter from a famous alumnus. A letter from anyone appealing to a midwestern constituency should have a different personality from a letter to an eastern constituency. This is not always easy to achieve in mass mail, but it can be done.

Personality becomes critical when you draft a letter for a celebrity. When Oram Group Marketing wrote a letter from Helen Hayes we endeavored to make it sound soft, caring, and dignified. When the letter was written from Bob Hope we attempted to make it sound like his televised appearances with the troops overseas.

Language

Writing the fund-raising letter is not like writing a newsletter or an annual report to donors or a bequest brochure or a funding proposal. Rather it is a combination of a letter to a friend, a hard-hitting political speech, and an irresistible sales pitch.

You will doubtless recognize the following phrases:

> And in just a moment, I'll tell you how . . . but first . . .
>
> I am writing to you not as an _____ but as a _____ . . .
>
> Here is what is at stake!
>
> Your help is desperately needed.
>
> If you have not yet decided whether to join, let me . . .
>
> Please don't delay . . . time is not on our side.
>
> And that's where you come in . . .
>
> If you agree with me (or if this idea touches you) please read on . . .
>
> Here is what I would like you to do . . .
>
> But what is even worse . . .
>
> My pledge to you is this . . .

There are hundreds of such phrases. You may call them hackneyed or trite. They may be. But the point is that this tried and true fund-raising language works. By using phrases like those above, you can draw the reader further into your appeal.

We encourage you to come up with new phrases of your own. But until such time as you have mastered the art of using proven fund-raising language, we caution you not to deviate too much. Besides, you will be surprised at how original you can be even when following the rules.

LESSON NUMBER 2: FORMAT

Now it's time to sit down at your typewriter and actually compose a fund-raising letter. Before you begin, however, please develop a plan. Call it an outline or a format, but do it first.

Following is our recommended guideline:

1. Create interest
2. State the problem
3. Arouse emotion
4. Offer hope
5. Offer participation
6. Induce response (ask for the gift)
7. Offer thanks

Let us for a moment compare this outline, or format, to that used by many novelists seeking to write best sellers. Both the novel and the fund-raising letter try to set the hook (*create interest*) in the very beginning. Then the novelist describes the hero's struggle for life against poverty, oppression, disease, loneliness, or whatever (*state the problem*); makes you identify with the story's characters by making them sympathetic (*arouse emotion*); gives you a tantalizing glimpse at the happy ending (*offer hope*); and makes you feel while you are reading the story that you are actually a part of it (*offer participation*).

In just a moment we will discuss each element of the format or outline. But first, let us show you an exceptional fund-raising letter.

The first thing you will notice is that it is not a long letter as we have been advocating. Let us be clear about long vs. short letters. A letter should be as long as is required to tell your story. This example is *exactly* as long as it needs to be.

The second thing you will notice is that the letter follows all of the seven rules for successful letter writing just stated. Moreover, it follows rules we haven't even discussed yet.

If you can write a letter that pays off as well as this one did for its author, you may already be an expert.

Figure 5-1: The Perfect Fund-Raising Letter

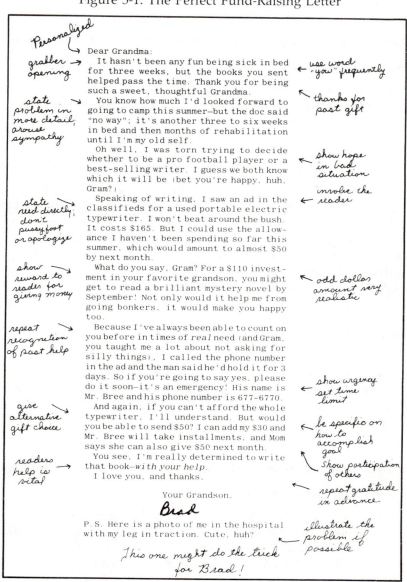

Personalized

grabber opening →

Dear Grandma:

It hasn't been any fun being sick in bed for three weeks, but the books you sent helped pass the time. Thank you for being such a sweet, thoughtful Grandma.

← use word "you" frequently

← thanks for past gift

state problem in more detail; arouse sympathy →

You know how much I'd looked forward to going to camp this summer—but the doc said "no way"; it's another three to six weeks in bed and then months of rehabilitation until I'm my old self.

Oh well, I was torn trying to decide whether to be a pro football player or a best-selling writer. I guess we both know which it will be (bet you're happy, huh, Gram?)

← show hope in bad situation

← involve the reader

state need directly, don't pussyfoot or apologize →

Speaking of writing, I saw an ad in the classifieds for a used portable electric typewriter. I won't beat around the bush. It costs $165. But I could use the allowance I haven't been spending so far this summer, which would amount to almost $50 by next month.

show reward to reader for giving money →

What do you say, Gram? For a $110 investment in your favorite grandson, you might get to read a brilliant mystery novel by September! Not only would it help me from going bonkers, it would make you happy too.

← odd dollar amount very realistic

repeat recognition of past help →

Because I've always been able to count on you before in times of *real* need (and Gram, you taught me a lot about not asking for silly things), I called the phone number in the ad and the man said he'd hold it for 3 days. So if you're going to say yes, please do it soon—it's an emergency! His name is Mr. Bree and his phone number is 677-6770.

give alternative gift choice →

And again, if you can't afford the whole typewriter, I'll understand. But would you be able to send $50? I can add my $30 and Mr. Bree will take installments, and Mom says she can also give $50 next month.

← show urgency set time limit

← be specific on how to accomplish goal

readers help is vital →

You see, I'm really determined to write that book—*with your help*.

I love you, and thanks.

← show participation of others

← repeat gratitude in advance

Your Grandson,

Brad

P.S. Here is a photo of me in the hospital with my leg in traction. Cute, huh?

← illustrate the problem if possible

This one might do the trick for Brad!

Create Interest

If you do not create strong interest in the first few sentences of your letter, your reader will never know how brilliant your second paragraph was. Here are two grabbers from highly successful campaigns.

- **Prospect letter for the Girl Scout Council of Greater New York, N.Y.**

    I am writing to you not as an actress—but as the mother of a Girl Scout and as a Girl Scout Leader. I know how valuable the Girl Scout experience is because I know how much happiness and personal fulfillment it brought me and my daughter Mary before she died of polio when she was just 19.

    (Signed by Helen Hayes)

- **Prospect letter for the Vietnam Veterans Memorial Fund, Washington, D.C.**

    I'm offering you the opportunity to take an active part in a project that is long overdue.

    It has been over seven years since America ended its involvement in the Vietnam war—the longest, and certainly the most controversial war in our nation's history.

    (Signed by Bob Hope)

(See Figures 5-2 and 5-3 for the complete letters.)

Writing an opening that keeps one reading is probably the most difficult thing to do in any form of writing. Look for your lead in the body copy of the letter. After you have written your entire letter, put it aside for a time and return to it fresh. In almost every case you will find a better opening sentence or paragraph buried in the body copy of your letter.

Following are five paired leads. The first of each is as originally written. The second lead (the lead actually used) was in each case "discovered" in the body copy of the letter. See whether you agree with our final choices (the complete letters—Figures 5-4 through 5-8—follow these examples):

- **Renewal letter for the Sea Turtle Rescue Fund, Washington, D.C.**

    Good: Every year, in Michoacan, Mexico, more than 20,000 breeding turtles are being slaughtered annually by Aztec Indian fishermen.

    Better: For just $15.67 you can "adopt" a nest of green turtle eggs and take part in a unique project designed to help rescue these wonderful creatures from extinction.

- **Prospect letter for membership in the Appalachian Mountain Club, Boston, Mass.**

    Good: Dear Outdoor Enthusiast,

    This is your invitation to membership in the Appalachian Mountain Club (AMC), the nation's oldest and largest outdoor recreation and conservation organization. We're made up of 30,000 members from Maine to Delaware who enjoy just about every wholesome and exciting outdoor activity you can imagine.

Better: Dear Outdoor Enthusiast,

This should be a very welcome letter . . .

You see, I've got something that I'm pretty sure you want—at the right time, place and price. I'm offering affordable, year-round outdoor recreation and vacation opportunities for you and your entire family.

Interested? Read on.

- **Prospect letter for Gallaudet College, Washington, D.C. (liberal arts college for the deaf)**

  Good: Helen Keller once said that if she could live again, she would dedicate more of her time to deaf people and their problems. "Deafness," she said, "is a much worse misfortune because of the loss of the most vital stimulus—the sound of the voice that brings language, sets thoughts astir, and keeps us in the intellectual company of man."

  Better: (A photograph precedes the following copy.)
  Dear Friend:

  You are looking at two of the best reasons I know why Gallaudet College needs and deserves your support: Doris Wilding and Ken Bader, students at Gallaudet, are both deaf. Yet in a few years they will take their places in a hearing society in careers that may surprise you . . . thanks to Gallaudet College.

- **Prospect letter for the ASPCA**

  Good: Dear Friend:

  The ASPCA—America's first humane society—has battled ignorance and cruelty for generations. We have turned the outrage of concerned citizens into a tough, hardworking program to protect and save animals of every kind . . .

  Better: Dear New Yorker:

  Were you aware that in last summer's brutal heat wave:
    - three horses collapsed and died in Midtown (July 18)
    - a fourth horse died in Central Park (August 5)
  And were you aware that: only one humane society took direct action—The ASPCA!

- **Prospect letter for the American-Israel Public Affairs Committee, Washington, D.C.**

  Good: Because you care about America, I appeal to you to help our government avert a political and military blunder that will jeopardize our own national interests.

  Better: AIPAC desperately needs your help to stop the sale of the AWACS to Saudi Arabia. And we need your help immediately because the Administration will begin the Congressional approval process *tomorrow!*

Do these revised beginnings *create interest*? Clearly they do, each in its own way, because each campaign has been markedly successful.

By studying each of the following sample packages, you will not only learn how to *create interest*; you will also learn how to *state the problem, arouse emotion,* and *offer hope.* What is more, you will discover a variety of ways to *offer participation, induce a response,* and *offer thanks.*

The last three elements cannot be over stressed for they are at least as critical as creating interest in the opening. A variety of closings are used in the letters exhibited on the next few pages, but all have one thing in common. They *induce response* by asking straightforwardly—even forcefully—for a gift.

We especially call your attention to the compelling closing of the Vietnam Veterans Memorial Fund letter (Figure 5-3) and to the P.S. in the AIPAC letter (Figure 5-8) that had the effect of generating an average gift twice the size of the requested $35.

The Vietnam Veterans Memorial Fund closing:

> If you can give $20 it will sponsor the name of one Vietnam War veteran who gave his life in service to our country. We intend to inscribe every single name—57,661 to be precise. A lot of names—a lot of lives. Won't you please help us to begin by sending your tax-deductible gift of $20, $40 or more today?
>
> Thank you for taking the time to read this letter. And bless you for your generosity.

The AIPAC P.S.:

> **P.S.** *Before you make out your check* will you search your heart? And if America has been especially good to you—has provided you with the means to be generous—then please won't you consider a gift larger than the basic membership. Can you send $100? $500? $1,000?
>
> And for your generous gift of whatever amount, thank you for playing an important role in this fight!

LESSON NUMBER 3: CREDIBILITY

Listing the Board of Directors

Some claim that a listing of the board of directors will not improve returns—that it only uses space and clutters up the look of the letter.

We disagree. With today's proliferation of competing direct mail appeals, people are forced to make hard choices. And, while they are still swayed by the heart, they read more carefully. They want to know exactly who is in charge of managing and spending their money. So list your organization's board somewhere in the package.

For several of our clients, rather than conventionally listing their very impressive board down the side of the letterhead, we grouped the names together at the end of the letter, on the fourth page, with the following introduction.

> Although I sign this letter to you as a concerned individual, many others join me in this appeal. Just read the list of Directors printed below. Rarely do you see such an outstanding alliance of respected, talented and influential supporters who have been mobilized to give time, energy and money to a cause in which they deeply believe. *Their support is meaningless without yours.* Won't you join with them today? Thank you.

Figure 5-2. Girl Scout Council of Greater New York
Prospect Letter

Please read all of this letter!

From the desk of Helen Hayes

Dear Friend,

I am writing to you not as an actress — but as the mother of a Girl Scout and as a Girl Scout Leader. <u>I know how valuable the Girl Scout experience is because I know how much happiness and personal fulfillment it brought me and my daughter Mary before she died of polio when she was just 19.</u>

Mary loved being a Girl Scout and I loved watching her blossom into a warm, respectful, responsible young woman. That's why I led a performing arts group for my daughter's troop. Using the marvelous magic of the theatre, my young Girl Scouts learned poise and self-confidence, friendship and generosity, honesty and reliability.

I have never written a letter like this before, but Girl Scouts of Greater New York has done so much for me and my family, I want to do everything possible to help them now in their time of need. <u>I hope my letter will inspire you to join me in supporting one of America's greatest traditions for young people.</u>

In fact, The Girl Scouts is this country's oldest and largest organization for girls. Since the first handbook was published in 1913, Girl Scouts have been helping others in their troops, neighborhoods, communities and countries. Here in New York City, Scouts work as volunteers in hospitals; work with senior citizens and religious groups making holiday gifts for the needy; work on clean-up drives, and so much more.

The Girl Scouts is also the only organization that teaches young women life skills for all environments. So, whether Scouts go camping in a forest or visit a retirement home, they know how to interact as a group, as team members, respecting their surroundings wherever they are.

<u>But we at the Girl Scouts also realize that in these turbulent, changing times, new skills must accompany the old.</u> Today, many women no longer have a choice — they <u>must</u> work to help support their families. In response, today's Girl Scouts offers programs in computers, mathematics, home repair, aerospace, and business — in addition to the traditional badges in cooking, sewing, child care, household budgeting, etc.

And that's what makes this organization so valuable. From household whiz to corporate executive, Scouting offers every girl a variety of ways to become a productive part of society. I say "every" because Girl Scouts reaches out to all girls of every race, creed, economic and social class.

(please turn over)

Girl Scout Council of Greater New York, Inc.
335 East 46th Street, New York, NY 10017

79

Right now, over 25,000 city girls are participating in Scouting programs. That's a lot — but it's not enough. There are many more girls who really need the support and guidance of Girl Scouting ... young girls who live in hard-core tenement neighborhoods ... who are often left unsupervised, alone to fend for themselves ... whose young eyes often view a cold, uncaring world of concrete and hopeless dreams.

Unless we win your support, and the support of other good friends like yourself, we will not be able to bring Scouting to those girls who need us most. That would be a terrible shame — because New York girls need and want Scouting programs. They want them so much, in fact, that these girls raise approximately 30% of the New York Council's total operating budget all by themselves!

How do they do it? Cookie sales. One particularly enterprising eleven-year-old named Markita sold 2,640 boxes of Girl Scout cookies last year, earning her way to summer camp! But even with remarkable Scouts like Markita, and the Council's stringent frugality, the offers are still coming up short.

That's why we're turning to you now. Please help us raise the $55.90 to send a New York inner-city girl to camp; the $34 to maintain a needy youngster in the Disabled Girls Program; the $20 a month to keep one girl in the After-School-Program.

I have pledged my lifetime support to the Girl Scouts. I have given time and money to help continue the valuable work of this incredible organization — and I ask you to join me by sending your tax-deductible contribution for as much as you can afford in the enclosed postage-paid envelope. In return, I give you my personal pledge that you are supporting a worthwhile cause totally devoted to helping our young daughters, nieces, neighbors — right here in our own metropolitan community.

Thank you, very, very much.

Helen Hayes

Helen Hayes

P.S. Please don't put my letter aside intending to make a contribution later. Do it now, before you forget, because, without your help, we won't be able to bring Girl Scout programs to girls who need them most. Some of those programs are described in the enclosed brochure. Won't you take a moment to read it, and give, today? Thank you.

Figure 5-3. Vietnam Veterans Memorial Fund
Prospect Letter

VIETNAM VETERANS MEMORIAL FUND

"I'm writing you today not as an entertainer, but as a fellow American who has something very important to share."

Bob Hope

May, 1980

Dear Friend,

I'm offering you the opportunity to take an active part in a project that is long overdue.

It has been over seven years since America ended its involvement in the Vietnam war -- the longest, and certainly the most controversial, war in our nation's history.

None of us can forget that this war provoked bitter debate here at home -- dividing generations and families, and severing friendships.

The impact of that war has changed forever the lives of many Americans, and most of all, it has changed the lives of the over 2½ million Americans who served in it.

The war subjected these Americans to unparalleled pressures. Moreover, the rancor and bitterness that the war caused created an atmosphere that in many cases denied the returning veterans the hero's welcome they so rightly deserved.

Some were volunteers, but most didn't ask to go and fight. Yet, when our country called because we needed them, they served.

Many of these veterans are left only with the feeling that their sacrifice was in vain and that they are the forgotten victims of an unpopular war.

But at this Memorial Day holiday it is time to remember. To remember the 57,000 who died, the 300,000 wounded, and the 100,000 handicapped or seriously disabled.

And that is why I'm writing to you today.

Recently, a group of Vietnam veterans formed the Vietnam Veterans Memorial Fund for the purpose of providing every American the opportunity to pay grateful tribute to all who served in that war, and especially to those who gave their lives.

... over, please

Vietnam Veterans Memorial Fund, Inc.
1025 Connecticut Avenue N.W., Suite 405, Washington, D.C. 20036 (202) 659-1151

When these veterans asked me to be their spokesman for the project, I didn't hesitate. I've spent a lot of time entertaining troops in the field and in hospitals all over the world, and it amazes me how many good people tend to forget our courageous veterans of Vietnam. Yet they served as honorably as did their fathers and grandfathers before them.

Take, for example, the experience of Jan Scruggs, one of the founders and now the president of the Vietnam Veterans Memorial Fund. When he graduated from high school, Jan enlisted in the Army. He was barely 19 years old when he was assigned to an infantry company in Vietnam. By the end of his tour, he had seen half the men in his company killed or wounded. Jan himself was seriously wounded, and was awarded the Purple Heart and decorated for valor.

Here, in his own words, is what happened when he came home:

> "On my return from Vietnam, still in uniform, a group of people my own age booed and made obscene gestures at us. This experience was painful, but others suffered far worse than I. One veteran -- an amputee -- was told straight out, 'It serves you right for going there.'"
>
> "We Vietnam veterans soon learned that having served our country in this particular war was a dubious distinction at best."

These and other heartbreaking episodes experienced by so many of the returning veterans must somehow be set right. We must show those who were hurt, rejected or just plain ignored, that this Nation -- however belatedly -- does care for its sons and daughters who served during a most difficult time.

It is our duty to show these heretofore unrecognized veterans and their families that you and I personally care.

The Vietnam Veterans Memorial Fund was founded with a single, specific purpose -- to build a permanent memorial in our Nation's Capital, honoring veterans of the Vietnam war -- especially those who gave their lives.

I am proud to tell you that over one half of the members of the United States Congress -- 270 Republicans and Democrats in all, including 96 of the 100 senators -- are now sponsors of the legislation to provide National Park land near the Lincoln Memorial for the site of the Vietnam Veterans Memorial.

And that's where you come in.

You see, I can't think of a better way to express to these young men and women that all Americans appreciate the sacrifice they made for our country. And I can't think of any more appropriate way to unite all Americans, regardless of how they felt about the war, than for them to participate in helping to build this memorial.

Just the knowledge that the people of the Nation -- liberals and conservatives, hawks and doves -- wish to honor those who served in Vietnam, will help restore the self-esteem of these thousands of returned veterans.

Similarly, this tribute will bring long overdue honor to the families of those who gave their lives in the war. But equally important to all Americans, this memorial will be a lasting symbol of our nation's determination to heal the divisions and differences generated by Vietnam, and to restore the unity which existed prior to that war.

IF THIS IDEA TOUCHES YOU, PLEASE READ ON...

Although this memorial will not bring back the dead, or heal the wounded, or erase the scars of war suffered by many thousands, it will stand as a perpetual symbol from a proud and grateful nation. That's why I am so enthusiastic about it.

The memorial is being planned around five basic elements:

- Inscription of the names of all of the 57,661 Americans who died in Vietnam.

- Sculpture symbolizing the experience of Americans who served in Vietnam.

- An overall landscaped design; a living memorial in harmony with its surroundings.

- A spacious garden setting that is inviting to passersby.

- Artistic integrity of design, components and materials.

The design and plans for the memorial will be subject to the approval of the National Commission of Fine Arts.

Aside from the gift of the land from the federal government, and the future maintenance by the Department of the Interior, the Vietnam Veterans Memorial will not require one penny of government assistance or support.

The funds for the design, construction and inscription of the names of the dead (and all other aspects of the memorial) will come from the generous contributions of grateful Americans like you and me.

Let me say right here that the memorial will make no political statement about the Vietnam war. Rather, it will symbolize our national unity and further the reconciliation of our country after the divisions caused by the war.

Through support of the memorial, Americans of diverse political beliefs and opinions regarding U.S. policy in Vietnam can unite in expressing their acknowledgment of the sacrifice of those who served there.

If you agree with me that it's time we did something to honor and recognize the sacrifice made by our sons and daughters who served in Vietnam, then here is what I would like you to do...

To make this memorial a reality, we have set a goal of $2.5 million. We can only reach that goal if you and other patriotic Americans from all walks of life, from all age groups, from all political persuasions, search your heart and make out a check for $10, $25, $50 or any amount you can afford to send. Your contribution is fully tax-deductible.

And, if America has provided you with the means to be very generous, then please won't you send a gift of $100, $500, $1,000 or more.

On my part, I know of no better way to show Vietnam veterans that a grateful nation has not forgotten them.

If you're undecided about contributing at this time, please read the letter I've enclosed. It was written by parents whose 20 year old son Robert died in Vietnam. If that letter doesn't convince you of how important this memorial is, then nothing will.

But I'm confident you'll want to join with me and other Americans in making the Vietnam Veterans Memorial a reality.

Thank you for taking the time to read this letter. And bless you for your generosity.

Sincerely,

Bob Hope

P.S. If you can give $20, it will sponsor the name of one Vietnam war veteran who gave his life in service to our country. We intend to inscribe every single name -- 57,661 to be precise. A lot of names -- a lot of lives. Won't you please help us to begin by sending your tax-deductible gift of $20, $40 or more today?

Receipt and deposit of contributions is the exclusive responsibility of an independent banking institution.

Financial report on the Vietnam Veterans Memorial Fund, Inc., will be available upon request. New York State residents may also obtain a copy through the Dept. of State, Office of Charities Registration, Albany, New York 12231

Figure 5-4. Sea Turtle Rescue Fund Prospect Letter

Sea Turtle Rescue Fund
Center for Environmental Education Inc.
624 9TH STREET, N.W.
WASHINGTON, D.C. 20001

A turtle hatchling finally breaks through his shell!

Fall, 1982

Dear Friend:

For just $15.67 you can "adopt" a nest of green turtle eggs in Mexico and take part in a unique project designed to help rescue these wonderful creatures from extinction.

You see, Mexico once possessed the largest and most diverse sea turtle populations on earth. There are seven species of sea turtles in the world, and Mexico has six of them. And of these six species, two are threatened and three (including the green turtle) are in imminent danger of extinction as a result of ruthless exploitation of the turtles and their eggs.

As recently as 1976, some 20,000 nesting turtles were being slaughtered annually in Michoacan, Mexico by Aztec Indian fishermen -- many of whom relied on selling the eggs and leather for part of their income.

(Black marketeers will pay an average of 16¢ per egg or about $11 per nest. And a motivated local can earn $54 for each female turtle he drags off the beach and delivers to smugglers).

Turtle poachers earned $54 for each adult female captured!

Then in 1976, sea turtle expert Kim Cliffton (who had witnessed the poaching of eggs and the slaughter of adult turtles first hand) devised the idea of offering the native people an alternative.

He reasoned that the Indians would be willing to sell exclusively to him if he could offer more than the going commercial rate. Moreover, if he could raise the necessary money, he could even offer employment to some of the locals to help him transport the eggs to protected nesting areas (and to watch over them until the newly hatched turtles could be safely released into the sea).

When Kim returned to the United States he presented his ideas to private and government wildlife organizations. The result of these meetings was an agreement that Kim's approach should be tried. And for the past four years, the Sea Turtle Rescue Fund, the World Wildlife Fund and the U.S. Fish and Wildlife Service have provided the funds to carry out this unique project.

continued...

Local fishermen gather turtle eggs for relocation to protected nest areas.

Turtle hatchlings in safety of holding tank.

The project's great success is graphically illustrated in the photographs on this page. Last year alone, more than 300,000 eggs were collected, and this year's goal is to collect at least 400,000 eggs! And after the eggs have incubated in the hatcheries, the local people help the biologists release the hatchlings into the sea where at least some of the tiny turtles have a chance of surviving their <u>natural</u> predators.

I hope that you share our enthusiasm for this exciting project, and that you will want to help us meet our financial commitment to this year's project which runs from October through February.

Remember -- poachers received $11 per nest for turtle eggs. <u>But for just a few dollars more -- for just $15.67 -- you can "adopt" an entire green turtle nest of some 80 eggs!</u>

(Incidentally, we arrived at that figure of $15.67 by dividing the total project cost by the projected number of turtle nests that will be saved.) Gifts of all sizes are needed and are fully tax-deductible. So if you possibly can, please "adopt" two turtle nests for $31.34 or three for $47.01. And as the holiday season approaches, why not consider giving a gift of a turtle nest for that hard-to-shop-for friend who shares your conservation interests? We'll send a personalized gift card in your name, and it will be a gift long remembered.

For your generous contribution of whatever amount, thank you very, very much.

A tiny turtle hatches and instinctively heads for the sea.

Sincerely yours,

Thomas B. Grooms

Thomas B. Grooms
Executive Director
CENTER FOR ENVIRONMENTAL EDUCATION

Figure 5-5. Appalachian Mountain Club Prospect Letter

FIVE   JOY   STREET,   BOSTON,   MASSACHUSETTS   02108

Spring 1983

Dear Outdoor Enthusiast:

    This is your personal invitation to join us outdoors -- for the time in your life!

    No, I didn't make a mistake.

    I'm writing to you about the leisure time _in_ your life -- time that you yearn to fill with activities that are exciting, fun and rewarding.   What's more, if you are like most people I meet, you are searching for a healthier life style -- one that combines physical and mental well being.

    If this describes your needs, I have good news! You can make your dreams come true right now by joining the Appalachian Mountain Club (AMC) -- the oldest and largest outdoor recreation and conservation organization in the nation.

    What's more, the time, place and price are right!

TIME: You can join AMC any time of the year, but with warmer weather and the promise of spring foliage just ahead, why not take advantage of the best nature has to offer?

PLACE: AMC is all over the Northeast with headquarters in Boston and chapters and facilities from Maine down to the Delaware Valley --

organized by chapters to serve
you close to home. (For chapter
listings, see the enclosed
membership application form.)

PRICE: Individual membership dues are
only $30 a year ($45 for families
regardless of size). And when
you have finished reading my
letter and realize just how much
you get for your investment,
you'll have to agree that the
price is right!

What's more, when you join AMC, you'll be joining a group of some 29,000
people who share your interests — people who enjoy just about every wholesome
and exciting (non-motorized) outdoor activity.

Who are we?

...We're hikers, backpackers and mountaineers

...We're canoeing and kayaking enthusiasts

...We're campers and trail-builders

...We're cyclists and cross-country skiers

...We're bird-watchers and outdoor photographers

...We're volunteer land managers

...And above all, we're conservationists who
believe in enjoying the out-of-doors while
diligently promoting its wise and careful
use for the enjoyment of future generations.

<u>...if that
describes you,
please read on...</u>

AMC MEMBERS ENJOY A WIDE VARIETY
OF BENEFITS INCLUDING...

A subscription to the APPALACHIA BULLETIN
— a monthly magazine that not only keeps
you informed of club-wide activities, but
which is also filled with "how to" articles
on a variety of outdoor activities.

Regular notices of trips, programs and workshops on such diverse subjects as outdoor photography, safety equipment, birdwatching, technical climbing, mountaineering and much more.

Discounts on an outstanding selection of publications (books, maps, trail guides, instruction pamphlets and much more).

Discounts at the club's many facilities (camps, lodges, huts, shelters and campgrounds).

Affiliation with one of twelve local chapters, providing members with the opportunity to be as active as they wish.

That's right. When you join AMC nationally, your name will be forwarded to the local chapter nearest you so that you may participate in a variety of local activities. (And don't be surprised if a fellow member telephones you to welcome you to membership even before your first chapter newsletter or activity notice arrives.)

The chapter aspect of AMC is an especially important and rewarding benefit of AMC membership. Just before I began this letter, I leafed through several chapter newsletters so that I could give you a preview ...

... from the Worcester Chapter Newsletter:

"Mid Year Meeting and Banquet at Greendale People's Church. Delicious oven pot roast dinner only $5.50 per person. The program, entitled 'Remember When,' will be a journey back in time to the 1920s using members' slides."

... from the Boston Chapter Newsletter:

"If you have extra gear to sell, or if you are looking for equipment at bargain prices, plan to attend our Used Equipment Sale in Cabot Auditorium. Items available will include packs, tents, stoves, sleeping bags, skis.... AMC leaders will be on hand to conduct a variety of workshops."

... from the New York Chapter Newsletter:

"The Conservation Committee urges AMC members to write to [their Senators and Representative] asking them to co-sponsor the legislation required to include Fire Island in the National Wilderness Preservation System..."

... from the Connecticut Chapter Newsletter [notes from a camp logbook]:

"Four friends spending the weekend here; perfect weather, bright sun, hiked to
the top of Bear Mountain; rested awhile and hiked to Sages Ravine; we must have
passed a hundred different cascades and rushing falls. Cabin warm, comfortable
and clean thanks to all those nice people we met going down as we were going up."

    I just wish there was enough space to quote from each of AMC's chapter
newsletters. But even if your state wasn't mentioned, you can be certain that
activity in all chapters is equally enjoyable. For it is at the local level
that your membership in AMC will be the most socially rewarding. AMC members
make firm and lasting friendships based on shared interests and experiences.
(And if you're not feeling particularly sociable, you'll be offered every
opportunity to get out and away from everything and everybody!)

                Earlier I mentioned that AMC members are entitled
                to substantial discounts at our various facilities.
                Now I want to take just a minute to describe some
                of the unique facilities operated by the club.

    THE FRIENDLY HUTS are probably the most famous of all AMC facilities and
there are eight of them -- simple and cozy -- spaced a day's hike apart, high
in the White Mountains of New Hampshire. And whether you plan a single day's
outing with one overnight or a full eight day mountain adventure, visiting each
of the huts, you will sleep bunk-style and share delicious hearty meals (prepared
by the hut crews) with people who share your enthusiasm for the outdoor life.

    PINKHAM NOTCH CAMP is located in the heart of the White Mountain National
Forest in New Hampshire with public transportation available right to the door.
In addition to serving as a base camp for thousands of hikers, climbers
and skiers each year, Pinkham has also become a recreational
and educational resource offering lectures, seminars and
workshops on a variety of subjects including
trail maintenance, bushwacking, backpacking,
winter mountain safety,
winter camping
and much
more.

MOUNTAIN GATE LODGE is located in the heart of the Catskill Mountains, 100 miles north of New York City — easily accessible by car or bus. Accommodations are bunk-style rooms, and delicious meals are served family style. The Lodge has a guest lounge with fireplace and a meeting room, reading room and game library. But most visitors to Mountain Gate spend their time exploring the nearby trails that wind through spectacular countryside.

AMC operates more facilities than space permits me to describe. But when you join, we'll include a free copy of our facilities brochure in your membership packet!

In the beginning of my letter I said AMC members are — above all else — conservationists who work to promote the wise use of our natural resources. That's an integral part of the club's philosophy, and I don't want to conclude this letter without touching on this important matter.

For over one hundred years, AMC as a club, and AMC member volunteers, have...

... worked closely with the National Park Service to build and maintain the Appalachian Trail in an environmentally sound manner.

... learned first-hand about the complexities of land management.

... fought for and are committed to the wise management of our national parks, forests and wilderness areas.

... cooperated with federal, state and local government agencies and with other private conservation organizations to obtain and/or protect threatened natural areas.

We're not just talkers — we're doers!

Thus when you join AMC, you will be adding your voice to a respected conservation organization — 29,000 members strong. And when environmental battles rage, that voice is strong, reasoned, balanced and effective!

Moreover, when you join AMC, you will be joining an organization that is as dedicated to safety as it is to outdoor adventure. Since the club's founding in 1876, AMC member-volunteers have traditionally --

> ... served on AMC's famous Search and Rescue Team which answers more than 100 calls for help each year.

> ... conducted safety programs and training workshops in mountaineering, canoeing, rock climbing and other potentially dangerous outdoor activities.

I hope you agree that AMC provides the answers for the leisure time in your life -- for outdoor recreation, social activity, adventure, learning experiences, relaxation and vacation opportunities. You see, we're not offering memberships in AMC on a random basis. We want and need people like you -- people who share our enthusiasm for outdoor recreation and who also share our commitment to the earth's conservation.

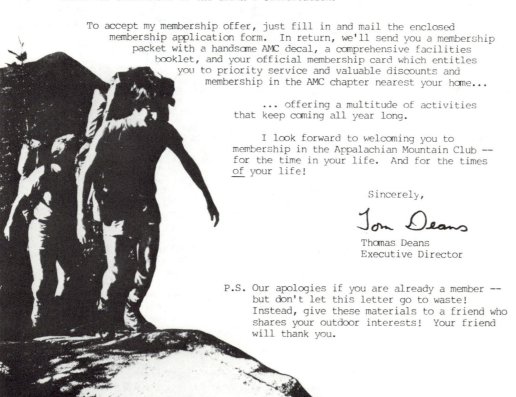

To accept my membership offer, just fill in and mail the enclosed membership application form. In return, we'll send you a membership packet with a handsome AMC decal, a comprehensive facilities booklet, and your official membership card which entitles you to priority service and valuable discounts and membership in the AMC chapter nearest your home...

... offering a multitude of activities that keep coming all year long.

I look forward to welcoming you to membership in the Appalachian Mountain Club -- for the time in your life. And for the times of your life!

Sincerely,

Tom Deans

Thomas Deans
Executive Director

P.S. Our apologies if you are already a member -- but don't let this letter go to waste! Instead, give these materials to a friend who shares your outdoor interests! Your friend will thank you.

Figure 5-6. Gallaudet College Prospect Letter

GALLAUDET COLLEGE
Kendall Green
Washington, D.C. 20002

September 1983

Dear Friend:

You are looking at two of the best reasons I know why Gallaudet College needs and deserves your support!

Doris Wilding and Ken Bader, students at Gallaudet, are both deaf. Yet in a few years they will take their places in a hearing society in careers that may surprise you.

Thanks to Gallaudet College -- the world's only accredited liberal arts college for deaf students, founded in 1864 -- Doris' and Ken's career choices will not be limited to jobs traditionally thought "suitable" for deaf people such as shoe repair, seamstress or piece worker, printing press operator, assembly-line worker in a factory, or any other routine, isolated occupation where only limited communication with co-workers and supervisors is necessary.

Gallaudet College does make a difference! Our 8,000 graduates have more career options, hold positions of greater responsibility and earn far more income than other deaf people.

Ken, for example, plans to be a clinical psychologist working with deaf people. Doris is interested in a career in education. Both students want to help other deaf people overcome their disabilities and go on to lead normal, productive lives.

Others of our 1,400 students -- from every state in the union -- are working towards degrees in business and social work (the two most popular majors), science, computer math, economics and in many other fields. Past statistics show that thirty-nine percent will earn master's degrees and three percent will earn doctorates.

I want to tell you more about Gallaudet and about how you can help deserving young men and women like Doris and Ken. But because I have come to realize that most people have great misconceptions about deafness (and are generally very curious to learn the truth), let us first take a moment to explore the world of deaf people.

Continued inside...

THE INVISIBLE HANDICAP

Because deaf people look the same as the rest of us -- without dark glasses or cane or wheelchair to identify their handicaps -- deafness is often regarded as less than serious -- not a real obstacle to living a normal life.

But if you have known a deaf child, you know better! The hearing child learns language effortlessly because he or she is bombarded by it. But for the deaf child, communication is tremendously difficult and frustrating. Never having heard sound, they cannot mimic it, and the speech they develop through long years of repetitious practice is often difficult to understand. Compared to the hearing child, who on the average has a vocabulary of some 5,000 words by the age of five, the deaf child who has not been taught sign language may know fewer than 50! Consequently, the deaf child has no effective way to communicate with his parents -- or perhaps more importantly -- with himself.

As for lip reading, it must be remembered that the child who is born deaf does not even know which words to look for. For that child, learning to lip read unknown words is like trying to understand someone speak a foreign language on TV with the sound turned off. Try it sometime! You will come away with a greater appreciation of the tremendous obstacles deaf people must overcome. (Incidentally, even the most fluent lip reader -- through intense concentration -- only grasps less than half of what is being said and must fill in the rest. Lip reading in an animated group conversation is virtually impossible.)

Helen Keller once said that if she could live again, she would dedicate more of her time to deaf people and their problems. She felt that of her two handicaps -- deafness and blindness -- that deafness was the greater problem. "Deafness," she said, "is a much worse misfortune because of the loss of the most vital stimulus -- the sound of the voice that brings language, sets thoughts astir, and keeps us in the intellectual company of man."

In addition to setting our students' thoughts astir, Gallaudet College teaches young people like Doris and Ken how to make their handicap a less limiting factor in their lives. They are given the opportunity to develop a positive, confident self-image, leadership skills and the art of self-expression. It is this part of the college experience that will, more than any other, prepare them to accept the challenges awaiting them in a hearing world.

KEN BADER -- Class of '84

Ken Bader was born into a family with no history of congenital deafness, but when he was four years old he was diagnosed as being hard-of-hearing. His hearing loss was to be steadily progressive.

When Ken was fitted with a hearing aid at the age of four, he walked over to a flower and tried to listen to it. "I did not even know," he says today, "which things made noise and which did not.

"When I was a child, my parents helped me learn to vocalize," he says, "but it didn't occur to them to teach me sign language. They hoped surgery would restore my hearing. But it didn't work out that way."

Ken's grades improved dramatically after transferring to Gallaudet!

(continued on Page 3)

Today, after numerous operations, Ken wears two hearing aids in order to maximize his residual hearing, explaining, "I hear the sound of your voice, but I can't understand the words without reading your lips."

Despite his handicap, Ken attended public schools. "The only special education I got," he says, "was sitting up in the front row. I fondly remember this one teacher who used to bend over me and emphasize her lip movements for my benefit." He laughs at the recollection. "I could see all the way into her tonsils!"

In 1978, Ken entered the University of New Mexico. Of that experience he says, "I missed those concerned teachers who put me in the front row. The university classes were enormous and the professors walked up and down, up and down -- many of them mumbling into their beards. It was impossible to lip read."

Frustrated, Ken transferred to Gallaudet where his Grade Point Average shot up from a 2.5 to a 3.54! At Gallaudet he has more friends than before, has participated in the National College Honors Council Seminar and is a past president of the Honors Students' Organization.

To earn money to help pay for his education, Ken tutors other students during the school year. One summer he worked at the Cape Cod Alcoholism Intervention and Rehabilitation Unit. He has also taken nursing courses and has worked in an alcohol detoxification center -- experiences that are helping to prepare him for a career in psychology.

Ken is concerned that there are only a handful of deaf psychologists in the entire country. "Many deaf people feel isolated from the rest of the world," he says. "It starts in childhood when kids are ostracized and even sometimes abused by members of their own family. I want to help change all that -- to impart to others some of the strength and confidence I have gained on my own as a result of the Gallaudet experience."

Doris works in the Development Office of Gallaudet, acknowledging the generous contributions from people like you.

DORIS WILDING -- Class of '86

Doris is one of nine children -- all of whom were born with a hearing loss. Unlike Ken, Doris learned to sign at an early age and at the same time was encouraged to vocalize. When meeting Doris today, one is impressed with her ability to communicate in spite of her deafness.

Doris grew up in Gooding, Idaho a small town 200 miles south of Boise. She attended both the Idaho School for the Deaf and public schools. In public school, Doris had an interpreter, enabling her to keep up with her hearing classmates.

After graduating from public high school in 1981, Doris was selected to be a foreign exchange student in Finland. Although she lived with a hearing family that spoke a different language, Doris became adept at com-

municating in her own special way. During her stay in Finland she taught at a school
for the deaf. In speaking about her year in Finland, Doris says, "This was one of
the most rewarding, educational, and fulfilling experiences I have had so far."
Doris and her "family" in Finland still write to each other.

Last year, Doris enrolled in Gallaudet College -- an experience she had long
looked forward to as she would be the fourth member of her family to attend Gallaudet.
Both her parents graduated in 1960 and her oldest sister graduated last spring.

To help defray the cost of her education Doris works as a clerk/typist in the
Development Office at Gallaudet. And, when she learned that Miss Deaf America won
a $500 scholarship, she immediately became eligible for the crown by entering and
winning the Miss Deaf Washington, D. C. pageant.

As Doris begins her sophomore year at Gallaudet, she has not firmly decided on
her major. She is interested in English, home economics and foreign languages. "I
am not sure which area I will choose," she says, "but I definitely want a career in
education."

Doris has never let her deafness be a handicap. "I have lived with it all my
life," she says. "It has never prevented me from participating fully in life. I
have been very lucky. I have travelled and met interesting people who now understand that deaf people are just like everyone else. And I feel very proud to represent the deaf community and the world's only liberal arts college for the deaf."

THE GALLAUDET EXPERIENCE

And just what is the "magic" of the Gallaudet experience?

As Doris Wilding puts it (and Ken agrees completely), "The best thing about
Gallaudet College is that it gives the deaf student the most normal college education
possible by being a special campus. Everything about Gallaudet -- from the size
of the classes to the facilities and the methods of teaching -- is barrier free."

"Barrier free" at Gallaudet means the use of sign language, captioned television
programs, ingenious "telephones" with a typewriter keyboard, specially trained staff
and faculty and much more.

Because some of our students have additional handicaps in addition to deafness
(including blindness or confinement to a wheel chair) Gallaudet has taken special
care that the physical facilities respond to these needs. Thus Gallaudet students
are able to concentrate on their studies and school life without having to constantly
be preoccupied with overcoming basic difficulties of communication!

Just for a moment, imagine the thrill of entering a classroom where -- for the
first time -- you are able to understand everything because your instructors and the
other students and even the staff communicate in sign language. Imagine the proud
feeling of self-reliance in being able to take your own notes at lectures. And
especially imagine knowing that you have an absolutely equal chance to make the
cheerleading or football team...or to become yearbook editor...or even class
president.

In short, imagine your own school experiences -- and the main advantage we all
took for granted -- the opportunity to learn with and compete with our peers!

In addition to our ongoing needs, we face an average increase of 66 percent in incoming enrollment each year over the next several years. That increase is the result of the 1963-1965 rubella (German measles) epidemic that swept through the United States causing deafness in more than twice the usual number of children!

And if that were not tragic enough, some 40 percent of these children were left with additional handicaps -- blindness being the most common affliction!

The first group of rubella-deafened students entered Gallaudet this fall. Next year our problem will be even worse as another large class enters. Despite our progress in expansion, we have not yet raised all the money necessary to adequately enlarge our facilities, to purchase all of the necessary equipment and learning tools and to hire and train sufficient new faculty.

We cannot wait until next year to know how many 1984 students we can take in! We must complete our expansion plans this year! And every week that goes by without our raising significant additional money means that another student may have to be turned away -- bright, talented students like Doris and Ken who need and deserve the special education only Gallaudet has to offer.

Will you help? If you will, Gallaudet will not have to say "no" to hundreds of students who are otherwise qualified to enter.

Your tax-deductible gift is urgently needed. Can I count on you to send it today?

A deaf student's tomorrow depends upon whether your answer is "yes."

Sincerely,

Edward C. Merrill, Jr.
President
GALLAUDET COLLEGE

P. S. Before deciding on the amount of your gift, please look at the enclosed leaflet which details some of Gallaudet's urgent needs ranging from $35 to $3,500. Thank you for your generosity.

ECM:tog

A

GALLAUDET COLLEGE
Where Ability Counts More Than Disability

- Founded in 1864, Gallaudet College is the world's *only* accredited liberal arts college for deaf students.

- 90% of all deaf college graduates in the world are Gallaudet graduates.

- Most Gallaudet students are born deaf, making learning even more difficult than for students who became deaf later in life.

- The average hearing loss of a Gallaudet student is 90 decibels. (A decibel loss of 70 or more is classified as deaf.)

- 85% of Gallaudet students need financial assistance in order to complete college.

- 85% of Gallaudet graduates are employed in professional, technical and managerial occupations.

- Gallaudet alumni families earn about 50% more than does the average deaf family in the U.S.

- The average yearly Gallaudet alumni family income is in the upper half of incomes earned by the U.S. population.

B

C

photos:

A—*Did you know that Gallaudet "invented" the football huddle to shield their signing of the plays from their opponents?*

B—*Proving that rhythm doesn't originate in the ear drum, but rather comes from long hours of practice, the famed Gallaudet Dancers perform all over the country.*

C—*Barbara Tubbs—a Gallaudet Dancer and cheerleader—won a $500 college scholarship last year when she was crowned* **Miss Deaf** *America in a national competition.*

Figure 5-7. ASPCA Prospect Letter

ASPCA
The American Society for the
Prevention of Cruelty to Animals

441 East 92nd St., New York, N.Y. 10128

June 1983

Dear New Yorker:

Hot weather is hard on all of us, but it is especially hard on the city's animals.

Were you aware that in last summer's brutal heat wave:

° three horses collapsed and died in Midtown (July 18, 1982)
° a fourth horse died in Central Park (August 5, 1982)

And were you aware that:

<u>Only one humane society took direct action — the ASPCA!</u>

We rushed to the scene in the 90-degree-plus heat with ambulances and medical attendants, ordered the other horses back to their stables and shut down the carriage operation until temperatures fell.

This is just one example of the essential work the ASPCA is doing all over the city — from Manhattan to the Bronx ... from Queens to Brooklyn ... and out to Staten Island — to protect the animals of New York.

This letter is your invitation to come with me on a tour of New York City — to learn more about the ASPCA, and also about the important role New Yorkers like you play in making our work possible.

You'll also meet several of the city's most interesting animals who have their own fascinating stories to tell. And you'll learn why summer is harder on city animals than any other season — and about what can be done to make animals' lives easier during the so-called "dog days" of summer.

All Working Animals Need Protection

The four horses just described were not the only animals worked to death. Earlier this year, a guard dog company was hired by the City to provide police dogs to protect the upper floors of a Centre Street building. This seems harmless enough. Who would suspect that valuable animals, hired to safeguard property, would not be well cared for?

But when ASPCA agents (responding to a tip) entered the building, they found one of the worst cases of neglect on record! The dogs, left without food for long periods — were emaciated and desperate. Some had cannibalized others, and one had jumped to its death as if committing suicide. Yet, even in the midst of all this horror, a gaunt, scrawny mother was nursing her pups....

The ASPCA rescued all of the animals and brought charges against the guard dog company, resulting in a substantial fine.

The Other Side of ASPCA Legal Services — The Human Side

The ASPCA provides legal advice to pet-owning tenants from Staten Island to Queens. Right now, we are working to put into law the "senior citizen pets in housing bill" which provides that persons 62 years or older many not be denied occupancy in or be subjected to eviction on the sole ground they have a dog or cat residing with them!

The bill made headway in the New York State legislature this past session — but the Assembly didn't take it to the floor for a vote. But we will not let up our efforts until we succeed — because we know how very important it is for most people to live with a pet. (It has already been proven that pets help sick people get well faster and even live longer!)

Another Reason for Legalities — The Rewards of Affection

The Pet Assisted Therapy Program was created in 1978 to help people in nursing homes, hospitals and other institutions. And just a few short years since the program was launched, it has received spontaneous praise from health care professionals who find that the affectionate spontaneity of a pet is the best tonic in the world for institutional residents. This program is projected to expand to help even more people. But we need your help to fund it.

WILL YOU HELP IN STATEN ISLAND?

In Manhattan, the ASPCA operates America's fourth largest veterinary hospital, the Bergh Memorial Hospital of New York. General health care for animals is just a part of this hospital's work, however. The medical staff also attends to numerous accident cases each year.

Open windows in the summertime are understandable — understandable, to you and me. But our animal friends do not always sense the potential danger, and last year alone there were 150 reported cases of cats accidentally falling from high-rise buildings. Dr. Gordon Robinson, hospital director, refers to cats falling from apartment building windows as "high-rise syndrome" and urges all who live in apartment buildings above the second floor to install safety screens or grillework to protect animals as well as children.

Not all falls are accidental. As hard as it is to believe, people throw dogs off rooftops during the summer! Here is one documented case from last year:

Some construction workers witnessed what looked like a child being thrown from a 5th floor window and called the police. But when they arrived they discovered, not a small child, but a critically injured puppy. When he was brought to the ASPCA Hospital, we didn't know if he'd make it, but "Lucky" was a strong little guy, and he pulled through. Then, through our adoption services, one of the workers, who'd seen "Lucky" fall, came to take him home.

As you know, the ASPCA never turns an animal away. But, hospital treatment is very expensive. Last year, despite every economy and the help of volunteers, the Bergh Memorial Hospital spent $1.1 million on the care of animals, and has a substantial deficit every year.

WILL YOU HELP IN MANHATTAN?

WILL YOU HELP IN THE BRONX?

Grand Concourse Blues

   What happened to "Lucky" is but one of many summertime miseries inflicted on animals. You will be shocked to learn that here in New York, thousands of domestic pets and farm animals are sacrificed in the name of "religion" every year! Yes — even in this day and age — pagan, sacrificial rites are performed on helpless animals. And although some claim that we are inter- fering with the rights of people to practice religion as they see fit, our law enforcement officials continue to rescue helpless, caged animals from death in sacrificial rituals.

   Some acts of cruelty are performed out of sadism, some in the name of religion, others out of ignorance. The idea of locking someone in a cage out- side in the blaring heat of the sun strikes all of us as a heinous form of torture. But how many times have you, yourself, seen dogs locked in parked cars (windows rolled up) in the summer?

   Trapped inside these solid, metal and glass cages, at least one to two dogs per week (that we know of) either collapsed or died in the summer of 1982.

   In the "Quinn case," 110 animals were kept in a hot, tiny, airless house by a 58-year-old woman and her mother. Although the animals were well-fed, sanitary conditions of the home (as reported to the ASPCA by distraught neighbors) were deplorable! The ASPCA picked up all 110 pets and put them up for adoption.

   Last year, the ASPCA investigated over 10,000 cruelty reports in New York City alone, spending one-half million dollars on law enforcement.

Frequent Flyers

   If you fly frequently, you know how uncomfortable and tiring flying can be. It's especially hard on animals: remember, they're flying with your baggage.

   Thanks to you, the ASPCA offers rest, food and care for animals passing through Kennedy and LaGuardia Airports. Acting as an inspection station, the "Animalport" checks carriers to make sure pets have enough space and ventilation when traveling. And you can take advantage of our Animalport boarding facilities, secure in the knowledge that your pet will be well cared for while you're away.

   And don't worry about changing your flight plans — the shelter remains open 24 hours a day to meet travelers' needs.

TWEETERS IN TRANSIT

"I like traveling with my family every summer and when we come through New York, the ASPCA's Animalport is just what I need after long hours of flying.
"Because of the ASPCA and friends like you, we flyers get the rest and care we need. I love you, New Yorker!"

WILL YOU HELP IN QUEENS?

Left on Vacation

In the summertime, many people are more concerned about long weekends and vacations than about their pets' welfare.

During the summer months, the ASPCA picks up more strays and abandoned animals than during any other time of the year. Unfortunately, in summer, fewer of these animals are adopted!

While we try to accommodate all animals, we cannot! Last year, we were forced to close three of our shelters — in Queens, Staten Island and in the Bronx — due to lack of funds!

On the bright side, the ASPCA's adoption centers at our two major animal shelters in Manhattan and Brooklyn offer free spaying and neutering services to all ASPCA adoptees.

WILL YOU HELP IN BROOKLYN?

– 5 –

Have you ever visited our headquarters at 92nd Street and York Avenue? If you have, chances are you have witnessed what I see every working day — numbers of happy people debating about which dog or puppy or cat or kitten to take home.

I will never forget one little girl in particular as she held a rather homely, scrawny kitten. The girl's mother suggested that several of the other kittens in the litter were cuter and stronger looking, but the child was insistent. This was the one she wanted!

When asked why she had not chosen one of the more attractive of the litter mates, the child replied, "Because I was afraid that no one else would ever want this one and that he would be left behind."

This scenario is a frequent one at the ASPCA Adoption Center, where there is always great joy in making both people and animals happy. And it is at moments like these when I feel especially proud to be a part of this fine organization — and grateful to the tens of thousands of New Yorkers and others from all over the country who contribute so generously to our work.

Will you join us in our campaign to protect and help animals? All it takes to become a member is a tax-deductible contribution of $20. Larger gifts help us accomplish even more.

Won't you send it today so that our Adoption Centers, Hospital Spay/ Neuter clinics, Emergency Rescue Service, Pet Assisted Therapy Programs, Law Enforcement and other ASPCA services can be maintained and improved throughout this long, hot summer — and beyond.

On behalf of all of the animals of New York, thank you for your generosity, and best wishes for a wonderful summer!

Sincerely,

John Kullberg

John F. Kullberg
Executive Director

P.S. I have enclosed some helpful hints which can make your pet safer and more comfortable in the summertime. Please share them with friends or neighbors who also have pets. And remember, our Emergency Rescue Service is available to you around-the-clock. Call us if you need us!

illustrations by Stephen Klinger

If this is a duplicate, please accept our apologies and pass this on to a friend!

Thanks, New Yorker!

Figure 5-8. AIPAC Prospect Letter

AIPAC Alert

444 NORTH CAPITOL STREET, N.W., SUITE 412
WASHINGTON, D.C. 20001 · (202) 638-2256

SEPTEMBER 8, 1981 -- 6:45 P.M. -- WASHINGTON, D.C.

Dear Fellow American:

AIPAC, the American Israel Public Affairs Committee, the only American Jewish organization registered to lobby in Washington on behalf of legislation affecting Israel, desperately needs your help to stop the sale of the AWACS to Saudi Arabia!

And we need your help immediately because the Administration will begin the Congressional approval process tomorrow.

Because you care about America, I appeal to you to help our government avert a political and military blunder that will jeopardize our own national interests.

And because you care about Israel, I appeal to you to help protect this small, embattled nation from perhaps the greatest military threat of the past thirty years.

At issue is the danger of America's selling its most sophisticated weapons technology to an inherently unstable regime -- a country that is the declared enemy of our friend, Israel.

You can help stop this potential foreign policy disaster, and in just a moment I'll tell you how. But first let me describe exactly what is proposed and what the implications of the sale are.

Here is what the Saudis would purchase:

-- Five Airborne Warning and Control Systems aircraft (AWACS), able to view all of Israel from safely within Arab airspace;

-- Over 1,100 Sidewinder missiles -- the same missile recently used by the United States Navy to shoot down two attacking Libyan fighters! In a letter to Congress, twelve American F-15 pilots have courageously opposed the sale of these, our most advanced air-to-air missiles, to the Saudis;

-- Fuel tanks and tankers which would vastly increase the range of the F-15 fighters sold to Saudi Arabia by the Carter Administration.

Congress will have a total of just 30 days after formal notification to "veto" this arms proposal by majority votes in both the Senate and the House of Representatives. We expect formal notification at the end of this month.

This coincidence of timing forces us to remember another autumn just eight years ago. The date was October 6, 1973 -- Yom Kippur. And on that holiest of days, as unsuspecting Israeli Jews prayed for the atonement of their sins, Egypt and Syria opened a surprise coordinated attack on the Golan Heights and along the Suez Canal.

You remember, of course. None of us can ever forget that moment of Arab treachery.

But perhaps you do not recall that among the nine Arab states which joined in the battle, it was Saudi Arabia that sent a brigade of some 3,000 troops to try to defeat Israel.

SEPTEMBER 8, 1981 -- 6:45 P.M. -- WASHINGTON, D.C.

And eight years later, Saudi leaders still vow to use all their weapons --
including the AWACS -- in the Arab war against Israel. They call for Jihad; a holy
war against Israel! They claim the existence of the "Zionist entity" is their
greatest threat. They seek to "cleanse Jerusalem of the Jews."

We at AIPAC believe that the Saudi threat to destroy the State of Israel is real.
Certainly these new arms -- and the many more to come -- are not intended by the Saudis
for use against the Soviet Union or other Arab countries. Against whom, then, are they
needed?

The target appears clear enough -- despite Administration claims that "Saudi
leaders have assured the United States that they have no offensive intentions against
any country including Israel."

Such assurances, of course, are absolute rubbish. Israel is now, as in the past,
Saudi Arabia's declared enemy -- and the United States well knows it. Even the Department of Defense admits to the threats inherent in the sale, and I quote from a Spring,
1981 Pentagon memorandum:

> "An AWACS aircraft...could conceivably be employed opposite
> Israel. Prudent Israeli planners will have to take the
> possibility into account in preparing their calculations
> for a possible future Arab/Israeli war."

We at AIPAC do not care to speculate as to whether such a war "might" result. We
intend to stop the sale in its tracks! But we have just one month after formal introduction of the proposed sale to accomplish this critical goal -- and we desperately
need your help!

We have not written to you before because we have been able to accomplish our goals
with a small budget -- a budget raised solely through contributions from private citizens
-- for AIPAC receives no monetary assistance from Israel nor from the national Jewish
agencies with which it works so closely.

However, the money and effort being put into this battle by the Arabs and their
supporters in this country are so enormous that we need additional help to succeed.

Already, AIPAC has devoted countless hours in a monumental lobbying effort to head
off this sale, for the Administration had planned to submit the arms package this past
April, then in June, and again in early July. But, because of heavy opposition in both
the House and Senate, it was delayed. This delay, however, is not in Israel's interests,
and we cannot even for a moment rest on past lobbying achievements.

We must not lose this fight! Israel's security depends on the outcome! So does
America's. We must not allow our technological advantage over the Soviet Union to be
jeopardized in any way. The experience of Iran remains fresh in our minds -- what if
a Saudi version of Khomeini overthrew the House of Saud with Soviet help? (Remember,
the greatest danger to the Saudi throne comes from within.) How long would America's
secret, sophisticated technology remain secret? How long would it take Soviet military
scientists to strip our defenses bare?

All of our interests would be best served by a true peace in the Middle East. But
irresponsible arms sales do not lead to peace accords! And it would be reckless to provide the Saudis arms with which to ignite a major conflict -- one that could easily and
rapidly escalate into an all-out-war.

106

AIPAC Alert

444 NORTH CAPITOL STREET, N.W., SUITE 412
WASHINGTON, D.C. 20001 · (202) 638-2256

SEPTEMBER 8, 1981 -- 6:45 P.M. -- WASHINGTON, D.C.

                    Will you help AIPAC stop this sale and
                    thus help avert tragedy?

                    Will you contribute $35 non-deductible
                    dollars -- or more -- towards this end?

     You see, AIPAC urgently needs your assistance to increase its lobbying efforts at
this critical time. For while we are an organization called by The New York Times
"the most powerful, best-run and effective foreign policy interest group in Washington,"
we are up against unusually formidable opposition on this one. For just as we are
determined that the arms sale will not go through, the Administration is determined that
it will.

     Why, you want to know, is your contribution to AIPAC not tax-deductible? The answer
is simple. AIPAC is not a charity and only charities and educational institutions are
tax-deductible. AIPAC is a lobby -- and only the direct lobbying of Congress can be
effective in preventing this potentially disastrous sale.

     Why, you also want to know, are we seeking gifts of $35? The answer is that member-
ship in AIPAC is just $35, and we want you to become a member and remain current on
events in Washington and the Middle East through the weekly newsletter, NEAR EAST REPORT.

     There's also another reason. Ironically, $35 is the equivalent price of a barrel
of Arab oil. We want to call the Saudi's bluff -- to show them that they do not have
Americans so terrified of an oil embargo that we are willing to sell out to the declared
enemy of our friend, Israel. The world must learn that American foreign policy will not
be held hostage to a barrel of oil!

     One last request.

     In addition to your contribution of dollars -- as much as you can afford -- your
voice is urgently needed in the upcoming fight. Congressional offices are paying special
attention to mail on this issue. That is why I have enclosed, for your signature, a
memorandum protesting the sale of AWACS and other sophisticated arms to Saudi Arabia.

     My pledge to you is this: If you will rush your signed memo together with your
contribution in the enclosed envelope, an AIPAC lobbyist will personally deliver your
protest to your two Senators -- with copies to your Representative.

     That's right -- AIPAC wants to deluge each and every Congressional office with the
protests of concerned Americans. We want them to realize how strongly their constituents
feel about this very real threat to peace and the perception of American strength.

     Remember -- from the time this sale formally goes to the Congress, we have just
30 days in which to be effective. So please don't delay in sending your signed memo
and urgently needed contribution.

SEPTEMBER 8, 1981 -- 6:45 P.M. -- WASHINGTON D.C.

Make no mistake about it -- the security of the United States and Israel is in grave danger if this reckless, irresponsible sale to the Saudis goes through.

We're counting on you.

Sincerely,

Thomas A. Dine
Executive Director
AMERICAN ISRAEL PUBLIC AFFAIRS COMMITTEE

P.S.   Before you make out your check will you search your heart? And if America has been especially good to you -- has provided you with the means to be generous -- then please won't you consider a gift larger than the basic membership. Can you send $100? $500? $1,000?

And for your generous gift of whatever amount, thank you for playing an important role in this fight!

READ WHAT TWO DISTINGUISHED AMERICANS AND TWO DISTINGUISHED NEWSPAPERS HAVE TO SAY ABOUT AIPAC...

"The most powerful, best-run and effective foreign policy interest group in Washington."
The New York Times

"Without AIPAC's persistent efforts over the past 20 years, Israel's security, and that of the western alliance in the Middle East might have been severely affected."
The Hon. Clifford Case

"A power to be reckoned with at the White House, State and Defense Departments, and on Capitol Hill."
The Washington Post

"When I needed information on the Middle East, it was reassuring to know I could depend on AIPAC for professional and reliable assistance."
The Hon. Frank Church

*   *   *   *   *   *   *   *   *   *   *   *   *

NOTE: Because it was critical that this alert be timely, it was impossible to eliminate all list duplications. Should you receive more than one appeal, please accept our apologies.

Even if the names on your board are not famous, list them. At the very least list the officers and perhaps the executive committee. A board listing says that you are responsible citizens and not fly-by-nighters.

The Honorary Sponsoring Committee

The easiest way to bring life to a board of directors whose members are not public figures is to establish a distinguished sponsoring group which is printed just above a listing of your board.

The endorsement factor is particularly suitable for organizations just starting up. It is often crucial to emergency appeals, for example, saving a great building from a flood, preventing a dam from being constructed, or rebuilding a landmark gutted by fire.

In choosing people for such a committee, do not look simply for the most famous names you can find, but for names that have *relevance* to the cause. For example, if you are saving a museum in Italy, it would make sense to have at least a third of the committee made up of famous Italians, including Italian-Americans. If you are saving a local cultural landmark—say a performing arts building—it is important that you not only invite those who have performed on your stage, but local social and business leaders who regularly attend performances and who support the enterprise as well. There is nothing more unbelievable than an entire committee comprised of famous names.

The Letter Signer

The signer is possibly the most debated element of the direct mail appeal. Some consultants advise organizations to stick with their own—the organization's chairman, president, or executive director. Others recommend celebrity signers as a rule.

The precedent for the celebrity signer stems from the use of celebrities in advertising. Who, for example, does not know that Bill Cosby plugs Coca-Cola, Jell-O, and Texas Instruments or that Bob Hope promotes Texaco or that sportscaster Don Meredith drinks Lipton Tea? But does the fact that "Wonder Woman" Lynda Carter uses non-smear Maybelline mascara actually cause women to buy that particular brand?

In the fall of 1983, *Advertising Age* commissioned the SRI Research Center of Lincoln, Nebraska, to conduct a poll on this subject. The poll concluded that while people have high recall for the names of celebrities endorsing certain products, they are rarely moved to purchase a product because of such endorsement.

Let's look at two of the more relevant questions asked in the poll.

1. *"In general, do you think most celebrity spokespersons use the products or services they represent?"*
   In fund raising, this question could be translated to ask whether they believe the celebrity is personally involved with and/or contributes to the cause they represent. In the SRI poll, about two-thirds (64 percent) said no, 25 percent said yes, and 11 percent didn't know.
2. *"When a celebrity appears in advertising for several different companies, do you believe that makes him or her more believable, less believable, or makes no difference?"*
   In fund raising, this could be important if you are considering a celebrity signer who already signs for another—albeit quite different—cause. In the SRI poll, more than half (54 percent) said it made no difference, 33 percent said the plugging of several products made the celebrity less believable, 8 percent said it made the celebrity more believable, and 5 percent didn't know.

From these sample questions, we learn that the average American is too sophisticated to place much faith in the recommendations of "hired" celebrities.

We agree with the conclusion of the SRI poll: that celebrity endorsements *for their own sake* make no sense whatsoever. However, we also know that a celebrity signer can vastly enhance many appeals—*provided that the signer has some affiliation with your cause or institution or widely known and accepted empathy for your goals*. Credibility, then, is the first rule.

It would not be credible, for example, for a famous movie or stage star to sign an appeal for war orphans—unless, of course, she had entertained troops abroad and/or had adopted children of her own.

Similarly, it would not be credible for a famous author to sign a letter to help the blind. But if the author had a blind child or parent, or if he is blind himself, then such an appeal would have credibility.

Many famous people have signed fund-raising appeals and we have ghost written many of their letters. Among those who signed letters for the World Wildlife Fund were Rachel Carson (author of *The Silent Spring*), Roger Tory Peterson (famed ornithologist and artist), and Charles Lindbergh. All were credible; all were successful. The *most* successful signer, as might be expected, was Charles Lindbergh. Partly it was because he was so genuinely passionate about conservation. But, more important, Lindbergh was one of America's all time great heros and because he had never endorsed *any* product or appeal in his long career, his plea for the world's vanishing wildlife and wild places was especially credible. Sadly, most people in the very beginning probably didn't realize that the signature at the bottom of the letter was real. Charles Lindbergh personally signed the first 2,000 letters that went out over his name because he thought a facsimile signature was not quite honest. (Later he succumbed to mass mail because he realized that he could not personally sign hundreds of thousands of letters.)

One of today's most famous letter signers—Katharine Hepburn on behalf of Planned Parenthood—explains very early in her letter exactly why she has taken a personal interest. The Hepburn letter is an all time great; it was executed by Craver, Matthews and Smith, an outstanding consulting firm. When Helen Hayes was asked recently to sign a letter for The Girl Scouts, a client of our firm, we knew that she had been a den mother and that her crippled child had been a Scout—facts included in the letter that made her appeal credible.

When we were mounting the direct mail campaign for the Vietnam Veterans Memorial Fund, one person immediately came to mind as the ultimate signer—the American entertainer who had distinguished himself for more than three decades in entertaining American troops abroad, Bob Hope. Not only did Mr. Hope's endorsement lend credibility, it also helped overcome the liability that the young veteran (Jan Scruggs) who led the memorial effort was an unknown at the time. Scruggs' signature on renewal appeals fared as well as Bob Hope's. But we continued to use the Bob Hope letter to get the *first* contribution.

Now you may ask, "Are people really naive enough to believe that Bob Hope and Katharine Hepburn and Helen Hayes are really writing letters to them?"

The answer is a qualified, "Yes, they do." They know, of course, that the letter isn't a one-of-a-kind. But they expect, *and they have a right to expect*, that the person is solidly behind the cause, and that he or she has read and edited, if not actually written, the copy.

If you cannot find exactly the right celebrity to sign your appeal, it is far better to have the president or chairman of your board sign the letter.

And even if you are lucky enough to have just the right celebrity signer for your cause, you should double check your instincts by testing the celebrity signer against a credible "in-house" signer. The results could be surprising.

The Letter's Length

In the good old days of direct mail fund raising—before merge/purge, before computerized lists, before window envelopes, before common use of nonprofit postage (would you believe most of our prospect appeals went first class?), and certainly before the kind of competition in the mails we see today—we were taught that the letter must be, above all, short.

In fact, the letter had to be so short that it would fit on one side of a piece of 8½" × 11" stationery which already included a letterhead, logo, and long board of directors listing.

It wasn't that the short letters were bad. Many of Harold Oram's were masterpieces. But as it was almost always impossible to tell the entire story on one page, we traditionally enclosed a separate brochure—six to eight panels, glossy stock, two colors, complete with photographs and the board of directors listing that was sometimes removed from the letterhead to save space for precious words of appeal.

As you are aware, the trend today is in the opposite direction. Today's letters are two, three, four—even six and eight pages. And we've actually seen—and read—12-page letters that didn't have a single photograph to relieve the copy.

But this trend didn't begin in direct mail fund raising. The way was paved by advertisers and commercial mailers.

In 1973, Kay Lautman attended an international conference for the World Wildlife Fund in Bonn, Germany, and participated in a day-long seminar on fund raising for the 15 or so countries that make up the Fund's chapters (called appeals).

David Ogilvy, head of Ogilvy and Mather, was attending. "Why don't you," he said to her following her presentation, "test a four-page letter without a brochure against your traditional package? Longer letters work much better for our commercial clients, and I know they will for you too."

"If he hadn't been David Ogilvy," Kay recalls, "I would have thought he was crazy. Maybe I still thought he was a *little* crazy because I didn't test it right away. But when I finally did—WOW! In almost every case, the longer letter outpulled the shorter version by a substantial margin. I've always been grateful to him."

It's true. If your longer letter is interesting, compelling, and well constructed and laid out, you can claim the reader's attention for just as long as any newspaper or magazine. (And once your prospect has committed himself to reading the entire letter, your chances of receiving a contribution increase dramatically.)

Why? Because if a prospective donor is initially interested in the subject, he or she will want to know more. And a longer letter not only imparts more information, it also provides numerous reasons for helping. A longer letter makes the subject seem more important than an additional brochure ever can. There are exceptions to this rule, of course.

While the longer letter (i.e., four to eight pages) works best for political candidates and social action causes (especially topical causes), it has been observed that certain types of causes can obtain equally effective results with briefer messages. These include well-known "household word" humane societies and other domestic animal welfare groups and major health organizations.

The American Cancer Society is a case in point.

The Society's list of more than 4.5 million donors was not built on direct mail, but rather on a long-standing door-to-door campaign conducted by volunteers and other non-direct mail methods. (This in itself makes the following story even more remarkable.)

To learn about the Society's new direct mail efforts, we interviewed John Seremet, Assistant Vice President. Here is what he told us.

To solicit renewals from past donors, the Society relies on a generic direct mail campaign in which 45 of the Society's 58 divisions currently participate. Combined, these 45 divisions drop 12 million pieces of mail annually in a series of three mailings (on the average). Each mailing realizes an average gift of $12 and a 6-9 percent return.

Until 1978, the Society's direct mail packages were fairly traditional, consisting of a computer-personalized letter and response card. The unit cost, at these levels, was 16¢ exclusive of postage.

In 1979, Seremet decided to test a package consisting of *only* a computer-personalized response card and a reply envelope. This unit cost was 5¢ exclusive of postage.

The result? Net income per thousand pieces mailed of the test package was 20 percent more than for the control package, resulting in savings of many thousands of dollars.

We asked Seremet why he thought the simpler appeal had performed better than the traditional package that included a letter. His response was that according to a recent Gallup Poll, the Society's recognition factor was 94 percent among all Americans. Further, the Society has a high credibility factor that enabled it to mail a simple, inexpensive piece that looks, purposely, like a bill (see Figure 5-9).

Encouraged by this success, Seremet decided to develop a similar package for acquisition mailings. In 1984 the Society executed a test of 600,000 names and a roll-out of 2.4 million pieces which overall produced over a 3 percent return. Demographic and psychographic test lists were used, with the psychographic lists accounting for most of the mailing's success.

Our comments. Most not-for-profit organizations cannot replicate the Society's inexpensive package and still maintain a high percent return and average gift. However, if your organization has extremely high national recognition and credibility, you may wish to conduct a carefully controlled test in which you match your control package against a simple bill. We do not think it necessary to do a 50-50 split on such a test, but would recommend that you initially split out 30 percent of your list and send the control package to 15 percent and the test package to 15 percent. Then, if results warrant, you can increase the test on your next mailing.

Above all, be completely honest with yourself as to whether your organization has the recognition factor that will make such a test worthwhile.

A final note on the length of the letter. Most professionals will agree that the letter should be as long as necessary to tell the story effectively and induce the desired response. To ascertain that which is right for your organization you must test, re-test, and re-test again. (In Chapter 9 we provide important guidelines for testing long letters against short ones.)

LESSON NUMBER 4: APPEARANCE

Letterhead

Look at your organization's letterhead. Is it attractive and up-to-date, or has everyone just gotten used to it? Is your logo something that immediately identifies you to the public (like the 4-H Club's four-leaf clover) or does it need revision? Is the typeface in your letterhead old-fashioned? (Perhaps it should remain somewhat old-fashioned if that is part of your image. But couldn't it use just a little jazzing up?)

Paper

White 50 pound offset paper is standard, and there's rarely a need to get fancy. Black type on white paper is not only traditional, it's easiest to read. But there are many kinds of 50 pound offset

Figure 5-9. American Cancer Society Renewal Package

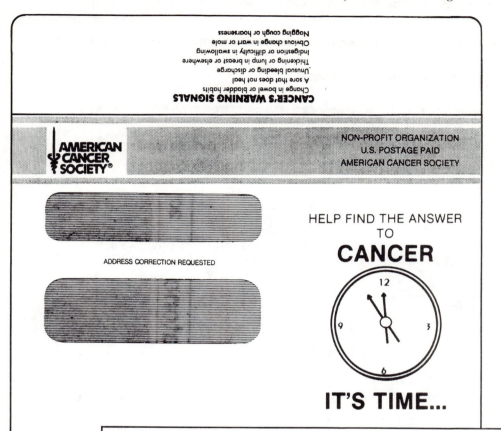

CANCER'S WARNING SIGNALS

Change in bowel or bladder habits
A sore that does not heal
Unusual bleeding or discharge
Thickening or lump in breast or elsewhere
Indigestion or difficulty in swallowing
Obvious change in wart or mole
Nagging cough or hoarseness

NON-PROFIT ORGANIZATION
U.S. POSTAGE PAID
AMERICAN CANCER SOCIETY

ADDRESS CORRECTION REQUESTED

HELP FIND THE ANSWER
TO
CANCER

IT'S TIME...

MOVE THE CLOCK FORWARD

506 SHOSHONI
CHEYENNE, WYOMING 82009

60000-011-00-01259-83G

CAR-RT-SORT** CR12

MRS. A HARRIS
505 VERDE ST
CHEYENNE, WY 82001

My tax deductible donation is:

☐$25 ☐$20 ☐$35 ☐ $_____
                              OTHER

WYOMING DIVISION, INC.
506 SHOSHONI
CHEYENNE, WYOMING 82009

Please make your check payable to The American Cancer Society, and return this form with your check.

Figure 5-9. American Cancer Society Renewal Package (Continued)

stock, so be sure that your printer uses one that doesn't drink the ink, making the entire job look smudged and messy, or uses paper that rejects ink, leaving you with a letter that looks like a fifth carbon copy.

Typeface

Do *not* typeset your letter. The brochure can be typeset. The reply card can be typeset. Even the envelopes can be typeset. But the letter—never. People do not send typeset letters to their friends and associates.

But not just any typewriter typeface will do, and you will be guided by several factors in making your selection. The first is size and the second is "image." Our basic advice is to select a large, easy-to-read typeface. If you want to get creative, many possibilities exist.

For example, if your letter is from a wildlife biologist writing from his tent site in the African bush, you might want to type his message on a portable typewriter, retaining some of his strike-overs and other errors. If you represent a small, struggling organization, you might even want to type your letter on an old-fashioned manual typewriter with an uneven stroke. But in this case, correct all typos. The writer in Africa didn't have the facilities to make corrections, but you do. To imply to the reader that you are so poor that you can't afford typewriter correction fluid or a dictionary is not credible. If you are writing for an established institution, such as a university, type your letter in modern typeface on an electric typewriter or word processor.

Margins

Margins are extremely important—especially in a letter which has no photographs or illustrations. There's no reason for even the unillustrated letter to look boring. The Bob Hope letter (Figure 5-3) is such a letter—far from boring, even though it's all copy.

Subheads

If your letter is long, four or more pages, subheads are a logical and inviting way to break up the copy. As in newspaper or magazine usage, the subheads should be short and attention getting. But don't overdo. Just as there can be too much underlining, so too can there be too many subheads. Generally, we recommend at least two, and no more than three, to a page. The Gallaudet College letter (Figure 5-4) is an excellent example of the use of subheads.

The Art of Underlining

Recently we received an appeal letter in which so much of the copy was underlined that the only parts that stood out were those that were not. Clearly, this is too much of a good thing. Underlining is important in that it makes your reader look at those pertinent messages in your letter, but there are other ways to do it effectively.

For example:

- Try using fat bullets at the beginning of indented listings.

( ) Use large parentheses around entire short paragraphs.

"Use a different typeface (bold italics, etc.) to set off cohesive sections such as quotes or reviews."

Once your letter is finally typed and you have inserted all bullets, parentheses, typefaces, underlinings, etc., put your letter aside for several days and look at it again as though for the first time. You probably will find something to cut. Do so.

Marginal Notations

Another way to get your message across and bring excitement to the look of your package is to use handwritten marginal notations, or call-outs. The prospect letter for the Appalachian Mountain Club (Figure 5-3) is an excellent example.

Marginal notations have a friendly, homespun look and, accordingly, are not appropriate for every organization or appeal. But for animal welfare, most children's appeals, and many membership appeals (especially those that offer fun and exciting benefits), they can enhance a letter's looks, as well as the response.

Here again, don't overdo. A letter with too many marginal notations becomes as difficult to read as a letter with too much underlining.

Use of Photography and Illustrations

Good illustration enhances most direct mail, but the wrong illustrations can spoil the very best copy.

Photographs are more effective than drawings. Photographs convey reality. Drawings convey impressions. Photographs say "this is really happening." Drawings say "maybe this happened, but no one really saw it happen."

Imagine a photograph of a starving child next to a drawing of the same subject. Or imagine a photograph of a frightened, trapped animal next to a drawing of one. Now try to imagine a drawing of the wilderness.

If your agency doesn't have good photographs, go out and take them. The investment of time and money will be returned many times over.

There is an art to using photos effectively in direct mail. Direct mail letters, brochures, and response devices should not look overly slick. Rather, they should look more like a well-kept family scrapbook.

The page position of photos is determined by what you are trying to achieve. You can use photos to break up copy; but be sure that position breaks up the copy at a natural stop—not in a place where continuity is critical.

One effective format is to use photographs throughout the letter as in the letter from the Sea Turtle Rescue Fund (Figure 5-2).

Another way to use photographs effectively is to omit them entirely from your letter and use them on your response device. This works best when your cause does not lend itself to story-telling through photographs, but rather demands a straight copy, serious approach.

In the letters included in this chapter, you will see varying uses of photographs which will be helpful to you in designing your own appeals.

Here is a list of basic rules to follow in choosing or taking photographs to be used in your direct mail package.

1. Be sure the photograph will reproduce well. It may be a great shot, but if it's blurry, what's the use?
2. Select people photographs with "eye contact" to the reader.
3. Avoid sexy photographs and generally shun those of men with beards or long hair.
4. Group shots should be interracial and show members of both sexes if possible. But be proportionate and honest. If, for example, your school has only 15 black students out of an enrollment of 250, don't show a group of two blacks and two whites.
5. In a "poverty" appeal, don't be overly graphic lest your reader discard your letter in despair.
6. In a health appeal, don't show open sores. Rather, show patients in the process of recovery—in wheelchairs or in physical therapy with a doctor or nurse.
7. Don't use funny photographs. Humor seldom works well in fund raising. This does not mean that you can't show people smiling.
8. If you are juxtaposing a hero and a villain, be sure your hero looks his clean-shaven best and that your villain looks as though he's been out all night. If your hero is unattractive, show him with his wife and children.
9. Photos of children and animals always have appeal. Combined, they're unbeatable.
10. Use captions—they are among the first things read. Keep them short and use them to describe the most critical aspects of your work or to illustrate items that a donor's contribution will help purchase.

Color

Of all decisions relating to the appearance of the package, those involving color are often the most difficult. People's response to colors has been the subject of many studies.

The use of color in direct mail can create many different reactions on the part of the recipient. The right color can enhance the mood of the written word. The right color, used properly, can help organize complex information. The right color can represent an idea or a product. And above all, it can claim the reader's attention.

Color isn't just a matter of taste. Psychological tests show that men respond best to blue while women prefer red shades, especially pink. Of the primary colors, yellow is the least favorite of both sexes, but don't discount it entirely. A soft, mellow yellow can evoke feelings of happiness and excitement in a reader. So can red, orange, and other warm colors. Cool colors, on the other hand, like blue, purple, and dark green bring a sense of serenity. Used in a headline, hot colors (intensified warm colors) will grab your prospect's attention—but the cool colors will hold onto it. Body copy is therefore best printed in blue, black, or dark green.

Let us examine the reasons certain colors are chosen for certain packages. (For obvious reasons, we were unable to reproduce our samples of direct mail packages using their original colors.)

National 4-H Foundation. When we mailed for the National 4-H, whose image evokes the green of the famous four-leaf clover (Head, Heart, Hands, and Help), we didn't spend a lot of time debating whether we should try red or orange for a change of pace. The letterhead and other typeset copy was produced in 4-H green, with the body copy set in black. Incidentally, we used the same color scheme for the Girl Scouts and Boy Scouts.

American Israel Public Affairs Committee. The choice of colors was dictated in this case by the colors of the American flag (red, white, and blue) and the Israeli flag (blue and white).

Vietnam Veterans Memorial Fund. The debate was between colors that evoked a feeling of peace (light blue and white) and colors that recalled war (greens and browns). We chose the latter (a buff-colored paper with black and khaki) because it was the *veterans* we sought to honor for their service. Peace was not the issue here.

Appalachian Mountain Club. Seasonality dictated this color choice. In the spring, when prospective members were yearning to get out of doors, we chose a light, spring green. In the summer we chose sky blue and in the autumn we chose golden colors.

Finally, we would like to stress two points:

1. Except in very rare circumstances, *never* screen or tint photographs in color. Blue, green, or red people (the red ones turn out pink) are exceptionally unattractive. Even if you are using a second or third color in your printing, print the photographs in black and white.
2. If you choose colored stock, if you tint your white stock to a color, or if you use a colored drawing or other graphics as background for copy, be sure that the tint is very light in the interest of copy legibility.

Color is important for good design, it is equally important in lending credibility and in generating the desired emotional response. There is hardly a color we have not used successfully on a package, but if we were forced to choose the one color that would work best for a variety of causes, that color would be blue.

PART II. THE RESPONSE DEVICE

The main purpose of the response device is to bear the donor/member's name and address, and allow the donor/member to indicate the size of his contribution. But if you let it go at that, you have not developed a complete package.

The response device should include the following:

- Name and address of the donor
- Name and address of the organization
- Statement about tax-deductibility (if applicable)
- Statement to enable donor to make a response such as:
    ☐ Yes! I want to help and enclosed is my tax-deductible gift of $_____.
- Listing of suggested gift amounts.

Suggested gift amounts generally should be listed in ascending order from smallest to largest. Some like to reverse this order or mix up the amounts. However, we have not found that this technique increases the average gift. On the other hand, the following *will* help you get the gift you are after:

1. listing it first
2. listing it in bold face
3. circling the gift
4. listing it in another color
5. having the computer print out that amount only.

Note: Be sure to leave space for what we call "other amount." No matter how many suggested gift categories you come up with—and we don't believe there should be more than eight—someone will always want to be different. (And that difference could be in your favor.)

The basics, as described above, are illustrated in the response device from Gallaudet College. But just look what happens when the Gallaudet response device (see Figures 5-10 and 5-11) unfolds along a perforated line—it turns into a "mini brochure," which

- Explains what suggested gift amounts will do.
- Illustrates the deaf student's world through photographs.
- Thanks the donor. The photograph of the Gallaudet students in cap and gown is particularly effective because it shows the end product—the grateful graduate.

There are many other things your response device can do to help improve results and increase the average gift. For example, if you are offering a premium for joining (or for gift upgrading) you can have the response device "re-sell" the premium which your letter has already described.

Offer Premiums

Figure 5-12, the Appalachian Mountain Club response device, shows how premiums were listed on the response device.

Explain Membership Categories

If yours is a membership organization, especially one with substantial basic dues, do not overlook the possibility that some people might wish to support your work, but are not in a position to join at the present time.

In such a case, be certain to include a line that says, "I cannot join at this time but enclose a tax-deductible gift of $," as the Appalachian Mountain Club (AMC) does (see Figure 5-12).

You will note that the AMC response device is a non-perforated double device (it folds just beneath the signature line to fit a number 10 envelope). The additional space is used to list Membership Categories and Preferred Chapter Affiliations.

Involve the Donor

The appeal for the National 4-H included the following instructions in the fund-raising letter:

> "You'll notice that I have enclosed a special stamp with *your* state's 4-H clover. Here is what I'd like you to do. Consider how large a gift you can afford to make to your state 4-H Foundation, then write out your tax-deductible check for that amount. Then place *your state's* stamp on the enclosed response card and return it with your gift."

Figure 5-10. Gallaudet College Response Device—Front

GALLAUDET COLLEGE   Kendall Green   Washington, D.C. 20002

☐ **Yes!**   I want to help a student receive a Gallaudet education. The amount of my tax-deductible gift is indicated at right:

Please read the attached leaflet for dramatic examples of what your gift can buy.

☐ **$35**
☐ **$55**
☐ **$100**
☐ **$325**
☐ **$400**
☐ **$500**
☐ **$984**
☐ **$1,500**
☐ **$3,542**
☐ **$** _____
  other

GALLAUDET COLLEGE— *Qualifies For Corporate Matching Gifts*

Detach here and return with your gift.

$55 *will buy a flashing light smoke detector that could save students' lives or a light relay to visually indicate a ringing telephone.*

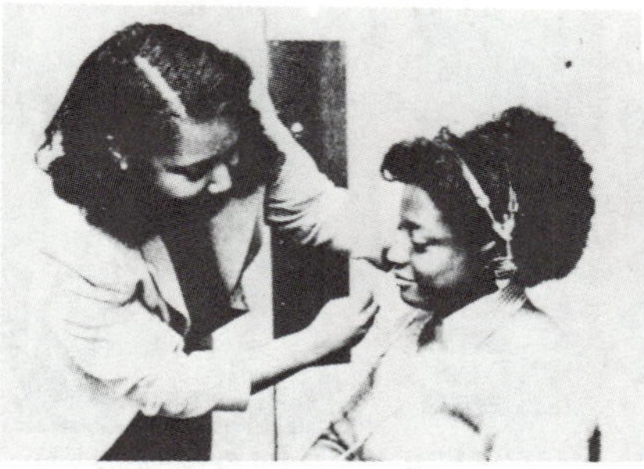

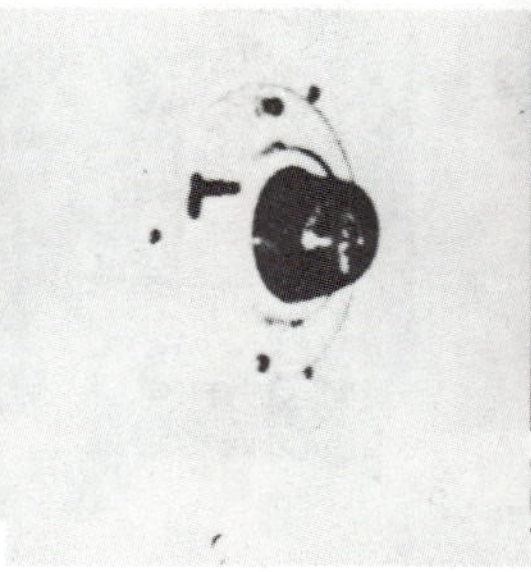

$35 *pays for a mandatory hearing evaluation for an incoming student to insure proper hearing aid adjustment to maximize use of residual hearing.*

$325 *will purchase a hearing aid for a student with limited resources.*

$100 *will pay for a full day of interpreting services—enabling students to "listen" to lectures and presentations by prominent educators, politicians, career counselors and philosophers. Interpreters are also critical when students represent Gallaudet in meetings with visiting dignataries.*

$400 *will purchase a basic computer terminal for individualized instruction in language and math.*

over . . .

119

Figure 5-11. Gallaudet College Response Device—Back

$1,500 *will pay for an intensive eight week course in sign language for a new faculty member whose expertise is in his or her subject area and not necessarily deafness.*

$500 *will purchase a TDD—a keyboard operated Telecommunications Device for the Deaf. The TDD, which often substitutes for the telephone, is invaluable to faculty, staff and students alike.*

$525 *will pay for a semester's braille materials for a deaf student who is also visually impaired.*

$984 *will pay for one student's tuition for one academic year.*

$3,542 *will pay for one student's tuition, room, board and fees for one year.*

Figure 5-12. Appalachian Mountain Club Response Device

APPALACHIAN MOUNTAIN CLUB

5 Joy Street, Boston, Mass.
Att: Thomas Deans, Executive Director

Dear Tom:

☐ ~~Yes~~ I want to join AMC and enclose my check for $_____
corresponding to the membership class indicated below.

☐ I don't wish to join, but enclose a tax-deductible gift of $_____
to help AMC keep the great outdoors great.

☐ I want to give a gift membership in AMC to the person(s) listed on the back.
Please send a notification in my name. My check is enclosed for $_____

_____
SIGNATURE

MEMBERSHIP APPLICATION

A one-time APPLICATION FEE OF $5.00 is included in the following categories except youth.

Membership Class	Dues
Check one:	
☐ Adult	$35.00
☐ Family	$50.00
☐ Youth (to age 23)	$20.00
☐ Senior (age 70 +)	$25.00

Additional categories of membership are provided so that members may support AMC's aims and goals to a greater degree whenever possible.

☐ Contributing (Individual)	$ 50.00
☐ Supporting (Individual/Family)	$100.00
☐ Sustaining (Individual/Family)	$150.00
☐ Life (Individual)	$750.00

Preferred Chapter Affiliation

Check one:
☐ Berkshire, Mass.
☐ Boston, Mass.
☐ Southeast Mass.
☐ Worcester, Mass.
☐ Connecticut
☐ Delaware Valley
☐ Maine
☐ Narragansett, R.I.
☐ New Hampshire
☐ New York — North Jersey
☐ Catskill
☐ Vermont
☐ I do not wish to be affiliated with a local chapter.

TRY US ON FOR SIZE!

If you join AMC as a member before June 30th, 1984, we will send you **FREE** the Country Walks Book (**$6.95 VALUE**) of your choice! Just indicate which one you prefer by checking the appropriate box. Then enclose this form with your check in the envelope provided and join the Adventure!

If you already are a member—DON'T WASTE! Please accept our apologies and pass this offer on to a friend. Thank you.

☐ COUNTRY WALKS Near Boston by Alan Fisher 180 pages!

☐ COUNTRY WALKS Near Montreal by William G. Scheller 152 pages!

☐ COUNTRY WALKS Near Baltimore by Alan Fisher 214 pages!

☐ COUNTRY WALKS In Connecticut by Susan D. Cooley 218 pages!

☐ COUNTRY WALKS Near Philadelphia by Alan Fisher 180 pages!

☐ COUNTRY WALKS Near New York by William G. Scheller 200 pages!

...AND WALK AWAY WITH A FREE GIFT!

Here is a reproduction (see Figure 5-13) of the back of the 4-H response card where the stamp was to be placed and a sample of the stamp designed for Texas (see Figure 5-14). The result of the test? It worked! Even people who wrote letters regretting that they could not send money, faithfully placed their state's stamp on the response card as had been requested.

Figure 5-13. National 4-H Foundation Response Device

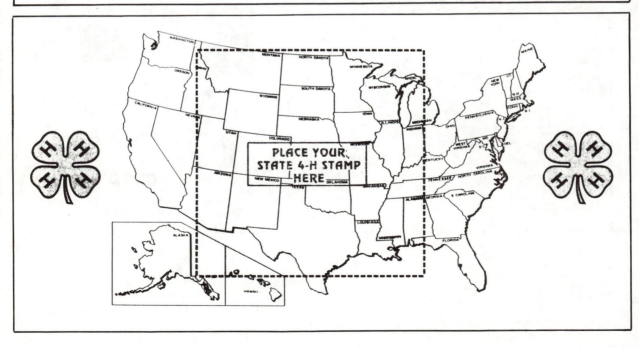

Figure 5-14. National 4-H Foundation Sample Stamp

Clearly, there are many things a response device can do. You have just seen how it can:

- Illustrate what the gift will do.
- Show those whom the gift will benefit.
- Offer premiums for larger gifts.
- List categories of membership.
- Ask for a gift even if the reader can't join at this time.
- Involve a donor by giving him something to do besides just writing a check.
- And much, much more.

The question you must address before you design *your* response device is "What do I want the donor to do?" Then set out to make it as easy as possible for the donor to do it. A bit of advice here: don't make your instructions sound patronizing and don't ask the donors to do too many things, lest they become confused and lose interest.

Some important technical advice:

1. The response device should be printed on stock slightly heavier than your letter so that it feels substantial. This is not necessary if you're using a double-folded reply.
2. The response device should fit the envelope and not slip around inside. It is critical for mail delivery that the name and address not slip out of the window.
3. Before you print, insert the blueline or proof of the response device into the envelope to make sure that the space you have allowed for the address label or computer fill-in is adequate and in the right place.
4. Make sure your response device fits in the reply envelope without the donor having to fold it.
5. If you use a folded response device, make certain that the fold is at the bottom. Should it be printed upside down, the machine inserter will not be able to grab the loose edges and you will be stuck with thousands of unusable pieces.

...onfession: When we did this to one of our clients, we extricated ourselves by printing thousands of "upside down window envelopes." But you can't always bail yourself out so easily—especially if your envelopes have already been printed right side up.

A few more hints about response devices:

- If you have a lot of information to pack in, use a double or even triple response device—and print on the back too—rather than making a single card difficult to read by using tiny type.
- If your package is in computer format, include a personal computer-generated message on the response device.
- Use the response device to sell an "add-on" gift. For example, if the smallest gift you are suggesting is $20, you might say something like the following: "Whatever the size of the check you are about to write, $25 or $250, won't you please add another $3.00 to cover the cost of (here you insert some modest but appealing item)." You'll be amazed how many additional $3 gifts you will get and how quickly they add up. But don't get greedy. If you ask for too much more, it won't work.

PART III. THE ENVELOPE

THE (OUTER) CARRIER ENVELOPE

Postage

To begin, we will assume that your budget, like that of most nonprofit organizations, prohibits the use of first class postage for prospect mail and that you reserve its use for renewing your major donors or for other special programs.

The use of nonprofit postage doesn't eliminate experimentation. There are at least four ways to vary postage.

1. You can have your lettershop "meter" your mail. This costs a few pennies more, but the look is far more personal than a pre-printed indicia. And, as so much of today's first class business mail is metered, few people will notice the difference in the actual amount of postage.

2. You can have your lettershop apply a nonprofit "live stamp." This costs a little more than metered mail, but can be extremely effective in increasing both percent return and average gift—especially when used on an envelope designed to look as personal as possible. We've also heard that the post office often moves this mail faster.

3. You can have a nonprofit indicia printed at the same time your envelopes are printed. This is the least expensive (and the least personal) of all, but if your envelope is highly commercial looking to begin with, it may not matter.

Size of Carrier Envelope

Most mailers use a number 10 (#10) carrier envelope because these are readily accessible and cheapest. But why not a larger envelope—or a smaller one?

The larger envelope has not fared well in direct mail fund raising. This is probably because the large format is psychologically identified with "hard sell" advertising promotions for books, records, insurance, and other merchandise. Moreover, it is extremely costly.

124

The smaller envelope—a number 9 (#9) size—is about the smallest you can use and still enclose a letter of sufficient length to convey your message. There is a great deal to be said for the #9 envelope. It looks more personal than the #10 envelope. In fact, were it personalized and not a window envelope, it might look like a letter from a close friend or relative, or even an invitation to a party.

We believe the #9 format has an important place in direct mail, especially in renewal and donor upgrading programs where the envelope *and* the letter are done on computer. This is not to say that the #9 format shouldn't be used on a prospect campaign. If you can afford to have your entire package re-designed to this size—and remember, this includes not just the carrier envelope but the letter, response device, and brochure—then by all means test it.

The fact that such a test requires all package components to be totally re-designed is, we believe, why more tests on #9 against #10 format are not conducted.

Whether to Use a Window Envelope

Whether you are using a #10 or a #9 carrier, you must decide whether to use a window envelope or a closed face envelope. Clearly, a closed face envelope looks more personal—or does it?

Does a label applied to a closed face envelope look personal? Or were you going to put the label on the response device? If you were going to do the latter, how were you going to address the envelope?

Certainly you can have two sets of labels run provided you can get the list owner to *believe* that you are using them for the stated purpose rather than using the second set for another mailing. But by the time you pay for affixing the label to both pieces, and then pay for a hand-match insert, you could have afforded the cost of a computer letter. No getting around it—you're going to have to make a decision between the two.

Some years ago, after our clients had converted to the use of window envelopes for prospect mail, one organization held out. They insisted that the labels be applied to a closed face envelope. This required the use of a wallet flap reply envelope where the donor had to fill in his own name and address.

Because these mailings were highly successful the client was reluctant to spoil a good thing. Finally they agreed to a small test of closed face versus window envelope. The results were almost equal. Then we made a larger test. The results showed that the window outpulled the closed face envelope by a small but not insignificant amount. When we began sending *all* their prospect mail in this manner, guess what happened? Clerical turnover in their membership department slowed to a standstill because the workers no longer had to struggle with illegible handwriting. And best of all, the accuracy of the donor list dramatically improved. As a result, they raised more money than ever before.

Designing the Carrier Envelope

Naturally, your carrier envelope has your organization's name and return address in the upper left hand corner or on the back flap. Where to put it depends on what else you put on the envelope and why.

Do you want to include, on the face of your carrier envelope:

- Teaser copy?
- A photograph or illustration?
- Nothing?

It's easier, of course, to design a plain envelope, and sometimes that's exactly the right thing to do. You've heard some people say that they *never* open envelopes with teasers. On the other hand, you've heard of many cases where a good teaser outpulls the plain envelope. How then do you know what is right?

The answer is that until you actually test the two envelopes you don't know for certain. But let's assume for now that you want to use an envelope with a teaser. First, ask yourself these questions:

- Do you really have a good teaser line or art? If not, do without.
- If your package contents don't live up to the tease, do without.

If you do decide on a teaser, here are some guidelines:

- If you are using a celebrity signer, use the name and/or photograph on the envelope. You'll need no other message.
- Use a strong photograph. It can even cover the entire face of the envelope, providing that you've made sure that the postage will be legible.
- Try a handwritten note.
- Put the beginning of your letter on the envelope—just the first few lines.
- Make your envelope look like a telegram or a foreign air mail letter—but be sure you follow through inside with an emergency situation.
- Put "PHOTO ENCLOSED: DO NOT BEND" on the outside of the envelope if you're enclosing a photograph or facsimile.
- Try a manila Kraft envelope for an official look.

Don't

- Use teaser copy if you are mailing first class.
- Tease about something you can't deliver—i.e., don't indicate that it's an emergency if it isn't.
- Use banalities such as "Open Immediately."
- Attempt teaser art or copy on a one-color envelope. Spend the extra money for two colors for optimum results.

Here are some of our favorite "teaser" envelopes from different campaigns.

For the American Israel Public Affairs Committee

The envelope in Figures 5-15 and 5-16 was used for a prospect campaign to enlist new members at the height of the fighting in Lebanon in 1983. Note the use of the hero/villain tactic described in Lesson Number 4.

Figure 5-15. AIPAC Teaser Envelope—Back

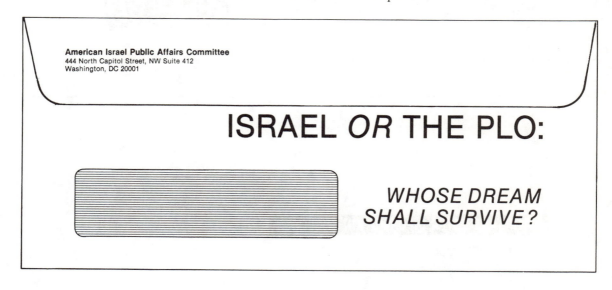

WHOSE DREAM SHALL SURVIVE?

"We shall not rest . . . until we destroy Israel."
—Yasser Arafat

"Peace is the dream"
—Golda Meir

Figure 5-16. AIPAC Teaser Envelope—Front

American Israel Public Affairs Committee
444 North Capitol Street, NW Suite 412
Washington, DC 20001

ISRAEL *OR* THE PLO:

WHOSE DREAM SHALL SURVIVE?

For Friends of the Earth

   Two envelopes (see Figure 5-17) were tested in a prospect campaign to recruit new members in FOE. The theme of both appeals was that citizen participation in 1983 is critical to the outcome of the elections to be held in 1984. In the top envelope, the photograph of the woman in the voting booth and the copy reinforce the point. In the bottom envelope, we "plagiarized" an official government envelope to get the reader's attention with the line, "IMPORTANT VOTER INFORMATION ENCLOSED."

   Question: Which envelope do you think won the test? Answer: The bottom envelope by 30 percent.

Figure 5-17. Friends of the Earth Teaser Envelope Test

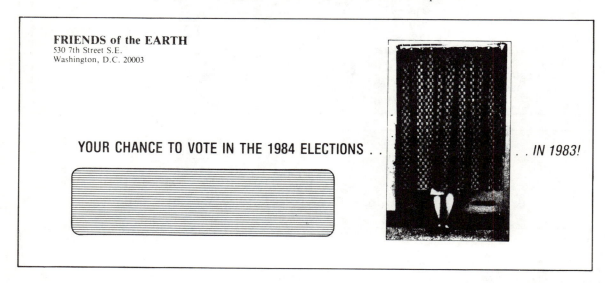

For the Animal Research and Conservation Center

This envelope (see Figure 5-18) is a good example of using a celebrity on the envelope to attract attention and increase interest. The use of Marlin Perkins' photograph increases the chance that he will be recognized, and his affiliation with the television show, "Wild Kingdom," enhances his credibility to speak for this cause.

Figure 5-18. Animal Research and Conservation Center
Teaser Envelope

For the Appalachian Mountain Club

This envelope (see Figure 5-19) was designed to recruit new members, whose outdoor interests are symbolized by the different footgear on the envelope.

Figure 5-19. Appalachian Mountain Club Teaser Envelope

For Wildlife Preservation Trust International, Inc.

The challenge this small organization faced was keen direct mail competition with larger and better-known wildlife conservation groups. The challenge was answered by dramatizing the plight of less popular animals—a theme epitomized by the outside envelope (see Figure 5-20). Here, the copy "We care about the animals nobody cares about" was accompanied by a photograph of a most unusual and appealing animal, an endangered black-footed ferret.

Figure 5-20. Wildlife Preservation Trust International Teaser Envelope

For the Center for Environmental Education (Sea Turtle Rescue Fund)

While we have stated that we prefer photographs to drawings, certain subjects are difficult (if not impossible) to photograph well. And sometimes, to make a strong statement, a drawing does work better. Clearly, the envelope pictured in Figure 5-21 (printed on both sides of a reverse-flap envelope) could not be photographed.

In an envelope test for the Sea Turtle Rescue Fund, the dinosaur envelope (Figure 5-21) was tested against the control envelope showing a sea turtle. The result? The dinosaur envelope with provocative teaser question won by 18 percent.

THE REPLY ENVELOPE

The direct mail appeal must include an addressed, postage paid return envelope (business reply envelope—BRE). The donor doesn't have to find a pen and envelope and address it. Nor does he have to scrounge for a stamp. Nor does he have to call an 800 number and provide detailed information. *All the donor has to do is to write out a check and put it in the mail.*

If you don't believe a BRE (prepaid) is important, try omitting the envelope from a test portion of your next mailing.

There are four things to consider in designing reply envelopes:

- Size
- Plain or wallet flap envelope
- Postage paid or not postage paid
- Color and copy

Figure 5-21. Center for Environmental Education Teaser Envelope

Figure 5-22. Sea Turtle Rescue Fund Envelope

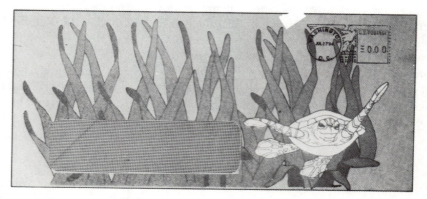

Size

The #9 size and the 6¾" size are standard. We prefer the #9 because even though it is a bit more expensive, the response device holds more copy and fits inside the carrier envelope without folding.

Plain or Wallet Flap?

The use of the wallet flap envelope came into vogue in the days before reply devices were in common usage. In those days, the donor generally filled in his or her own name, address, and gift amount on the inside of the reply envelope, and the "wallet flap" covered that personal information.

When window carrier envelopes and separate response devices came into common use, wallet flap envelopes declined in popularity. However, the flap can be useful for other things such as providing a place for donors to write the names and addresses of potentially interested friends (the flap is on the fold line so it tears off easily).

We sometimes use a wallet with an extended flap, or tongue, called a bang-tail, which permits a longer message.

Postage Paid or Not Postage Paid?

Because it currently costs a nonprofit organization 25¢ to receive a reply-paid contribution, some organizations are testing reply envelopes without prepaid postage.
Our advice:

- Always pay return postage on first-time "pilot" mailings. If you wish to find out if you can be successful without paying for postage due, test a portion of your own donor file and then test again.
- If your donors give just as readily when they pay the return postage, you then may wish to test this on prospect mailings.
- Be cautious. For example, on a mailing of 100,000 pieces, we would advise testing only 10,000 pieces (2,000 from each of five lists).
- If you haven't time to undertake an incremental testing campaign, play it safe and pay the postage.

Color and Copy

Few organizations add "promotional" copy to their reply envelopes, but it can be extremely effective. The best use we know of is when raising money for an emergency. In such a case you might find it effective to put a phrase on your BRE such as EMERGENCY RESPONSE ENCLOSED: RUSH PROCESS! And if you are appealing for a special fund or project, you might want to have your reply envelopes indicate that the gift is for that purpose.

When it comes to choosing a color for your reply envelope, we generally recommend white because it is standard and therefore more economical. Also, an all white BRE will usually stand out in a package where you have used a lot of color on the letter, response device, and brochure. Here, too, you can experiment.

PART IV. OTHER ENCLOSURES

Now that you have written and designed a letter, response device, carrier envelope, and reply envelope, do you have a complete package? Doubtless, if you put it in the mail exactly as it is, it would be sufficient. Still, you wonder: could a little extra something enhance results?

Here again, you will have to test an extra enclosure to learn whether the results would be worth the additional cost. Here are six items worth testing as additional enclosures.

1. **Outside endorsements.** This seal of approval usually takes the form of an editorial or news story about your organization that has appeared recently in a leading newspaper or magazine. Or, it could be part of a more general story where your president or executive director was quoted. The thing that makes it especially valuable is that it is not propaganda written by you, but an endorsement by an outside party.

   If you are fortunate enough to have one or many such clippings, reprint them simply on plain white stock; newsprint is even better. And do not fail to get permission from the media in which they originally appeared.

2. **The endorsement letter or "lift note."** Even if you have access to the perfect celebrity signer, it sometimes makes more sense to have the president of your institution sign the main letter and have the celebrity sign a brief letter of endorsement, sometimes termed lift note, or hanger. The reason for this is that it is more believable for the president to know all the details and statistics about your organization while the sympathetic celebrity underscores the emotional appeal. (see Figure 5-23).

   There's another reason, too, for asking the celebrity to sign the shorter letter, generally printed on monarch size stationery. It will take less time and headache to get his or her approval of shorter copy.

   One celebrity turned down a client when we submitted a four-page letter. But when we presented him with a short note, approval was immediate

3. **The petition.** If your organization is raising money to get something accomplished politically, a petition to a local or national government official can be an effective involvement device. It is regrettably true that politicians pay very little attention to "form" petitions (as compared to handwritten letters of protest). Nonetheless, petitions can be effective fundraising devices. Needless to say, you will receive a lot of return mail from people who sign the petition only and fail to send any money. What's more, this mail will come back first. Don't be too dismayed. The mail with the money will follow soon after. Note: The same is true of surveys and questionnaires of the type often enclosed in political or cause mailings (see Figure 5-24).

   Because such enclosures produce more names and addresses than money, some organizations and political candidates, seeking to build lists, resort to surveys and questionnaires solely to capture the names for later mailings. Their interest in the information elicited, other than name and addresses, is nil.

4. **The brochure.** As we said earlier, we construct very few packages with a short letter and an accompanying brochure because we have found that in most cases a longer letter with no brochure outpulls the alternative.

   However, there are exceptions. Some cases where this makes sense include:

   - A membership organization offering numerous membership benefits such as publications, products, trips, discounts, etc., might list them more effectively in an illustrated brochure that accompanies a shorter letter. Similarly, a mailing for an arts organization—listing events, performances, subscription series, or ticket prices—cries out for a separate brochure (see Figure 5-25).

- Special educational brochures—not for fund raising—telling how the donor can help in other ways.
- Case histories of those your organization seeks to help. (However, we generally prefer to include them in the letter.)

5. **The decal.** Certain organizations, especially those in the conservation field, have found that inclusion of a small decal increases results. When we tested a decal against a non-decal in a mailing for the Sea Turtle Rescue Fund, the decal outpulled the control package by 18 percent (see Figure 5-26).

A word of warning. The National Charities Information Bureau (formerly the National Information Bureau), in New York City, sometimes regards decals as unordered merchandise. To circumvent this problem, the NCIB suggests that you state that the donor is under no obligation to pay for or return the decal.

6. **The newsletter or magazine.** We do not advocate sending your organization's publication with an appeal to join. However, newsletters and annual reports can be effective if they are used in conjunction with annual or special appeals to your own file. Enclosing your publications can also be helpful in your appeals to renew lapsed donors.

7. **Unordered merchandise.** Some organizations include items—such as bookmarks, pencils, greeting cards, tokens, stamps, key chains, and so on—with the appeal letter.

Our advice about this technique can be summed up in one word: *Don't*. Not only will such items make your mailing look tacky, their inclusion will almost certainly lower the average gift. You will generate "guilt" money in the form of many $1 and $2 contributions which cost a lot to record and are impossible to upgrade. Consider the additional cost to your mailing and the fact that inclusion of such material is against the code of ethics of the National Charities Information Bureau and the Better Business Bureau.

Certain items (educational in nature and relatively inexpensive to produce) such as decals and small bumper stickers *can* enhance the success of a mailing. For such items, you can satisfy the requirements of the watchdog agencies by stating in your letter that the recipient is "under no obligation to pay for or donate in response to receiving the enclosed decal [or bumper sticker]."

PART V. THE PACKAGE AS A WHOLE

You've worked hard trying to make each component in the package look just right—from the teaser copy on your envelope to the special lift note from a credible celebrity. You can now rush to the printer, right? Not just yet. Each part of your package may be good, but how do they all look together? Do the pieces complement one another? Is the whole more (or somehow less) than the sum of its parts? To find the answers to these questions you should take a hard look at the package as it will be seen by the potential contributor. Here are some things to ask yourself.

Does the envelope fit well with the letter?

If you are using teaser copy, make sure that the reader who has been "teased" has his curiosity satisfied. For example, if you have a picture of an abused animal on the envelope with copy that reads, "This dog was in danger of dying, until . . ." don't wait until page three to mention the dog.

Figure 5-23. Berea College Endorsement Letter and Lift Note

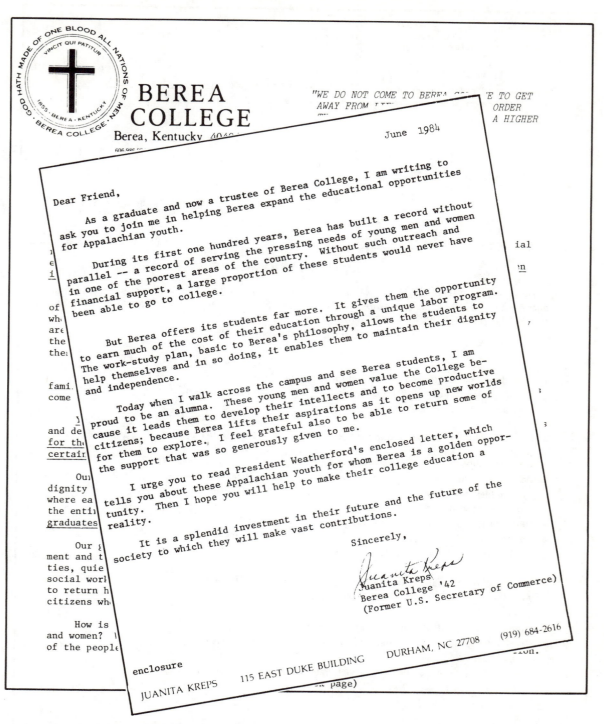

BEREA COLLEGE
Berea, Kentucky 404__
606-986-__

"WE DO NOT COME TO BEREA ___E TO GET
AWAY FROM ___ ORDER
___ A HIGHER

June 1984

Dear Friend,

As a graduate and now a trustee of Berea College, I am writing to ask you to join me in helping Berea expand the educational opportunities for Appalachian youth.

During its first one hundred years, Berea has built a record without parallel -- a record of serving the pressing needs of young men and women in one of the poorest areas of the country. Without such outreach and financial support, a large proportion of these students would never have been able to go to college.

But Berea offers its students far more. It gives them the opportunity to earn much of the cost of their education through a unique labor program. The work-study plan, basic to Berea's philosophy, allows the students to help themselves and in so doing, it enables them to maintain their dignity and independence.

Today when I walk across the campus and see Berea students, I am proud to be an alumna. These young men and women value the College because it leads them to develop their intellects and to become productive citizens; because Berea lifts their aspirations as it opens up new worlds for them to explore. I feel grateful also to be able to return some of the support that was so generously given to me.

I urge you to read President Weatherford's enclosed letter, which tells you about these Appalachian youth for whom Berea is a golden opportunity. Then I hope you will help to make their college education a reality.

It is a splendid investment in their future and the future of the society to which they will make vast contributions.

Sincerely,

Juanita Kreps
Juanita Kreps '42
Berea College '42
(Former U.S. Secretary of Commerce)

enclosure

JUANITA KREPS   115 EAST DUKE BUILDING   DURHAM, NC 27708   (919) 684-2616

(___ page)

As a graduate and a trustee of Berea College, former U.S. Secretary of Commerce, Juanita Kreps, is a credible celebrity signer for the lift note included in Berea College's fund-raising package.

135

Figure 5-24. AIPAC Questionnaire and Reply Form

Thomas A. Dine
Executive Director
AMERICAN ISRAEL PUBLIC AFFAIRS COMMITTEE
444 North Capitol Street, N.W., Washington, D.C. 20001

Dear Mr. Dine:

I WANT MY VOICE TO BE HEARD THROUGH AIPAC!

☐ Enclosed is my/our membership contribution of ☐ **$35*** ☐ **$100** ☐ **$500** ☐ **$1,000** ☐ **$**_____

☐ I am already a member of AIPAC but enclose a special contribution of $_____

Check One:
☐ Please begin sending the *Near East Report* to the address at left.

☐ I already receive the *Near East Report*.

*Remember, a gift of $35 can mean as much $42,777 in U.S. aid to Israel.

- -

AIPAC QUESTIONNAIRE

Please take just a few minutes to answer the following questions and return the form together with your contribution to AIPAC. The questionnaire will be detached from the contribution form, and your opinions will remain anonymous and confidential.

Thank you for taking the time to help us.

1. What do you believe to be at the *core* of the Arab-Israeli conflict?
   ☐ Palestinian issues   ☐ Religious hatred   ☐ Soviet expansionism
   ☐ Arab refusal to recognize Israel
   ☐ Other _____

2. Do you favor U.S. negotiation with the PLO today?   ☐ YES ☐ NO
   Would you favor such negotiation if they accept Israel and
   U.N. Resolution 242 which recognizes Israel's right to exist?   ☐ YES ☐ NO

3. Do you favor the Israeli extension of civil law to the Golan Heights?   ☐ YES ☐ NO
   Did you feel the bombing of PLO headquarters in Beirut was justified?   ☐ YES ☐ NO
   Did you support the bombing of the Iraqi nuclear reactor?   ☐ YES ☐ NO

4. Have you ever contributed to a political campaign?   ☐ YES ☐ NO

5. Do you vote
   ☐ By party   ☐ By candidate regardless of party affiliation

6. Are you Jewish?   ☐ YES ☐ NO

7. Do you believe the sale of AWACS to the Saudis constitutes a threat to:
   America ☐ YES   ☐ NO   ☐ DON'T KNOW
   Israel ☐ YES   ☐ NO   ☐ DON'T KNOW

8. During the AWACS/F-15 debate did you communicate on the subject with:
   ☐ Your Senator   ☐ Your Representative   ☐ The White House
   ☐ By Phone   ☐ By Mail   ☐ In Person   ☐ Through AIPAC

9. Are you affiliated with a Zionist or Jewish fraternal organization? Please list:
   _____   _____
   _____   _____
   _____   _____

This questionnaire was more than a donor involvement device; it elicited valuable information about AIPAC's supporters.

IN RETURN FOR YOUR SUPPORT OF AIPAC, YOU WILL RECEIVE...

For gifts of

$35 *or more*

A one year subscription to *Near East Report*, the authoritative Washington weekly that keeps you informed on Middle East events, Arab propaganda, Washington policy-making and much more.

$100 *or more*

Near East Report subscription PLUS an autographed copy of *Israel's Defense Line: Her Friends and Foes in Washington*, by I. L. Kenen, founder and Honorary Chairman of AIPAC—a book called "fascinating and informative" by Henry A. Kissinger.

$500 *or more*

Near East Report subscription, autographed copy of *Israel's Defense Line* PLUS quarterly legislative updates from AIPAC.

$1,000 *or more*

All the above PLUS private briefings by the director or a member of AIPAC's senior legislative staff whenever you visit Washington, D.C.

Because AIPAC is a registered lobby, contributions are not tax-deductible.

- -

10. Are you a member of AIPAC? ☐ YES ☐ NO

If "NO", had you previously heard of AIPAC? ☐ YES ☐ NO

11. Do you subscribe to the *Near East Report*? ☐ YES ☐ NO

12. Do you subscribe to any of the following publications?

☐ Jerusalem Post   ☐ Midstream

☐ Jerusalem Quarterly   ☐ Commentary

☐ Moment

☐ Other _____

☐ Local Anglo-Jewish Newspaper _____

13. Which aspect of AIPAC's work do you deem most important?

☐ Lobbying for financial   ☐ AWACS Watch
   aid to Israel

☐ Lobbying against U.S. arms   ☐ Countering Arab propaganda
   sales to Israel's enemies

☐ Promoting the political   ☐ Other _____
   involvement of the American-
   Jewish Community   _____

14. Compared to five years ago, do you believe American-Israel relations are:

☐ Better ☐ Worse ☐ The same

15. Special comments, if any: _____

_____

_____

_____

_____

_____

_____

_____

_____

_____

_____

Thank you for taking the time to help us.

Figure 5-25. Appalachian Mountain Club Membership Brochure

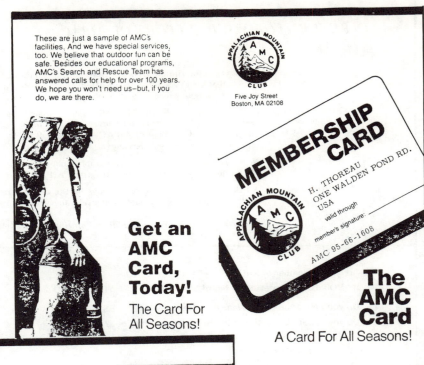

These are just a sample of AMC's facilities. And we have special services, too. We believe that outdoor fun can be safe. Besides our educational programs, AMC's Search and Rescue Team has answered calls for help for over 100 years. We hope you won't need us—but, if you do, we are there.

Five Joy Street
Boston, MA 02108

MEMBERSHIP CARD

APPALACHIAN MOUNTAIN CLUB

AMC

H. THOREAU
ONE WALDEN POND RD.
USA

valid through

member's signature:

AMC 95-66-1608

Get an AMC Card, Today!

The Card For All Seasons!

The AMC Card

A Card For All Seasons!

Pinkham Notch

Camp is located in the heart of the White Mountain National Forest in New Hampshire with public transportation available right to the door. In addition to serving as a base camp for thousands of hikers, climbers and skiers each year, Pinkham has also become a recreational and educational resource offering lectures, seminars and workshops on a variety of subjects including trail main-tenance, backpack-ing, winter mountain safety, winter camping and much more.

The Friendly Huts

are probably the most famous of all AMC facilities. and there are eight of them—simple and cozy–spaced a day's hike apart, high in the White Mountains of New Hampshire. And whether you plan a single day's outing with one overnight or a full eight day mountain adventure, visiting each of the huts, you will sleep bunk-style and share delicious hearty meals (prepared by the hut crews) with people who share your enthusiasm for outdoor life.

Mountain Gate

Lodge is located in the heart of the Catskill Mountains, 100 miles north of New York City—easily accessible by car or bus. Accommodations are bunk-style rooms, and deli-cious meals are served family style. The Lodge has a guest lounge with fireplace and a meeting room, reading room and game library. But most visitors to Mountain Gate spend their time exploring the nearby trails that wind through spectacular countryside.

By including this brochure in its fund-raising package, Appalachian Mountain Club is able to illustrate and describe facilities that are available to members—information that would have otherwise interrupted the flow of the covering letter.

Figure 5-26. Sea Turtle Rescue Fund Decal

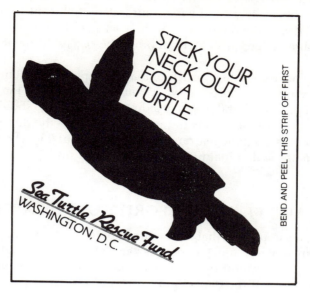

STICK YOUR NECK OUT FOR A TURTLE

BEND AND PEEL THIS STRIP OFF FIRST

Sea Turtle Rescue Fund
WASHINGTON, D.C.

The enclosure of this decal in prospect mailings not only increased returns by 18 percent, it is also an attractive reminder of the donor's support of the Sea Turtle Rescue Fund.

If you are constantly revising the envelope and/or the beginning of the letter, it's important to make sure that you don't decide on the "perfect" envelope and the "perfect" opening, only to find the two have little to do with each other.

Does your appeal have a theme?

As with most popular songs, a good letter has a "hook" that it keeps coming back to. That's why you'll want to make sure each part of the package relates to it. If your theme is "Give a kid a break" by sending him to summer camp, mention it on the response device by writing, "Yes, I want to give a kid a break! Please use my enclosed contribution for your Summer Camp Financial Aid Fund." On the BRE, instead of just having the name and address of your organization, you might include something like, "Summer Camp Financial Aid Fund Contribution: Process At Once." Even if your appeal isn't this specific, you should still make sure its theme is clear throughout the package.

Do you try to include too much information?

When you're doing preliminary research for your appeal, you may find that you have more information than you know what to do with. It may be tempting to try to include everything. But you have to be careful that you don't barrage the prospect with too much information at once. You also don't want to make your appeal visually unattractive by lengthening margins and avoiding pictures and sub-headings so you can get every last word in about your organization's programs. All the information in the world won't mean a thing if it is too difficult to read or be absorbed by the prospect.

Does the lift note or enclosure complement the appeal?

If you can get a credible celebrity to write a lift note you'll want to make sure that what the celebrity is saying relates to the other parts of the package. If your signer tells how one of your organization's programs helped his elderly mother, be certain to mention that program in the appeal.

Similarly, if you're enclosing a news article or magazine piece describing your group, the image that enclosure conveys should represent what you've presented in the rest of the appeal.

Like the pieces of a puzzle, all the pieces of a direct mail package should fit together to create a picture of what your organization is about, and why it merits the donor's support. That might mean you have to spend some time rearranging the pieces, but it will be worth it when the entire package is as good as the individual pieces which make it up.

PART VI. THE INTEGRITY OF THE APPEAL

Before concluding, it's important that we mention how crucial it is that your appeal be presented honestly. As important as it is to conceive of a package which will motivate people to support your organization, you must be careful not to damage your credibility by using false or misleading statements. Here are some of the dangers to watch out for.

Taking credit for something you didn't do.

Often, an organization will work on a problem with other groups. While you should highlight your role in such work, you also want to be careful not to hog all the credit. For example, if yours is a group fighting hunger in East Africa, and you coordinate your efforts with other relief agencies, you would not want to write:

> "Our organization has saved over one million lives which would have been cut short by famine."

A better and more honest statement would be:

> "Our organization has played an important role in fighting hunger in the region. We're proud to take part in relief efforts that have saved over one million lives which would have been cut short by famine."

For a politically active organization, the dangers are even greater. Everyone wants to think they alone have achieved something significant in the political arena, but don't claim exclusive credit for yourself when others have shared the burden.

Using misleading information to support your case.

One of the most effective ways to grab a prospect's attention is to use a startling statistic or fact to shock him into reading further. However, if you use this technique, make sure you get your facts right. When writing political direct mail, you have to be especially careful not to fall into this trap. For example, you might want to claim:

> "Last time Bob Harding ran for the Senate, he tried to buy his seat. But this time the voters aren't going to stand for it. They're not going to let another ten million dollar campaign con them into voting for Harding again!"

This implies that Harding spent $10 million on his last campaign, when in fact he spent $2 million. An aggressive researcher had come up with the $10 million figure after adding Harding's campaign expenditures from the last *four* elections.

A revised version of the copy could read:

"Did you know that Bob Harding has spent over $10 million dollars to keep his seat in the Senate over the past four elections? Isn't it time that we showed him that the people of our state can't be bought?"

If you think that such modifications don't make the statistic that startling, then you should find another alternative. But don't try to mislead the prospect. Even if he or she doesn't catch the deception, your opponent will.

Creating a false sense of urgency.

Another often misused technique is trying to convey a sense of urgency where absolutely none exists. If your organization has a particular urgent need, by all means play it to the hilt. But don't cry wolf. Not only is this dishonest, it will weaken your credibility when you really do have an urgent problem.

One example is the claim of an organization which states, "A cure for disease X is so close, we need just a little more research to put us over the edge. Won't you help us so we can do it?" even when a cure isn't in sight, let alone as close as the organization claims. (While we were writing this book, a group involved with cancer research made an exaggerated claim in its mailing and when it was discovered, had to explain itself in a front-page *Washington Post* story.)

Using extreme scare tactics.

It is to your advantage to point out the real dangers your group is fighting. What you want to avoid is an unrealistic depiction of these dangers. For example, a group fighting for an improved educational system for our children could declare,

"Without your help, our children soon won't be able to even add or read! The only thing they'll know how to do is watch television and play video games."

Instead, you could make your point by saying,

"Such dangerous trends, if allowed to continue, will cripple our children's interest in learning. Children *do* want to learn, but are too easily distracted by television and video games. With your support, we can turn such distractions into learning tools. Children can spend their time watching educational TV and playing video games which teach them arithmetic or English!"

Personal integrity can keep you from crossing the thin line between raising legitimate concerns in an exciting way and using unnecessary scare tactics.

Making false claims about how contributions will be spent.

When asking for a contribution, you must tell the prospective donor why his gift is needed by an organization and the people it serves. However, this can be dangerous if it leads to exaggerated or false claims. For example, if your organization's overall program includes one project that feeds malnourished children, you will want to highlight it in your appeal. But you do not want to overstate the case so that the donor comes to believe that it is the sole purpose of your organization. Thus, instead of claiming,

"Your gift will insure that Bobby will not go to bed hungry."

you may write,

"Our 'Meals for Children' program is just one way in which your contribution will help the people of _____."

Your credibility depends on delivering what you say you will. You have an obligation to your organization and to your donors to ensure that contributions are used for the projects described.

Organizations also must take care that their total fund-raising costs are not so excessive that little if any money reaches those the appeal claims it will. We don't have to remind you of the many investigative reports (some fair and some not) exposing nonprofit organizations that spend too little on the programs for which they request support.

These five dangers aren't the only ones you're likely to encounter when writing your appeal. But most of the time such dishonesty can be avoided simply by casting a discerning eye on what you're sending out and asking yourself if what you're claiming is really true. If the answer is no, it's best to change it. Not only is this the moral thing to do; it also is the most practical. Even if deceptive tactics can generate a few more contributors—a questionable assumption—such gains will be more than wiped out if such deception is discovered. It isn't worth it to risk your organization's integrity.

PART VII. CONCLUSION

In concluding this chapter on the direct mail package, we want to leave you with a few key words that will help you construct your next fund-raising appeal. They are:

Entrance	Make a strong entrance with an arresting opening paragraph.
Emotion	Appeal to the reader's heart first; intellect second.
Excitement	Build the tempo of your letter to an exciting climax.
Example	Talk about real people—their suffering and their hopes. Use case histories if possible.
Emphasis	Underscore or set off what absolutely must be read.
Endorsement	Have an appropriate celebrity write a short endorsement letter or sign the entire letter. Or, include a favorable newspaper clipping about your organization's work.
Education	Give the reader a comprehensive education about your organization but do not confuse education with dull, boring rhetoric.
Emergency	Use this approach only if you have a true emergency. If you do, play it up strongly.
Encouragement	Explain how, with the reader's help, something can be done about the problem.
Exit	Make a strong appeal for money. If you don't, the rest of your letter, however good, is largely wasted.

CHAPTER 6

Packages We Wish We Hadn't Done . . . and One We're Glad We Did

In addition to sharing our successes, we want to share some of our failures to help you avoid repeating the same mistakes.

Looking back at some of our less than successful campaigns we recall that in almost every case we took them on against our better judgment, at the insistence of the client. Some organizations are determined to try their cause in the mail, even though we or other consultants advise against it.

We cannot pass the buck to the clients, of course. In hindsight, it becomes clear that such failures were equally our responsibility because we could have declined to take on these jobs. (We're getting better at saying no.)

TYPES OF UNSUCCESSFUL PACKAGES

Examples of packages we wish we hadn't done fall into four basic categories:

- The too clever package
- The much too much package
- The institutional package
- The identity crisis package

The Too Clever Package

The direct mail copywriter's job is not to write clever copy, but to write copy that sells. The artist's job is not to design a package that will win an award, but to design a package that sells. The account executive's job is to keep both on target. In just a moment we will show you an example of one of our very clever failures.

The Much Too Much Package

This package confuses the prospective donor because it asks him to do more than two things. For example, the *ultimate* much too much package asks the donor to:

- Send a contribution.
- Sign a petition.
- Send the names of interested friends.
- Purchase merchandise.
- Answer a questionnaire.
- Give a gift membership.
- Ask a friend to join.
- Attend a fund-raising benefit.
- Vote in an election.
- Find and use his own postage stamp.

And so on.

While we have never seen, much less written, a package that encompassed *all* of the above, we have seen some that come close—including one of ours. We'll show it to you in this chapter.

The Institutional Package

Many organizational directors have a difficult time accepting the style in which direct mail copy is written. Presidents and executive directors may protest, "I just don't talk like that." Moreover, if directors don't actually insist that you include their photographs in the appeal, they may at least feel it necessary to include a lot of unnecessary material about the history of the organization, perhaps phrased in technical jargon certain to put the direct mail recipient to sleep. In short, they may want the appeal to focus on the organization and not on those it serves. We don't have an institutional package, *per se*, to show, but we will show you its first cousin—"the identity crisis package."

The Identity Crisis Package

The organization with an identity crisis isn't certain what it is or what it wants to be when it grows up—or even who its market is. As a consequence, such an organization sometimes tries to be all things to all people. And what is worse, it insists that the fund raiser produce a package that proves it.

The organization that got us to write not just one but several such packages held us accountable when they didn't work. They were right to blame us. Our sin was that we tried to make it work *more than once.*

SAMPLES OF DIRECT MAIL PACKAGES THAT FAILED

Sample I: The Too Clever Package

In the 1970s, a women's organization, which we will not name, hired us to launch them in direct mail. At the time, several women's organizations were beginning to experience success in the mail, and our friends were eager to follow suit. The problem was that this particular organization's basic program just didn't lend itself to a mail appeal. There was no question that they did important work, but their appeal was not visceral.

The organization didn't want to hear that, however. It was our job, they insisted, to package their cause in a way that would make it attractive to the direct mail donor. Thus challenged, try we did. In fact, we tried too hard. After writing the best letter we were capable of at the time, we found it sadly lacking. Instead, we decided to do something clever. *We invented a board game* the size of a small poster, and enclosed it with the appeal (see Figure 6-1).

Figure 6-1. Game Board as Part of Appeal

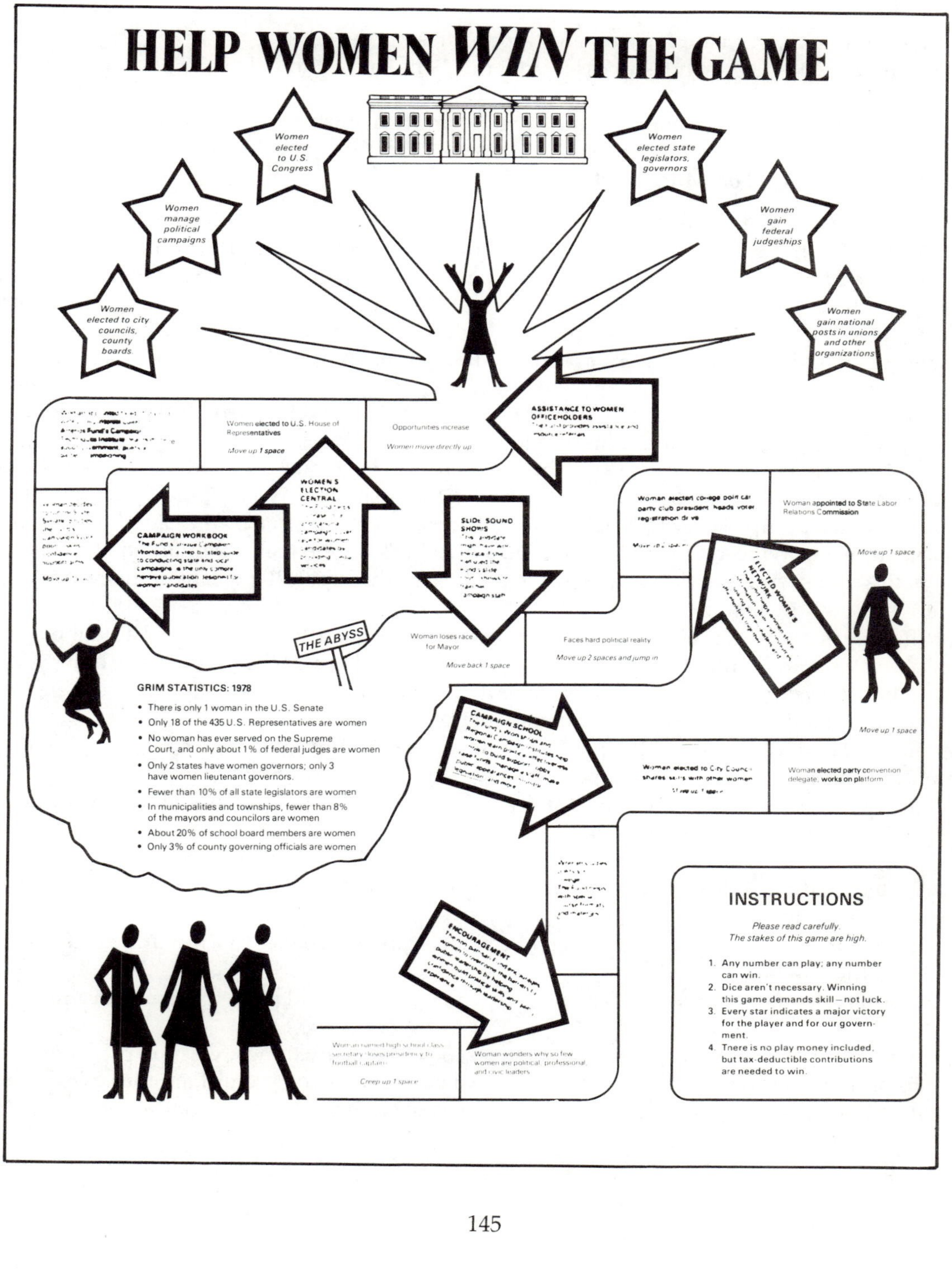

Yes, it was a real game with moves and penalties and rewards. It even had instructions. Our favorite instruction was "There is no play money included, but tax-deductible contributions are needed to win."

It didn't work. Do you know why? It was certainly clever—see for yourself. But could people take seriously a message that included a game? Clearly not. They didn't give in droves.

Today this cause might have a better chance in the mail. At least it would have three things going for it.

1. The fund-raising climate for women's groups has improved.
2. The organization has some successes under its belt that would help sell the program on its own merits.
3. No one, least of all us, would include a game in their fund-raising package.

Sample II: The Much Too Much Package

As much as we would like to tell you that all our mistakes were made long ago, the one we are about to describe happened in 1983 when we undertook a membership recruitment mailing for Friends of the Earth (FOE) (see Figure 6-2). Like many nonprofit organizations, FOE dreamed of a campaign in which each of its members (well—half of them anyway) would enlist just one more member, thus increasing its membership by 50 percent. Sounds wonderful, doesn't it? The problem was (and is) that this entails asking the most difficult thing one can ask of a friend—to spend his money on something *you* believe in.

When we agreed to do this mailing we were not altogether babes in the woods. We had tried this technique (without success) for another organization.

We took heart, however, in the fact that several organizations do conduct member-get-a-member campaigns successfully. An example is the National Rifle Association—an organization with a committed group of closely-knit, like-thinking members. So, fired by the client's contagious enthusiasm, we convinced ourselves that FOE's members were equally committed and equally passionate about saving the environment. We postulated that up to 10 percent of them would go out and enlist a new member.

But there was another problem to confront. FOE could not afford the cost of a mailing that wouldn't make a net profit. Thus we were charged with creating a package which not only would ask members to recruit new members, but one that also would ask members to make their own special contribution above and beyond membership dues.

Should we have refused to do the mailing? We might have done so had we not been inspired with an idea on how to make the appeal unique, clever, and *compelling*.

And it was all those things. We loved it. The client loved it. The client's staff and volunteers loved it. How could it fail when we had:

1. Created a cut-out letter for members to literally cut out and send to a friend? All members had to do was sign it.
2. Offered premiums for getting new members, including the chance to win a drawing for a trip down the Colorado River?
3. Made a really strong argument as to why each member should participate in the campaign?

Knowing that it is dangerous to ask the member to do too many things, we took precautions to keep him from being confused. In the letter that asked the member to enlist another, we did not ask that he also make his own contribution. That request was made in a separate letter (smaller in size and different in color) which, because it bore the member's name in large type, would automatically give him credit for soliciting the new member when he or she responded (see Figure 6-3).

Brilliant! Then we put the entire clever mailing into an equally clever envelope with teaser copy that said "One Good Friend Deserves Another" (Friend of the Earth—get it?) and mailed it off to FOE's membership list.

Then we waited. And waited. And waited.

Well, the results weren't as bad as all that! Some members actually did go out and recruit other members. Some more affluent and/or reticent members *gave* gift memberships to their friends. But it certainly didn't increase the membership by 10 percent or even come close.

Worse still, the mailing did not work as a fund raiser because members were accustomed to receiving straightforward appeals on specific environmental issues. This particular appeal simply got lost in the complexity and cleverness of the package.

The client was kind. Despite our failure, he still liked the package. In fact, we still liked it. But liking doesn't count. The only thing that counts is whether it works. *This may be the most important sentence in this book. Read it again.*

Sample III: The Identity Crisis Package

In the mid-1970s a venerable conservation organization focused on an important single issue became a client. Unfortunately, it became a client at a time when its president was intent on expanding its interests to include a multitude of other conservation issues.

Fund raisers should not be placed in the position of defining an organization's programs. Sometimes, however, we are encouraged to give our point of view as to how program changes will effect fund raising. In this case, our point of view—to stick to the narrow—was rejected.

Instead, we were charged with creating direct mail prospect packages that would show the organization to have a broadly comprehensive series of programs dealing not only with the issue they were best known for, but also with wildlife, forestry, wilderness, oceans, energy, national heritage, industrial pollution, farming, and even population.

The organization's management insisted that our membership recruitment campaign show that the organization could deal effectively with *all* environmental problems. The effect was that not only did the public not buy this premise, but the organization lost its unique identity in the process.

The prospect mailings we developed for this organization over a period of several years were not total failures. But because they never drew more than a .7 percent return, the client was always angry and perplexed that we could not generate better returns. His answer to the problem? To send us back to the drawing board to come up with yet another multi-issue appeal. He could never translate the fact that the appeals we developed to the membership based on single issues were dramatically successful, thus we were never allowed to try this approach in recruiting new members.

After we parted company with the client, its administration changed and the organization began concentrating once again on the area for which it was known to be expert.

Figure 6-2. Friends of the Earth Member-Get-a-Member Campaign Letter

Friends of the Earth

May, 1983

TO: Friends of the Earth Members and Supporters

FROM: Jeffrey Knight, Executive Director

RE: FOE's NEW MEMBERSHIP CAMPAIGN

Today there are 32,000 Friends of the Earth and another 15,000 non-member supporters — allied together out of respect and affection for the dwelling place of mankind, joined in a commitment to effective political action to save our planet. Our only planet. Our only earth.

If we are to succeed in preventing this earth from being poisoned, plundered and polluted beyond endurance, we must change the policies being pursued by the administration now in power. To accomplish this, we must build our membership in order to increase our lobbying power in Congress and to prepare for a major role in the 1984 elections.

That is why Friends of the Earth has launched an all-out campaign to increase our membership to at least 50,000 by the summer of 1984!

And we need your help to do it!

Let me explain how important an additional 18,000 members will be to FOE — and to the world. It would mean at least $500,000 we could use to be more effective advocates for the environment in Congress and around the country. And our larger membership would allow us to double our 1984 election efforts as compared to 1982.

What is more, if you and other Friends will accept the challenges to recruit at least one other member, almost all of the money will go directly to the cause. (As you probably know, it is expensive to search for new members in the mail. We do it, of course. And we do it as economically as possible, but it is a slow and costly process.)

That is why I am asking you to write, phone or visit one or two (or more) friends and personally urge them to join Friends of the Earth. When we have achieved our goal, not only will we have more money with which to do battle, but our sheer numbers will give us more political clout in Washington, D.C., and across the country.

Will you help?   Let me tell you about our exciting membership plans.

You have probably noticed that I have enclosed six membership application forms — each imprinted with your name and address and personal I.D. number.

The first thing I would like you to do is sit down with your address book or your Rolodex or your holiday card list and come up with at least one ... better six ... and possibly more names of friends, relatives and associates who share your environmental concerns.

(Continued on Page 3)

1045 SANSOME STREET, SAN FRANCISCO, CA 94111
530 7th STREET, SE, WASHINGTON, DC 20003

YOU CAN WIN
A TRIP DOWN THE COLORADO RIVER
THROUGH THE GRAND CANYON!

If you recruit one or more new FOE members* in our 1983 membership campaign, you will automatically become eligible to win the grand prize of an all-expense paid trip for two (including transportation) to Grand Canyon National Park—for a vacation to be remembered!

Entries will be based on the number of new members recruited (i.e., if you recruit six members, you get six chances in the grand prize drawing.)

THERE ARE NO LOSERS — ONLY WINNERS!

Even if you don't win the grand prize, you will receive a gift of appreciation just for participating.

HERE IS HOW IT WORKS:

IF YOU RECRUIT . . . .

. . . *ONE new member,* you will receive a handsome Certificate of Appreciation suitable for framing.

. . . *TWO or more members,* you will receive the Certificate of Appreciation AND a FOE cloth patch to sew on your jacket or backpack.

. . . *FOUR or more members,* you will receive the Certificate of Appreciation, AND the FOE cloth patch AND a FOE T-Shirt.

. . . *SIX or more members,* you will receive the Certificate of Appreciation AND the T-shirt AND a handsome poster depicting the "American Peaceable Kingdom" reproduced from the collection of Mr. and Mrs. Robert Redford.

Friends of the Earth

To be eligible for the prizes and for the drawing, you MUST use the official membership application forms enclosed. (Identical forms appear in the June issue of Not Man Apart). Contest ends December 31, 1983.

Then I would ask you to visit or write them and tell them about FOE and our campaign to defeat this administration's policies over the next year. I know you are very busy, so I have taken it upon myself to make it easier for you by writing a letter which you can simply photocopy and send to your friend(s) along with one of the enclosed membership application forms.

Of course, the letter is only a suggestion. Your own letter (or better still, a personal visit or call) will be even more effective.

(over)

Send this letter to a friend with the enclosed membership card!

You fill in the salutation →

Remember - one good friend deserves another!

Cut letter out here

I am writing to you about FRIENDS OF THE EARTH, an environmental organization which I support.

Friends of the Earth is the organization that — in addition to defending our national parks and wilderness areas — leads the fight to stop acid rain, reduce nuclear weapons, protect the nation's coastlines, and promote safe energy alternatives to nuclear power.

FOE has now launched a campaign to reverse the disastrous environmental policies of the Reagan Administration — a campaign based on the recognition that while Watt's wrong and EPA's Anne Gorsuch Burford was a disgrace, that the real puppeteer of the past two years — the man whose policies Watt and Burford were (and are) dutifully following -- is the President of the United States.

As a fellow environmentalist, I believe that you will agree with FOE's position. That is why I am sending you this letter urging you to join FOE and therefore join us in a national campaign to prepare for a major role in the 1984 elections.

When you join Friends of the Earth, you will be joining a growing body of concerned Americans for whom FOE is their advocate for effective environmental action. And you will be kept informed of that action through a subscription to the highly acclaimed monthly magazine, NOT MAN APART, which The San Francisco Chronicle says "provides the best overall news coverage of both regional and global environmental matters".

FOE is a leader, not a "jump-on-the-bandwagon" follower. Thus you will be joining the first environmental organization to become involved in the arms control/military procurement field and the only one to employ a full-time arms control lobbyist among all the conservation organizations.

over ...

But however you choose to do it, I urge you to participate in FOE's member recruitment campaign. Everyone who helps will receive a gift from us and will qualify for an all-expense paid Colorado River trip through the Grand Canyon.

But your greatest reward will be in knowing that you personally helped change the government — that you made it more responsive to the needs and desires of the American people. Thank you for your time. If you need more information or materials to help recruit members, please let me know.

Sincerely,

Jeffrey W Knight

Jeffrey W. Knight
Executive Director

FOE is affordable. Basic membership dues are only $25. However, it is only fair that I point out that membership is not tax-deductible. And for a very important reason essential to our unusual effectiveness: FOE is not a charity, it is an organization of activists which uses all legal means — including lobbying, legal action and elections — to accomplish its goals.

Another reason membership is not tax-deductible is because of FOE PAC, FOE's Political Action Committee. In its first major effort last year, FOE PAC succeeded in 34 of 48 races. (But unless I miss my guess, tax-deductibility isn't your main concern when it comes to protecting the environment.)

To join FOE, simply fill out the enclosed application card and send it with your check for $25 or more to Friends of the Earth. The address is on the back of the card.

I'll get credit for having recruited you as a member. But more importantly, you will have the satisfaction of knowing that — despite your very busy schedule — you are in the fight.

Will you let me know that you have agreed to be a Friend of the Earth? Or, if you have any questions, please call me.

With best personal regards,

P.S. Knowing you, you already support one or more environmental organizations. So do I — because it is critical to have a variety of forces at work, each with a different focus.

But I put FOE at the top of my list because they have the courage to lead. I hope you will put them high up on your list too.

Don't be afraid to say this. If tax-deductibility were a deterrent to membership, we wouldn't be in business!

Sign your name here

Thanks!

Figure 6-3. Friends of the Earth Member-Get-a-Member Campaign Personalized Response Device

To: **FRIENDS OF THE EARTH**, 1045 Sansome Street, San Francisco, California 94111

☐ Enclosed is my special contribution to FOE of $ _____ .
☐ Enclosed is my tax-deductible contribution of $ _____ to FOE Foundation. I understand that donations to the Foundation do not include membership in FOE.

☐ $20
☐ $50
☐ $100
☐ $500
☐ Other _____

Mr. Sam T. Moran
568 Maple
Sleepy Hollow, IL 60218

276144V

1G

You Can Count On Me!

THE EARTH NEEDS NEW FRIENDS!

Six recruitment forms are attached for your use in soliciting new members (or alternatively, for giving a gift membership).

THANK YOU for participating in this important membership drive.

I'll be a FRIEND OF THE EARTH!
My membership dues of $25 (regular member) or more – or $12 (student, retired member) are enclosed. ☐ Check here if this is a gift membership.

name _____ Mr. Sam T. Moran
address _____ 568 Maple
Sleepy Hollow, IL 60218
Recruited by Friends of the Earth Member:

276144V

I'll be a FRIEND OF THE EARTH!
My membership dues of $25 (regular member) or more – or $12 (student, retired member) are enclosed. ☐ Check here if this is a gift membership.

name _____ Mr. Sam T. Moran
address _____ 568 Maple
Sleepy Hollow, IL 60218
Recruited by Friends of the Earth Member:

276144V

I'll be a FRIEND OF THE EARTH!
My membership dues of $25 (regular member) or more – or $12 (student, retired member) are enclosed. ☐ Check here if this is a gift membership.

name _____ Mr. Sam T. Moran
address _____ 568 Maple
Sleepy Hollow, IL 60218
Recruited by Friends of the Earth Member:

276144V

I'll be a FRIEND OF THE EARTH!
My membership dues of $25 (regular member) or more – or $12 (student, retired member) are enclosed. ☐ Check here if this is a gift membership.

name _____ Mr. Sam T. Moran
address _____ 568 Maple
Sleepy Hollow, IL 60218
Recruited by Friends of the Earth Member:

276144V

I'll be a FRIEND OF THE EARTH!
My membership dues of $25 (regular member) or more – or $12 (student, retired member) are enclosed. ☐ Check here if this is a gift membership.

name _____ Mr. Sam T. Moran
address _____ 568 Maple
Sleepy Hollow, IL 60218
Recruited by Friends of the Earth Member:

276144V

1G

I'll be a FRIEND OF THE EARTH!
My membership dues of $25 (regular member) or more – or $12 (student, retired member) are enclosed. ☐ Check here if this is a gift membership.

name _____ Mr. Sam T. Moran
address _____ 568 Maple
Sleepy Hollow, IL 60218
Recruited by Friends of the Earth Member:

1G

ONE WE'RE GLAD WE DID

By pounding away at the basics, we do not mean to discourage you from trying to be creative. We don't want to make it sound as though creating successful direct mail fund–raising packages is done only by rote and rules that only sameness follows. Because every once in a long while someone has a truly clever idea—*and it still works!*

Kay Lautman had such an idea on behalf of the World Wildlife Fund in 1973. The idea struck her that the list of rare and endangered species was an exceedingly long one. She envisioned a prospect package that would list every endangered species on a very l-o-n-g, narrow paper (3″ wide) folded into a tiny envelope (3½″ × 4½″), with the smallest possible reply envelope folded to fit the carrier envelope (see Figure 6-4).

The exciting aspects, as she foresaw them, were:

1. People certainly would open the tiny envelope that looked like an invitation or thank you note.
2. The dramatically long list of endangered species made its point as well or better than the usual copy.
3. The likelihood of its being thrown away was less than usual, because many people would keep it for reference or curiosity or as a teaching aid.

She also saw the following possible drawbacks in the design:

1. The package was expensive to produce. It had to be printed and folded on special presses, and hand inserted into the tiny envelope.
2. The package was expensive to mail. Because of its unusual dimensions, the post office required that it be mailed *first class*.
3. The diminutive size of the envelope precluded enclosing a fund-raising letter. To compensate, the list of endangered species was prefaced with the words, "Dear Friend." And some 12 feet later, the listing ended with a one paragraph appeal made over the signature of World Wildlife Fund's president.

But the returns more than justified the additional costs. And for several years, no other single World Wildlife Fund package outpulled the six–foot, two-sided listing that began with the white-fronted wallaby and ended with the Seychelle Island tree frog.

Figure 6-4. World Wildlife Fund Appeal Letter

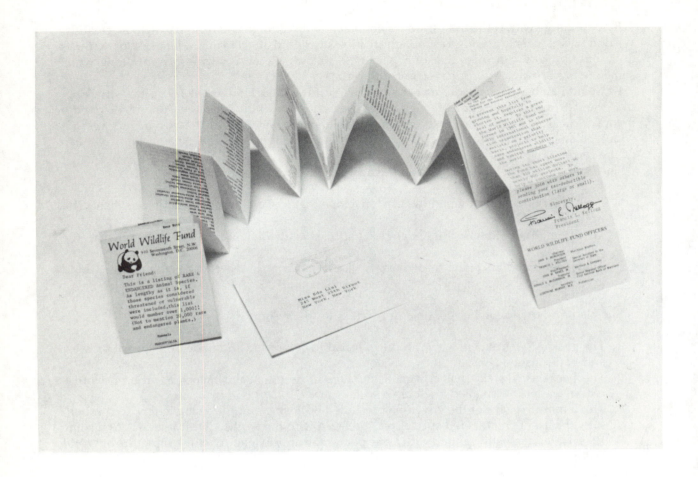

CHAPTER 7

Successful Direct Mail Packages by the Pros

Let's face it. There are some people who are going to be so receptive to your cause, they will give whether your appeal is exceptional or merely adequate. On the other hand, there are those who will not donate no matter how compellingly you present your information because they simply are not interested in your cause. (Yes, even with good list selection).

But in between the pre-sold donor and the you-can't-sell-me-anything types exist thousands of prospective donors who *can* be convinced to contribute—*if* your envelope compels them to open your appeal and your opening paragraph compels them to read your letter. For once a letter is read through, the chances of the prospect making a contribution increase dramatically.

That is why, with rampant competition in the direct mail marketplace, it has become increasingly critical to design and produce not merely a good appeal, but an exceptional one. In Chapter 5, and elsewhere throughout this book, we have shown you samples of letters and other package elements written and designed by our firm. But because we recognize that there's an awful lot of talent out there, we wanted to share some of the best work executed by some of our competitors.

Following are eight packages produced by six different firms for a variety of causes. The style and substance differ from one sample to the next. But all have one thing in common—they worked exceptionally well. And their success in motivating people to give (including those previously undecided about the issue or cause) is testimony to their authors' creativity.

Opposite each sample, we've provided background information about the package and a commentary. But as you pore over the envelopes, letters, response cards, and inserts, undoubtedly you'll agree that these appeals speak for themselves—just as they spoke to the millions of people who received them in the mail—and gave generously in response.

ORGANIZATION   Alton Ochsner Medical Foundation Society
REPRESENTED: New Orleans, Louisiana

DESIGNED/   Endata, Inc.
PRODUCED BY: Nashville, Tennessee

DATE OF   1982
APPEAL:

TYPE OF   Special Membership
APPEAL:

PURPOSE OF   To develop a membership structure which would increase volunteer
APPEAL: support and participation among donors and prospects to Alton Ochsner
                    Hospital and the Ochsner Clinic.

CAMPAIGN   The series of three letters shown was part of a test campaign. The first letter
RESULTS: was mailed to 1,263 previous contributors of $100-$499, with the two
                    follow-up letters sent to those who did not respond. The final results
                    included a response rate exceeding 30 percent with an average gift of
                    $220.13 and a net profit of $79,853. The overall campaign of which this test
                    was a part consisted of nearly 50,000 appeals mailed to different audiences
                    made up of donors, former patients, and selected prospects. The entire
                    campaign brought in $187,548 in net income, and earned Endata, Inc. a
                    Bronze Echo Award from the Direct Marketing Association in 1983.

COMMENTS: Through a carefully conceived, highly personalized campaign, the Alton
                    Ochsner Medical Foundation Society was launched to commemorate the
                    life and advance the work of Dr. Alton Ochsner.

                    The "society" theme was well executed throughout the appeals, suggest-
                    ing prestige, selectivity, and the high standards of Dr. Ochsner. As one
                    letter puts it, "Membership in our society . . . is a distinct honor."

                    The different levels of giving also provided an excellent means to upgrade
                    donors within the context of society membership. In the letter, donors are
                    reminded of their past contribution to Ochsner and asked to join the
                    appropriate membership category at a level of giving one or two notches
                    higher than where they are currently.

                    Other factors contributing to the success of the campaign included follow-
                    up letters which established continuity in the request for support; benefits
                    such as a commemorative lapel pin consistent with the prestige of society
                    membership; and the descriptive brochure on the Society and "The Och-
                    sner Heritage." Finally, the credibility and sincerity of the campaign was
                    enhanced by the letter signer, none other than Dr. Ochsner's son, seeking
                    to carry out his father's legacy.

Initial Appeal

Mr. David A. Sampleperson, Jr.
Endata, Inc.
421 Great Circle Road
Nashville, Tennessee 37228

1516 Jefferson Highway, New Orleans, Louisiana 70121

Special Donors

April 26, 1982

April 26, 1982

Mr. David A. Sampleperson, Jr.
Endata, Inc.
421 Great Circle Road
Nashville, Tennessee 37228

Dear Mr. Sampleperson:

It gives me great pleasure to inform you that your name has been placed in nomination for Charter Membership in the newly formed Alton Ochsner Medical Foundation Society.

Since my father's death last fall, we've been seeking an appropriate way to commemorate his exceptional life and work.

I personally believe no tribute could be greater than the formation of a society of farsighted individuals committed to advancing the tradition of excellence in patient care, medical education, and clinical research to which he dedicated his life.

And I use the word "advancing" advisedly. For today--more than at any other time in Ochsner's 40-year history--private contributions of every size are vital if we are to continue providing the finest medical care.

You will notice in the enclosed brochure that seven levels of membership in the Alton Ochsner Medical Foundation Society have been established, each carrying valuable benefits.

Because of your $100 gift in March 1981, it is my sincere hope you will accept this special nomination to the Alton Ochsner Medical Foundation Society by becoming a member at the ADVOCATE or perhaps even the ADVISOR level.

You will have the satisfaction of knowing your annual membership contribution is helping protect and strengthen Ochsner's heritage of caring and healing. I await your early reply.

Sincerely yours,

John Ochsner, M.D.

JO:laa

P.S. Simply indicate your level of membership on the enclosed Enrollment Form and return it with your membership gift today.

1516 Jefferson Highway, New Orleans, Louisiana 70121

157

ALTON OCHSNER MEDICAL FOUNDATION SOCIETY

May 24, 1982

Mr. David A. Sampleperson, Jr.
Endata, Inc.
421 Great Circle Road
Nashville, Tennessee 37228

Dear Mr. Sampleperson:

I am pleased to report that response to the Alton Ochsner Medical Foundation Society has been overwhelming!

Already more than 500 individuals have accepted nomination as Charter Members. I sincerely hope that you, as a valued friend and supporter of Ochsner, will join, too.

Membership in our society, formed in tribute to my father's life and work, is a distinct honor. I say this because the resulting contributions will provide the essential financial support necessary to maintain the important work of the Ochsner Medical Institutions.

Specifically, your participation will help us to continue offering the highest quality health care. Additionally, you will be indirectly responsible for educating the physicians of tomorrow in the most sophisticated specialities of health care. Also, you will be aiding Ochsner in discovering new answers to medical questions through clinical research.

Again, I urge you to select an appropriate level of membership from those listed on the enclosed Enrollment Form. Because of your previous gift of $250, I suggest the level of ADVISOR or even DIPLOMATE.

Ochsner is recognized as one of the world's great medical institutions. You can enjoy the lasting satisfaction of helping to protect and advance this heritage of caring through your participation as a Charter Member of the Alton Ochsner Medical Foundation Society. Please join today.

Sincerely,

John Ochsner, M.D.

JO:hlb

P.S. Please note the special benefits listed on the enclosed Enrollment Form that you receive as a Charter Member.

1516 Jefferson Highway, New Orleans, Louisiana 70121

Second Follow-up

ALTON
OCHSNER
MEDICAL
FOUNDATION
SOCIETY

June 21, 1982

Mr. David A. Sampleperson, Jr.
Endata, Inc.
421 Great Circle Road
Nashville, Tennessee 37228

Dear Mr. Sampleperson:

As you know, your name has been placed in nomination for membership in the Alton Ochsner Medical Foundation Society.

The deadline for acceptance is approaching and in order to become a Charter Member, I must have your answer by July 15.

Let me emphasize that nomination for Charter Membership in our society is only being extended to a select group of friends--persons like yourself who are committed to advancing the health care excellence of Ochsner and to ensuring that it continues to grow and to expand as medical knowledge and technology develop.

Through your membership, you will contribute directly to the strengthening of patient care at Ochsner, which my father so aptly described as "the court of last appeals for those suffering from difficult and unusual illness or injury."

Also, as a Charter Member, you will have the satisfaction of knowing you are helping to support Ochsner's superb medical education program as well as its important clinical research that seeks new answers to life-saving medical questions.

Please note the membership levels listed on the enclosed Enrollment Form. Your gift of $100 in September 1978 indicates you may wish to become an ADVOCATE or an ADVISOR. But whatever level you choose, please respond promptly. I must have your decision by July 15. I look forward to welcoming you into the Alton Ochsner Medical Foundation Society.

Most sincerely,

John Ochsner
John Ochsner, M.D.

JO:llc

P.S. Just as soon as I receive your Enrollment Form, I will send you complete details of your membership benefits.

1516 Jefferson Highway, New Orleans, Louisiana 70121

159

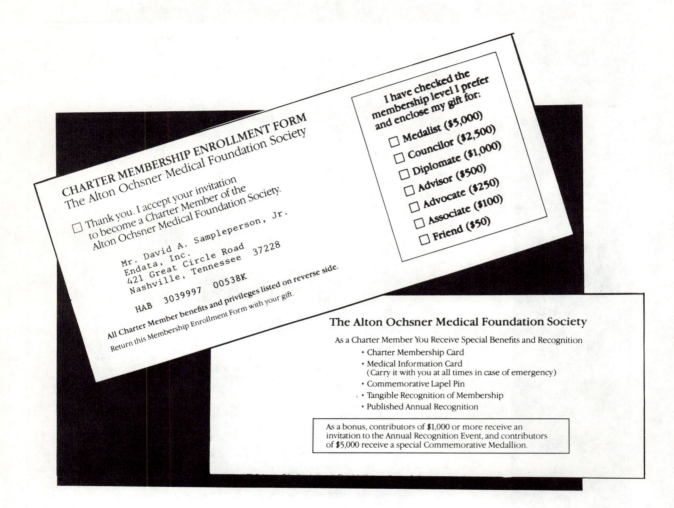

CHARTER MEMBERSHIP ENROLLMENT FORM
The Alton Ochsner Medical Foundation Society

☐ Thank you. I accept your invitation
to become a Charter Member of the
Alton Ochsner Medical Foundation Society.

Mr. David A. Sampleperson, Jr.
Endata, Inc.
421 Great Circle Road
Nashville, Tennessee 37228

HAB   3039997   00538K

All Charter Member benefits and privileges listed on reverse side.

Return this Membership Enrollment Form with your gift.

I have checked the
membership level I prefer
and enclose my gift for:

☐ Medalist ($5,000)
☐ Councilor ($2,500)
☐ Diplomate ($1,000)
☐ Advisor ($500)
☐ Advocate ($250)
☐ Associate ($100)
☐ Friend ($50)

The Alton Ochsner Medical Foundation Society

As a Charter Member You Receive Special Benefits and Recognition

· Charter Membership Card
· Medical Information Card
(Carry it with you at all times in case of emergency)
· Commemorative Lapel Pin
· Tangible Recognition of Membership
· Published Annual Recognition

As a bonus, contributors of $1,000 or more receive an
invitation to the Annual Recognition Event, and contributors
of $5,000 receive a special Commemorative Medallion.

ALTON
OCHSNER
MEDICAL
FOUNDATION
SOCIETY

BROCHURE

This philosophy was the guiding principle of the life and work of the late Alton Ochsner—physician, surgeon, teacher, researcher, civic leader, and humanitarian.

Today it is the legacy that endures at the medical institutions bearing his name. The first of these, the Ochsner Clinic, was opened in 1942.

Just three weeks before the doors of the clinic opened, the U.S. entered World War II and the Great Depression was stubbornly hanging on. Telling the story years later, Dr. Ochsner related how he and the other four founders had difficulty getting money to start: "The bank required us to put up our homes and other personal property as security for a loan, even my beat-up old Buick!" he said.

From the beginning, the five founders shared a common vision of creating a unique medical center where patients—especially those with difficult illness or injury—could receive the highest level of professional care in diagnosis and treatment—all in one central location.

None foresaw how successful their concept would be.

In 1944, led by Dr. Ochsner, the founders created a permanent, not-for-profit foundation dedicated to three primary objectives:
• providing the highest quality health care to patients;
• educating the physicians of tomorrow in the most sophisticated specialties of medical care;
• and seeking new answers to medical questions through clinical research.

The Ochsner Heritage...

"In this clinic and this hospital, the patient and the patient's family come first."

—Alton Ochsner, M.D.
1896-1981

ORGANIZATION   Democratic Congressional Campaign Committee
REPRESENTED   Washington, D.C.

PRODUCED/   Craver, Mathews, Smith & Company
DESIGNED BY: Falls Church, Virginia

DATE OF   1983
1st APPEAL:

TYPE OF   Acquisition
APPEAL:

PURPOSE OF   To generate new donors to the Democratic Congressional Campaign
APPEAL: Committee (DCCC).

CAMPAIGN   This package generated 80,000 new donors to the DCCC, resulting in a
RESULTS: gross income of $1,250,000. In addition, survey results were forwarded to
                       the Congressional delegates as stated in the letter.

COMMENTS: This appeal was mailed in the early stages of the 1984 election campaign
                       (March 1983-March 1984). It involved the recipients by allowing them to
                       "vote" for the Democratic Presidential candidate they would like to see
                       nominated. In addition, it provided a way for them to touch base with the
                       campaign of the candidate of their choice. The personalization on this
                       package is of particular interest, in that it is designed to enhance the effect
                       of a personal, audited survey. Authenticity is reinforced by the letter,
                       which explains the "advanced computer technology" used to obtain accu-
                       rate results.

                       After involving the prospect with the survey, the DCCC then presents a
                       compelling request for support of a strengthened Democratic House of
                       Representatives. The "Democratic Victory Campaign" allows prospects to
                       help defend Democratic members of Congress from defeat by Republicans.
                       The letter points out what a Democratic House has done to protect "the
                       interests of the average citizen. . ." and why it is important to gain
                       financial support even early in the campaign.

                       Both aspects of the appeal are represented in the enclosed survey and
                       attached contribution form. By allowing donors to add $5 to their con-
                       tribution to help pay for the effort, the average gift was raised by 25
                       percent. Perhaps the most important aspect of the appeal was that it
                       provided an excellent donor base which could be solicited for additional
                       support throughout the rest of the 1984 election year.

Appeal Letter from Congressman

OFFICIAL 1984 DEMOCRATIC PRESIDENTIAL SURVEY

Dear Friend,

Although the enclosed survey contains but <u>one</u> question, it is imperative that we know <u>your</u> answer.

You see, the answer to the question asked in this survey -- who is today the preferred Democratic candidate for the 1984 presidential election -- is of such vital importance to us, that you and the tens of thousands of other registered voters who were selected to participate were <u>not</u> just chosen at random.

Instead advanced computer technology was employed to ensure a cross section of voters from every state. Each survey ballot was assigned an individual number which will enable us to accurately weigh the tabulated responses from each section of the nation.

And that is why it is imperative that you and every one who receives a survey respond immediately. In fact, I must ask that you return your survey <u>within</u> <u>the</u> <u>next</u> <u>10</u> <u>days</u>.

The 1984 Democratic National Convention will be different than any other in the history of the United States. For the <u>first</u> time ever, Democratic Members of the House of Representatives and Senators will <u>directly</u> elect delegates to the national presidential nominating convention.

The reason for this change is to ensure that members of Congress -- who are responsible for enacting legislation proposed by our presidents -- have a direct voice in selecting the Democratic nominee for president.

Of course, the Congressional delegates will listen to the people they represent.

And, no doubt, they will also pay attention to the various "straw polls" being conducted this year in various places.

But that's not enough....

The Democratic Members of Congress must also know that the results of this poll are not just a small random sampling -- sometimes an important poll utilizes only a couple of thousand respondents -- but a vast, yet scientifically selected cross section of those with a Democratic preference.

In addition to the value of your choice to us, the enclosed survey form also can be of great value to you in learning more about the announced Democratic candidates. If you wish, you can be put in touch with the campaign

(over, please)

DEMOCRATIC CONGRESSIONAL CAMPAIGN COMMITTEE
400 N. Capitol Street, N.W., Washington, D.C. 20001
Paid for and authorized by the Democratic Congressional Campaign Committee

organization of your favored candidate. Or, if you are undecided, you can use the survey form to obtain information directly from the candidate about whom you wish to learn more.

This survey and the opportunity we offer you to become more involved in the presidential election at this critical early time is a service of the Democratic Congressional Campaign Committee. Because we Democratic Members of Congress know that <u>Ronald Reagan</u> <u>must</u> <u>be</u> <u>defeated</u> <u>in</u> <u>1984</u>.

However, as members of Congress we also are aware that ...

... CHANGING ADMINISTRATIONS IN WASHINGTON WILL <u>NOT</u> BE ENOUGH.

We must also ensure the election of a Congress responsive to the critical needs we face. A Congress which will work with our next Democratic president instead of blocking him.

I'm sure you realize that regardless of the 1984 presidential campaign, the special economic interests and their allies in the militant New Right intend to raise massive funds to hold their majority position in the U.S. Senate <u>and</u> <u>to</u> <u>work</u> <u>with</u> <u>all</u> <u>their</u> <u>might</u> <u>to</u> <u>gain</u> <u>back</u> <u>the</u> <u>ground</u> <u>they</u> <u>lost</u> <u>in</u> <u>the</u> <u>House</u> <u>of</u> <u>Representatives</u> <u>in</u> <u>last</u> <u>year's</u> <u>elections</u>.

You and I must not let them succeed. A House of Representatives controlled by Democrats has proven to be the only defense we have against the often unfair, sometimes greedy, and often wrong-headed notions of the Republicans.

Just look at what a strong Democratic majority in the House of Representatives has meant in protecting the interests of the average citizen against the narrow, self-serving interests of the rich Republicans:

-- We successfully blocked Reagan Administration attempts to inflict massive and unfair cutbacks in critical areas like nutrition, education, health, and housing.

-- We stood firm against dangerous policies which would escalate the nuclear arms race and give a virtual free hand in wasteful military spending.

-- We worked night and day to save the Social Security system and are now turning to the defense of Medicare.

-- We held the Republican special interests accountable when their shocking actions at the Environmental Protection Agency revealed their true interests. Interests which lie in protecting those who pollute the air you breathe and the water you drink.

(next page, please)

If the Republicans, with their millions and millions of dollars in campaign funds, succeed in regaining numerous seats or winning control of the House of Representatives, even a strong and effective Democratic president could be thwarted in his efforts to lead the nation.

You and I must begin working right now to ensure that our next president has a fair chance to succeed. That means giving him a working, progressive majority in Congress.

That's why this letter to you is so important.

Because ... in addition to seeking your opinion on the Presidential Survey, I want also to ask you to help us prepare for the critical 1984 Congressional elections.

The Democratic Congressional Campaign Committee has planned an effective campaign to ensure that Democrats continue to control the U.S. House of Representatives. It's called the Democratic Victory Campaign.

This is the most comprehensive campaign plan we have ever developed. A plan which must be implemented whether or not a Democrat wins the White House.

The Democratic Victory Campaign seeks to defend Democratic Members of Congress who are being targeted for defeat by the New Right's extremist political action committees. Groups like Jesse Helms' Congressional Club and Terry Dolan's National Conservative Political Action Committee.

A key to successful campaigning involves getting an early start on the next election season. The key to defending the Democratic House of Representatives rests in our ability to raise the money needed early to implement our campaign plans. To do that we've set up our special 1984 Victory Fund.

I hope you will make a special contribution of $15, $25, $50, or even $100, to this 1984 Victory Fund. Without your contribution we'll be unable to launch the critical, early stages of our Victory Campaign.

Your special contribution at this time will make it possible for us to get started now. Too often in the past -- because we didn't have the funds -- we were simply too late in developing strategies, registering voters, organizing volunteers, mounting media campaigns and taking all the early, critical steps necessary to ensure victory at the polls.

The Republicans' campaign war chests are already overflowing. Yet they continue to raise even more money. They know from past experience that in close races money makes all the difference in the world.

We don't have to match the Republicans dollar for dollar. The results of the 1982 Congressional elections proved that.

(over, please)

BUT ... we must at least have the funds needed for close races where money makes a great difference. And those funds must come from caring, concerned citizens like you.

That's why it's so important that I hear from you today. Please do the following while my letter is in front of you:

1. Cast your vote on the 1984 Presidential Survey. It's crit-
    ical that we select the best Democratic presidential candi-
    date so that we can defeat Ronald Reagan and his special
    interest allies.

2. Send a special contribution to launch the 1984 Victory
    Campaign. Every citizen contribution -- regardless of size
    -- is important to us. Please contribute whatever you can.

Your contribution of $15, $25, $50, or even $100, will help make the critical difference in the 1984 elections.

Only a Democratic Congress can ensure that the needs of all our citizens -- not just the privileged -- are met with fairness and respect.

Please help me put our 1984 Victory Campaign into motion by sending your contribution today.

                                     Sincerely,

                                     Tony Coelho

                                     Congressman Tony Coelho
                                     Chairman

P.S. When you make your contribution to the Victory Fund, please consider
      adding an additional $5 to help pay for the cost of processing your
      Survey and for distributing additional Surveys nationwide. Thank you.

PRESIDENTIAL SURVEY ENCLOSED

BUSINESS REPLY MAIL
First Class Permit No. 11372   Washington, D.C.

Postage will be paid by addressee

1984 DEMOCRATIC PRESIDENTIAL SURVEY

Congressman Tony Coelho, Chairman
Democratic Congressional Campaign Committee
P.O. Box 57090
Washington, D.C. 20037

No Postage
Necessary
if Mailed
in the
United States

OFFICIAL DEMOCRATIC PRESIDENTIAL SURVEY
prepared by
THE DEMOCRATIC CONGRESSIONAL CAMPAIGN COMMITTEE

SURVEY NUMBER   051899
TABULATION DEADLINE   10 DAYS AFTER RECEIPT

1984 PRESIDENTIAL BALLOT
My choice for the 1984 Democratic nomination for President is:

☐ Reubin Askew   ( )   Jesse Jackson
☐ Alan Cranston
☐ John Glenn
☐ Gary Hart
☐ Ernest Hollings
☐ George McGovern
☐ Walter Mondale
☐ Other_____

PRESIDENTIAL INFORMATION BANK
Please forward my name to the following candidate and ask him to send me information on his campaign:

☐ Reubin Askew   ( )   Jesse Jackson
☐ Alan Cranston
☐ John Glenn
☐ Gary Hart
☐ Ernest Hollings
☐ George McGovern
☐ Walter Mondale
☐ Other_____

Your name will not be used in tabulating this Survey. Only totals of the results will ever be released.

Please initial here: _____

Please return this entire Survey Form along with your contribution to: The Democratic Congressional Campaign Committee, P.O. Box 57090, Washington, D.C. 20037.

FOR OFFICE USE ONLY

Date Survey tabulated: _____

Information forwarded to
appropriate campaign: _____

CONTRIBUTION REPLY

Yes, Congressman Coelho, I want to make sure we have a Democratic Congress in 1984. If we elect a Democratic President he will need our help. And, if we don't, we will need — more than ever — a Democratic Congress to defend us against the self-serving interests of the Republican Party which seeks to favor the few over the many.

I have decided to send a special contribution to help launch the 1984 Victory Fund in the amount of:

☐ $15   ☐ $20   ☐ $25   ☐ Other $_____

Please tabulate my Presidential Survey and release the results to the press and the entire Democratic leadership. I am enclosing a contribution to help pay for this effort in the amount of:

☐ $5.00

My total contribution to the 1984 Victory Fund and to help underwrite the cost of the Presidential Survey totals:
$_____

Please make your check payable to the Democratic Congressional Campaign Committee (DCCC).

22101CAV2039R   173D

ORGANIZATION REPRESENTED:	Help Hospitalized Veterans San Diego, California
DESIGNED/ PRODUCED BY:	The Viguerie Company Falls Church, Virginia
DATE OF 1st APPEAL:	1983
TYPE OF APPEAL:	Acquisition
PURPOSE OF APPEAL:	To raise funds to send arts and crafts kits to veterans in military and Veterans Administration hospitals.
CAMPAIGN RESULTS:	This appeal was mailed to more than 1.8 million prospects, resulting in a 3.4 percent response rate and a net income of nearly $500,000.
COMMENTS:	The success of this appeal may be traced to its compelling emotional message evident throughout the various package components. In the letter from National Coordinator, Lola Tracey, the prospect is asked to empathize with the suffering of one vet forced to spend Christmas alone in a hospital. Then the prospect is shown a tangible means of relieving this suffering through the purchase of arts and crafts kits for veterans. (By purchasing arts and crafts materials in large quantities at volume discounts, the organization was able to distribute more than 167,000 arts and crafts kits with the net income from the mailing.)

The credibility and emotional impact of the appeal was enhanced significantly by the four-page letter from a hospitalized veteran. This letter not only dramatized his plight and that of other vets, it also testified to the benefits of the kits. Like Lola Tracey's letter, the writing is simple and direct.

Other features of the package include the personalized closed face carrier, reply device, and director's memo. The pre-cancelled nonprofit stamp also increases personalization. The enclosed prayer card also serves as an effective way to involve the prospect in the efforts of the organization on behalf of hospitalized veterans.

Finally, it is interesting to note that an effective acknowledgment program (not shown) allowed veterans receiving the kits to send a pre-addressed, stamped thank you card to a particular donor. This established direct donor-to-receiver contact and helped to reinforce commitment of the donor to the cause.

Appeal Letter from Help Hospitalized Veterans Director

HELP HOSPITALIZED VETERANS

SPECIAL CHRISTMAS APPEAL

708 W. Redwood St.   San Diego, CA 92103

National Coordinator
and Liaison Officer:
Lola Tracey

URGENT DIRECTOR'S MEMO

DEAR MR LOCKLIN,

**FRIENDS OF
HOSPITALIZED
VETERANS**

Lance Alworth
Lucille Ball
Pat Boone
Phyllis Diller
Bob Hope
Debbie Reynolds
Brooks Robinson*
Roger Staubach
Lee Trevino
John Wayne
  Great American
  1907-1979
Andy Williams

What is the one day of the year you're <u>sure</u> you don't want to be alone?

What day has the happiest memories for you?

What day do you most want to share with those you love -- relatives and close friends?

I think you and I would agree that day is... <u>Christmas</u>.

Please take the time to read the enclosed letter from a very special young man, Gary Belhumeur.

Gary, a hospitalized veteran, is suffering. But he asked me if he could send his letter to you.

He's asking that you help his buddies America's hospitalized veterans -- the same way he was helped.

And his plea for your help is especially important with Christmas in mind.

Because for them, this beautiful holiday will not be spent with loved ones, around the family Christmas tree.

But Gary Belhumeur wants to tell you how you can make this Christmas a very special one for these hospitalized American heroes.

Having spent long, lonely hours in the hospital. Gary knows

over, please

Help Hospitalized Veterans—serving our
hospitalized veterans since 1971.

Page two

the agony and despair other hospitalized veterans go through.
Especially on Christmas Day.

I urge you to read Gary's appeal for your help for his buddies.
I urge you to think about the 83,000 hospitalized veterans who will
still be in hospitals on Christmas Day.

And I ask you to do these two things today:

FIRST, please sign the enclosed Christmas Prayer Card to
Gary Belhumeur, and rush it back to me in the enclosed postage-
free envelope.

Let's let Gary know you're praying for him.

SECOND, please use your Urgent Reply Form to send a gift
of $12, $18, $24 or whatever you can afford, for Help Hospitalized
Veterans to provide more Arts and Crafts Kits to Gary's buddies
as he asks.

But I urge you not to delay. I'd like to be able to tell
Gary that, thanks to his appeal, HHV will have enough Arts and
Crafts Kits to give to all 83,000 boys who will be in the hospital
this Christmas.

So please act today. Gary's illness is already so advanced.

And please let your generous Christmas contribution for
HHV Arts and Crafts Kits be in honor of Gary Belhumeur...
a true friend of his buddies.

God Bless You,

Lola Tracey

Lola Tracey
National Hospital Coordinator

P. S. Again time is urgent. I want to be able to tell Gary
       he's made a beautiful Christmas gift of his own to
       his buddies, through his appeal to you. Please sign your
       Prayer Card and send your gift of $12, $18, $24 or
       whatever amount you can to HHV today.

Backup Appeal from a Hospitalized Vet

Dear Friend,

    I need your help.

    It's not help for me I ask. Rather I need your help for thousands of other hospitalized veterans like me.

    I really want to help my buddies in the hospital while I still can. You see, I'm dying of terminal cancer.

    A few years ago, my doctors gave me 24 hours to live.

    But something special happened to me I want to tell you about.

    That "something special" was an organization called Help Hospitalized Veterans (HHV).

    And the special thing they did for me was to give me one simple gift -- an Arts and Crafts Kit.

    Your first reaction is probably the same as mine was: what good is a Craft Kit to a dying man?

    To me it made all the difference in the world. And I've seen these HHV Craft Kits do the same thing for other hospitalized veterans too.

    So please let me tell you my story.

    I'm Gary Belhumeur. I'm a 30 year old U.S. Army Veteran who served in Vietnam. And I'm dying of incurable bone cancer.

    I've been face to face with death since January of 1979. That's when I first learned from the doctors

(Over, please)

about the cancer in my left leg.

I've had several operations since then and been treated with chemotherapy. But the cancer still spread.

It was April, a few years ago, wracked with fever and hemorrhaging, my family was told I had 48 hours to live. They tell me I was given my last rites.

Maybe it was the prayers, but I pulled through that time.

The doctors still say I could go at any time, and I'm reconciled to that now.

But my mother told me after I recovered from the fever,

> "Maybe you didn't die that day because
> you haven't finished all God intends
> for you to do."

That's a heavy thought, but I got to thinking about it when I received a very special gift.

I had been lying in my bed at Bay Pines Veterans Hospital near St. Petersburg, Florida. For days I had just been staring at the walls, totally despairing.

A physical therapist came in and handed me a wood-craft kit. He said it had come from a group called Help Hospitalized Veterans.

To this day I don't know why I started working on the kit. I remember thinking, "I can't build this; I'm too weak."

Then, I recall fiddling with the pieces of the kit, just out of boredom I guess. I found it required not

(Next page, please)

Page three

strength, but concentration.

In just three hours, I had built a wooden birdhouse from the kit!

I heard from some buddies in the V.A. hospital that a lady named Lola Tracey with Help Hospitalized Veterans (HHV) had been providing needy veterans with woodcraft kits, plastic models, paint by number sets, leather tooling and other kits for years.

In fact, I now know after meeting Mrs. Tracey that HHV has given over 5,000,000 Arts and Crafts Kits to hospitalized veterans over the past 13 years.

Most of these guys had the same reaction I did at first.

Their morale was down due to their long, lonely hours in the hospital. Many despaired of ever coming home to a normal life. Many thought that their injured limbs and impaired senses would stop them from doing anything productive.

Time and time again, the HHV Arts and Crafts Kits were what snapped them out of their boredom and despair.

When I left the hospital to go home, I felt like a different person, I had a reason to live.

I've continued working on HHV woodcraft kits, sometimes 8 or 12 hours a day. I spend so much time working on them, I don't have much time to think about my illness.

I do, however, think a lot about my buddies back in the V.A. hospital.

Some of the guys have been in the hospital since being wounded in World War II, Korea or Vietnam.

And my new friend, Mrs. Lola Tracey of HHV, has told me that there are 83,000 veterans like them in

(Over, please)

Page four

V.A. and military hospitals each day.

I've come to believe there really is a reason
I've survived my illness this long.

I feel it's so I can write to ask you to help
HHV send more Arts and Crafts Kits to veterans in
the hospital.

There are so many lonely, needy hospitalized
veterans that I know I'll be leaving behind. Some of
these guys will be able to leave the hospital some day.
Others may be there for the rest of their lives, and
still others know they haven't much longer to live.

But all of them will only face loneliness, despair,
and less hope of rehabilitation unless you help.

If an HHV Kit helped me in my state of illness
and despair, I know more kits can help more of them too.

Will you help HHV provide more Craft Kits to my
buddies? It would give such peace of mind to know
they're being helped.

Thank you for reading my letter.

Sincerely,

Gary Belhumeur

P.S.   Mrs. Tracey tells me it costs HHV only $12 to
       provide 2 Craft Kits to needy hospitalized
       veterans. For $18, you can give 3 Kits, and
       for $24, you can give 4 Kits.

       So please help a couple of my buddies today.
       I'm counting on the goodness of your heart to
       help.

174

708 WEST REDWOOD STREET
SAN DIEGO, CALIFORNIA 92103

Sleigh 1880s
USA 5.2c Nonprofit

MR W H LOCKLIN
9 CRAFT ST
GUILDER, NY 12084

RF9P2

HELP HOSPITALIZED VETERANS

SPECIAL CHRISTMAS APPEAL
URGENT REPLY FORM

FROM:

MR W H LOCKLIN
9 CRAFT ST
GUILDER, NY 12084

53J

TO: Lola Tracey
National Hospital Coordinator
Help Hospitalized Veterans
708 W. Redwood Street
San Diego, CA 92103

____**YES,** Lola, I've signed my Christmas Prayer Card to Gary Belhumeur. It's attached below. Please rush it to him.

____**YES,** I'll respond to Gary's plea to help HHV provide Arts and Crafts Kits to all our hospitalized veterans on Christmas Day. I want my contribution to be in honor of Gary.

I've enclosed:

____**$12 for 2 Kits**   ____**$24 for 4 Kits**   ____**$72 for 12 Kits**
____**$18 for 3 Kits**   ____**$48 for 8 Kits**   ____**Other $**_____

Please make your check payable to: Help Hospitalized Veterans.
PLEASE DO NOT DETACH CARD BELOW.

My Prayer Card To You

TO: GARY BELHUMEUR

Dear Gary,

I want you to know I'm praying for you.

I appreciate the good you're doing for America's hospitalized veterans this Christmas. And I'm sure the Lord blesses you for it. May God Bless You and Keep You.

Signed:_____

MR W H LOCKLIN

HHV's Guarantee: Every dollar you give to HHV will provide an equal dollar's value of Arts and Crafts Kits to hospitalized veterans. All gifts to HHV are tax-deductible.

175

ORGANIZATION
REPRESENTED:

KCET Channel 28
Los Angeles, California

DESIGNED/
PRODUCED BY:

Epsilon
Burlington, Massachusetts

DATE OF
APPEAL:

1980

TYPE OF
APPEAL:

Emergency to House File

PURPOSE OF
APPEAL:

To erase a $726,000 debt faced by KCET through a special appeal and follow-up to 146,974 donors who had contributed between $15 and $500 in the previous 12 months. Coordinated TV support in the form of 30-second spots was developed as a back-up to strengthen the campaign.

CAMPAIGN
RESULTS:

This campaign, which won "Best of Show" honors at the New England Direct Marketing Association, generated an amazing response rate of over 30 percent, with an average gift of $37.63. The net income from the campaign was over $1.5 million, more than twice the original goal.

COMMENTS:

The highly personalized look makes the first appeal stand out. The first class stamp, computer-addressed envelope, mention of the contributor's first name, personalized suggested gift in the body of the letter, and the high-quality offset printed signature all help to convey a genuinely personal feeling. This is enhanced by the emotional, sincere, and urgent copy of the letter, which makes the potential contributor feel personally needed.

In the follow-up "Urgent-Gram" sent ten days later, the urgency of the appeal is re-stated. Both the letter and reply form again highlight the desired contribution. Bold graphics, pithy writing, and the use of upper case print all combine to make the appeal resemble an actual telegram.

Community Supported Television

James L. Loper
President

PERSONAL   October 10, 1980

Mr. John D. Sample
Epsilon Data Management
24 New England Executive Park
Burlington, Massachusetts 01803

Dear John:

This is a very difficult letter for me to write.

You've been one of this station's most generous and loyal friends. That's why I feel compelled to write you this special letter...to share a very serious problem with you.

Right now KCET is faced with a financial emergency so critical -- so severe -- some of your favorite programs may be forced off the air.

To put it simply, I must raise at least $726,000 by November 24th.

Unless this money can be raised, we may not be able to make commitments to buy many of the programs you are expecting to watch on KCET this year.

This is why I'm turning to you, John, asking if you can possibly see your way to make an emergency gift of $35 right now.

I know $35 is more than you have ever given to us before, but I want to be perfectly frank with you; this debt has a stranglehold on the station.

Last year we invested a great deal of money in broadcast equipment. We bought new cameras, a new antenna, and much more ... in order to bring you programs and viewing of the highest quality.

But skyrocketing costs of interest payments alone -- not to mention the incredible jump in all our other expenses -- made our bills increase as never before.

I assure you we've done everything possible to avoid asking for your help. I've cut back on our broadcast

KCET · 4401 SUNSET BOULEVARD · LOS ANGELES, CALIFORNIA 90027

Mr. John D. Sample
Burlington, Massachusetts 01803
Page Two

hours... I've slashed budgets... My staff even pulled out
all the stops during our recent TV pledge drive -- hoping
that gifts from our viewers would wipe out the debt.

Even after all these measures I simply have no
alternative but to ask if you can send $35 or more.

With your help - and the help of other loyal friends -
I won't have to cut back on regular shows like SESAME
STREET, MASTERPIECE THEATRE, WALL STREET WEEK, NOVA, or
other favorites.

There is no other way to do it.

Your gift of $35 is needed to get us through this
emergency period.

I'm very proud to say that KCET has produced some of
the finest programs to be seen anywhere. In fact, two of
the major prime-time shows to be aired on PBS this year
have been produced right here at your station.

Programs like COSMOS, MEETING OF MINDS, and others,
will bring in the money we need to maintain a balanced
budget -- and produce more local programs for you.

This is one of the reasons I'm so confident we'll be
successful if we can make it through November. In fact,
our future looks very bright if we can just get over this
hurdle.

We have made a firm commitment to operate this
station with a balanced budget -- without sacrificing the
quality of local and national programming during the
coming year.

But this will be impossible unless our debt is erased.

Your response to this letter is a vote of confidence
in KCET's future. It is needed right now! I'm certain
your gift of $35 or more may be the single most important
gift you'll ever send to this station.

I know you'll do whatever you can.

Sincerely,

James L. Loper, President

P.S. Please respond today -- we must clear up this
     debt by November 24th.

Carrier Envelope and Response Card

James L. Loper, President
KCET
4401 Sunset Boulevard
Los Angeles, California 90027

Mr. John D. Sample
Epsilon Data Management
24 New England Executive Park
Burlington, Massachusetts 01803

EMERGENCY Reply Form

From:

Mr. John D. Sample
Epsilon Data Management
24 New England Executive Park
Burlington, Massachusetts 01803

I want to help with this urgent problem!
Here is my special gift to help keep KCET on the air.

ENCLOSED IS: ( ) $35   ( ) $.......   *please mail immediately!*

065434H   1A   Please make your tax-deductible check payable to:
KCET · P.O. BOX 128 · LOS ANGELES, CALIFORNIA 90051

Urgent-Gram

TO:	REPLY REQUESTED BY:
MR. JOHN D. SAMPLE EPSILON DATA MANAGEMENT 24 NEW ENGLAND EXECUTIVE PARK BURLINGTON, MASSACHUSETTS 01803	IMMEDIATELY

FROM:

JAMES LOPER
KCET - CHANNEL 28
4401 SUNSET BLVD.
LOS ANGELES, CA 90027

X129LMO2:35PMKCET

```
EMERGENCY APPEAL FROM JAMES LOPER AT KCET.

IF YOU CAN HELP WITH AN EMERGENCY GIFT --
NOW IS THE TIME TO SEND IT.

I WROTE TO YOU LAST WEEK AND EXPLAINED WE
ARE IN DEBT -- PROGRAMS ARE SUBJECT TO
CANCELLATION.

PLEASE CONSIDER THE GIFT OF $35 I MENTIONED IN MY
LETTER.

GENEROUS GIFTS FROM FRIENDS LIKE YOU ALREADY
COMING IN.  IF YOU HAVE NOT YET SENT YOUR GIFT I
AM URGING YOU TO DO SO NOW.

WE NEED TO RAISE THE MONEY IMMEDIATELY.
PLEASE HELP NOW IF YOU CAN.



FROM:   JAMES LOPER KCET
        08505440
```

DETACH BOTTOM PORTION AND RETURN IN THE ENCLOSED ENVELOPE.

Urgent-Gram

FIRST CLASS

MESSAGE REPLY

MESSAGE CODE: 08505440 3B	**REPLY REQUESTED BY:** **IMMEDIATELY**

FROM:	RETURN TO:
MR. JOHN D. SAMPLE EPSILON DATA MANAGEMENT 24 NEW ENGLAND EXECUTIVE PARK BURLINGTON, MASSACHUSETTS 01803	JAMES LOPER KCET - CHANNEL 28 PO BOX 128 LOS ANGELES, CA 90051

RETURN YOUR CHECK WITH THIS FORM IN THE
SPECIAL ENVELOPE PROVIDED.

PLEASE INDICATE THE AMOUNT ENCLOSED:

(   ) $35   (   ) $..........

Make your tax-deductible check payable to: KCET
P.O. BOX 128 • LOS ANGELES, CALIFORNIA • 90051

ORGANIZATION REPRESENTED:	The Nature Conservancy Arlington, Virginia

WRITTEN BY:	Frank Johnson, Copywriter New York, New York

DATE OF 1st TEST:	1982

TYPE OF APPEAL:	Acquisition

PURPOSE OF APPEAL:	To enlist new members for The Nature Conservancy at the yearly dues of $10.

CAMPAIGN RESULTS: When this appeal was first tested, it produced a higher response rate and average gift than the control. It has remained the most successful package, with 4.2 million pieces mailed for a 1.26 percent response rate, adding over 53,000 new members to the Conservancy's membership. (It is interesting to note that when the bumper sticker was not included in the appeal, the response dropped by 30 percent.)

COMMENTS: This package is a charming example of how a potentially dry subject such as land conservation can be treated with warmth and personality. The four-page letter reads as if the writer were talking to the prospect in his or her own living room. In doing so, it simply but convincingly describes the importance of the Conservancy, while making no less than nine allusions to the $10 requested gift. The letter is an example of one of the few cases in which a sense of humor is effectively employed to enhance an appeal.

Other factors which make the package successful include a wonderful, visually striking envelope that not only arouses curiosity, but also offers the bumper sticker enticement and mentions the $10 requested gift. The lift note from the Conservancy's President re-emphasizes the importance and urgency of the cause, while attractively displaying the animals helped by the organization. While the appeal does not make the prospect feel obligated to contribute in return for the bumper sticker, it does serve as a visual reminder of the Conservancy and its work. Finally, the response card cleverly includes an interim membership card.

Oversized Envelope

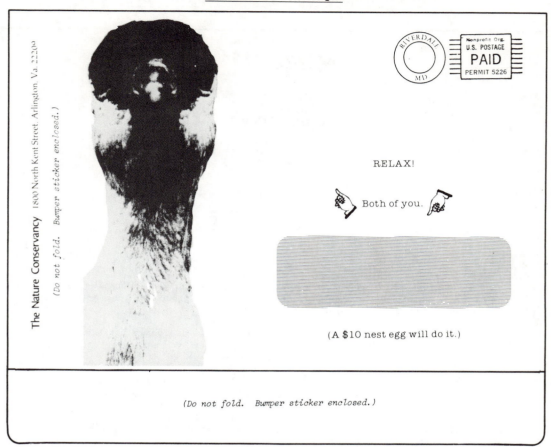

The Nature Conservancy 1800 North Kent Street, Arlington, Va. 22209

(Do not fold. Bumper sticker enclosed.)

RIVERDALE MD

Nonprofit Org.
U.S. POSTAGE
PAID
PERMIT 5226

RELAX!

☞ Both of you. ☜

(A $10 nest egg will do it.)

(Do not fold. Bumper sticker enclosed.)

Interim Membership Card and Response Card

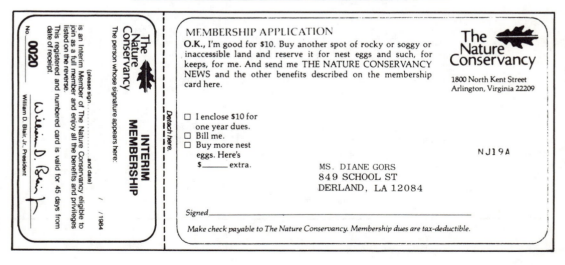

No. **0020**

This registered and numbered card is valid for 45 days from date of receipt.

William D. Blair, Jr., President

The Nature Conservancy

The person whose signature appears here:

is an Interim Member of The Nature Conservancy eligible to join as a full member and enjoy all the benefits and privileges listed on the reverse.

(please sign)

and date)

/   / 1984

INTERIM MEMBERSHIP

Detach here.

MEMBERSHIP APPLICATION

O.K., I'm good for $10. Buy another spot of rocky or soggy or inaccessible land and reserve it for nest eggs and such, for keeps, for me. And send me THE NATURE CONSERVANCY NEWS and the other benefits described on the membership card here.

☐ I enclose $10 for one year dues.
☐ Bill me.
☐ Buy more nest eggs. Here's $_____ extra.

Signed_____

Make check payable to The Nature Conservancy. Membership dues are tax-deductible.

The Nature Conservancy
1800 North Kent Street
Arlington, Virginia 22209

NJ19A

MS. DIANE GORS
849 SCHOOL ST
DERLAND, LA 12084

Letter of Appeal from Membership Director

Nancy C. Mackinnon
Membership Director

The Nature Conservancy

1800 North Kent Street
Arlington, Virginia 22209

Dear Investor:

The bug-eyed bird on our envelope who's ogling you with such dis-
temper has a point. He's a native American sandhill crane and you may be
sitting on top of one of his nesting sites.

As he sees it, every time our human species has drained a marsh,
and plowed it or built a city on it, since 1492 or so -- there went the
neighborhood. It's enough to make you both edgy.

So give us $10 for his nest egg and we'll see that a nice, soggy
spot -- just the kind he and his mate need to fashion a nest and put an
egg in it -- is reserved for the two of them, undisturbed, for keeps.
Only $10. (Watch those cranes come in to land, just once, and you're
paid back. Catches at your throat.) Then the cranes can relax, and so
can you. A bit.

> How will we reserve that incubator with your $10?
> Not by campaigning or picketing or suing.

We'll just BUY the nesting ground.

That's the unique and expensive and <u>effective</u> way The Nature Conservancy goes about its non-profit business. We're as dead serious about
hanging on to nature's precarious balance as the more visible and vocal
conservation groups. But our thing is to let money do our talking.

> And we buy a whopping lot of land: starting with
> 60 acres of New York's Mianus River Gorge in 1951
> (now 395 acres), we have protected 2,000,000 acres
> -- about the area of Rhode Island and Delaware.
> The plots are spotted coast to coast and from
> Canada deep into the Caribbean, 3,157 of them
> sized from a quarter of an acre to hundreds of
> square miles.

All of it is prime real estate, if you're a crane or a bass or a
sweet pepperbush or a redwood. Or a toad or a turtle. And a lot of

it's nice for people, too -- lovely deserts, mountainsides, prairies, islands. (Islands! We own huge Santa Cruz, off the California shore, and tiny Dome Island in Lake George, and most of the Virginia Barrier Islands, and dozens more.)

So besides being after your $10, we invite you to see a sample of our lands. We have 38 chapters in 32 states. Check your phone book. If we're not there yet, call me at (703) 841-5388. We'll guide you and yours to a nearby preserve where you're most welcome to walk along one of our paths, sit on one of our log benches, look about, and say to the youngster we hope will be with you, "This will be here, as is, for your grandchildren." Nice feeling.

We do ask that you don't bother the natives. E.g., there's a sign in one preserve that says "Rattlesnakes, Scorpions, Black Bear, Poison Oak/ARE PROTECTED/DO NOT HARM OR DISTURB." For $10, you're privileged not to disturb a bear or stroke a poison oak. Bargain.

> Bargains in diverse real estate are what we look
> for and find. Not just any real estate. We've
> been working for years to make and keep a huge
> ongoing inventory of the "natural elements" in
> each of the United States (so far, 30 are done).
> These "State Natural Heritage Programs" identify
> what's unique, what's threatened, what's rare or
> a rare natural sight to see in each state: ani-
> mals, birds, plants, bugs, lakes, river systems,
> swamps, waterfalls, woods ... and cranes' nests.

Then we try to acquire those places that desperately need protec-tion and preservation. We think big. Early last year, the Richard King Mellon Foundation gave us the largest single grant ever for private conservation: $25,000,000 to launch the National Wetlands Conservation Project.

We expect to match that grant over the next five years and create a $50 million revolving fund to protect outstanding examples of threatened aquatic and wetland systems from the Atlantic coast to Alaska. The work has already begun, copying successful projects like the protection of Elder Creek in Northern California, the preservation of the endangered manatees' wintering habitat in Crystal River, Florida, and the acquisi-tion of the whole Canelo Hills cienega (desert spring marsh) in Arizona.

But we don't just shovel cash at these projects. We buy some lands, trade for others, get leases and easements, ask to be mentioned in wills. Then we give or, preferably, sell up to 40 per cent of what we buy to states, cities, universities, other conservation groups -- any respon-sible organization which wants and loves the land so much that it doesn't mind our clever lawyers making it very difficult for <u>anyone</u> to "improve" any part of it, ever. Unless the someone can build nests or eat acorns.

That cash flow replenishes our revolving fund, every dime of which is plowed into the unpaved and as yet unplowed. All this activity generates a lot of fascinating true stories, and lovely photos. These we put into a small (32 pages) but elegant, sprightly and adless magazine, our report to our 180,000 members every other month: <u>The Nature Conservancy News</u>.

Here you may find that the land you and the rest of us have just bought is harboring a four-lined skink, or a spicebush, or boreal chickadees, or kame and kettle topography. You've a lot to learn and see that's most intriguing, as you'll discover.

<u>The Nature Conservancy News</u> also describes well-led tours of our various properties, tells you what we're doing in your state, and shows you how you can help and have some healthy fun at the same time.

You see, the millions of acres we own are mostly watched over by volunteer stewards -- wonderful men and women who are proud to show off their lovely charges. These likely include bats, salamanders, toadstools and such. Or cranes. You'll be invited to Nature Conservancy chapter meetings nearest you.

And if you paste the complimentary white-oak leaf sticker we've enclosed with this letter on your bumper, back pack, boat, hang glider, pool, bicycle, wheelchair ... wherever, you'll attract grateful grins from your fellow cognoscenti.

> Now, you may think it's disproportionate to brag about how we're raising millions for our projects and then ask you for only $10. Who needs you?
>
> <u>We need you, very much!</u> Those hard-headed foundations and corporations and ranch owners and such who give us money or property must be convinced that our ranks include a lot of intelligent, concerned, articulate citizens: people who know we ought to let nature alone to tend to much of this finite earth and all its creatures ... if we're to be among the creatures.

Yes, we need you and your ear and your voice -- <u>and</u> your $10 ($10 times 180,000 members buys a lot of acres). Please join us today, like so: Get a pen. Check and initial the "membership application" form that your hand is touching. Tear off the Interim Membership stub, sign and pocket it, and wait six weeks or so for your first magazine and permanent

card. Enclose a check for $10 in the return envelope (more, if you can
spare it) or ask us to bill you. NOTE that it's tax-deductible. Mail
the form. Go.

Thank you, and welcome!, dear wise fellow investor in nest eggs.
For your fanfare, listen for the wondrous stentorian call of that sandhill crane*.

Sincerely,

Nancy C Mackinnon

Nancy C. Mackinnon
Membership Director

* We borrowed his picture from Country Journal magazine where he
  illustrated an article about the International Crane Foundation of
  Baraboo, Wisconsin. The photo is by brave Cary Wolinsky. And we
  don't actually know if the crane is as upset as he looks. Maybe
  he's smiling? Certainly he will if, when he leaves the Foundation,
  his first motel stop has been reserved with your $10.

NCM/km

The
Nature
Conservancy

1800 North Kent Street
Arlington, Virginia 22209

Dear Skeptical Investor:

If putting a landing pad under a crane's egg, as Ms. Mackinnon's letter urges, seems too dank an investment for your $10, the other side of this note illustrates some different fauna which can use all the acreage we can buy for them. Because right now, they're losing ground.

Please help, by joining us today. There's reason to hurry. At least one of the world's five to ten million species is dying out every day, and soon it will be one an hour, and then when will it be our turn? We simply don't know.

Nor do we know, any of us (yet), just how our lives and survival may rely on the survival of hackberry trees and piping plovers, Indiana bats, wild orchids, golden-cheeked warblers, needle-and-thread grass, an insignificant little fish called the Panaca Big Spring spinedace (*Lepidomeda mollispinis pratensis*), or most of the tens of thousands of other rare living things now thriving on the lands we care for.

But you and I both know we must treasure that diversity of nature -- and we're losing ground. If enough of us get together, fast, maybe we can gain it back. The Nature Conservancy -- as you'll learn when you read our magazine and talk to any of our people -- is doing an intelligent, large-scale job of identifying and locating threatened species, as well as finding and buying the lands and waters they occupy.

Yet we're still not big enough, not fast enough. Most seriously, we need your voice, your thought, your contribution. Now. And thank you!

Sincerely,

William D. Blair Jr

William D. Blair, Jr.
President

WDB/ga

If you prefer other kinds of feathers or furs...

A Florida panther kitten, a river otter, a Pine Barrens tree frog, a brown pelican—all hanging on for and to dear life in Conservancy preserves.

A BUMPER STICKER WAS ENCLOSED---

BEND AND PEEL HERE

THE NATURE CONSERVANCY

ORGANIZATION   New York Zoological Society
REPRESENTED: Bronx, New York

DESIGNED/   Sanky Perlowin Associates
PRODUCED BY: New York, New York

DATE OF   1983
1st APPEAL:

TYPE OF   Special Acquisition
APPEAL:

CAMPAIGN   81,000 pieces of this appeal were mailed. Of this, 55,000 were prospects
RESULTS: and 26,000 were past donors who had contributed to institutions affiliated
                      with the New York Zoological Society. The appeal produced a 2.3 percent
                      response rate and a very impressive net revenue exceeding $185,000. Much
                      of this sum can be attributed to the large gifts ($100 and over) generated by
                      the package.

COMMENTS: Throughout the appeal, the copy successfully allows the prospect to
                      empathize with the many animals who need medical treatment. The
                      animals are shown to have very human problems to which the prospect
                      can relate. This theme is symbolized by the endearing envelope which
                      shows the doctor making the proverbial request to "SAY 'AH-H-H'" of a
                      large rhino. When reading the letter, it is hard not to sympathize with "a
                      giraffe with a sore throat, a baby camel that refuses to nurse, a gila monster
                      with a tummy ache . . ."

                      After involving the donor in this way, the letter then goes on to explain
                      why a new expanded and modernized hospital is needed, and how the
                      potential donor can help reach this goal. A special effort is made to attract
                      large donors by offering prestigious premiums recognizing different levels
                      of support. In all cases, the prospect is assured of a lasting reminder of his
                      or her contribution. The response device reinforces the request for larger
                      gifts by showing six suggested gift amounts, five of which are $100 or
                      more. Further, the matching gift incentive assures donors that their contri-
                      bution will be worth even more.

                      The brochure accompanying the package is an excellent addition. It reiter-
                      ates the themes outlined in the letter, while providing more information
                      about the animals and hospital. Of course, the best selling points of all are
                      the wonderful pictures of the animals themselves!

NEW YORK ZOOLOGICAL SOCIETY

Bronx Zoo
Bronx, New York 10460
Telephone: (212) 220-5090

New York Zoological Park
New York Aquarium
Animal Research and Conservation Center
Osborn Laboratories of Marine Sciences

Dear Friend,

What happens when a snow leopard catches a cold, a walrus has a toothache, or a 3,000-pound rhino comes down with an intestinal disorder? If the animal happens to be one of the 3,500 mammals, reptiles, amphibians and birds at the Bronx Zoo, the chances are good for a speedy recovery. Veterinarian Emil P. Dolensek -- family physician to the Zoo's 570 species -- makes a hurried house call or has the patient brought to the Zoo's Animal Hospital for more extensive medical or surgical treatment.

The Hospital is the oldest zoological hospital in the world. Built in 1916 by the New York Zoological Society to care for its animal collections at the Bronx Zoo and New York Aquarium, the modest one-story facility tends to over 600 animal patients a year and is known throughout the world for its zoological research and contributions to captive breeding.

Seeing to the health care needs of hummingbirds and elephants, pythons and gorillas is no easy task. Every morning Dr. Dolensek and his hospital staff make their rounds -- checking on a giraffe with a sore throat, a baby camel that refuses to nurse, a gila monster with a tummy ache. Those that cannot be treated in the exhibition areas -- a lioness in need of a Caesarean or a ringtailed lemur with a broken leg -- are moved to the Hospital.

All the animals in the Zoo -- from anteaters to zebras -- are under constant surveillance. Periodic examinations and vaccinations help forestall illness and major outbreaks of disease. Environmental conditions, animal behavior and diet are carefully monitored to ensure health and well-being.

Because animal species are vanishing from the earth at an ever-accelerating rate, zoos like ours may prove to be the last hope for hundreds of our world's most magnificent creatures. That's why two major concerns of the Animal Hospital are preventive medicine and applied research in reproductive biology -- to improve the survival chances of imperiled species in zoos and in the wild.

Our work in captive breeding is not confined to the Zoo, or even to the United States. Dr. Dolensek has traveled to far-away China to set up breeding facilities for the endangered giant panda, and to Chile and Argentina to help save two nearly extinct species of deer. Increasingly, our world's threatened wildlife will depend on long-range research and professional training like that being done here at the New York Zoological Society.

But our Animal Hospital is being stretched beyond its capabilities, and in a few short years, it will also be responsible for the medical care of 1,000

(over, please)

191

more animals in the Central Park, Prospect Park and Flushing Meadows zoos, which will come under the supervision of the New York Zoological Society.

That's why the Society has begun construction of a brand new Animal Hospital -- seven times larger than the present one, and equipped with the latest in medical technology. For example, the new x-ray equipment will be capable of examining an elephant or the tiniest shrew; and closed-circuit TV will permit observation and recording of surgical procedures, as well as 24-hour monitoring of convalescent animals.

The City of New York has recognized the need for expanding and modernizing our Animal Hospital and is underwriting $3.3 million of the $4.9 million budget. But the rest must come from concerned animal lovers like you. I know you'll want to help ensure the finest veterinary care for all the animals in our zoos and aquarium, and at the same time help ensure the survival of threatened species at the Zoo and in the wild through captive breeding programs.

We'll show our appreciation for your support by recording your name and those of all donors of $25 or more in our Book of Health, which will be on permanent display in the reception area. Donors of $100 or more will be invited to the dedication ceremony in 1984, and will also receive a beautiful memento of the occasion. Contributors of $250 will have their names inscribed on a plaque in the Hospital entrance, and donors of $1,000 or more will be honored with individually inscribed bronze medallions located at the Hospital.

And there's a special incentive. A donor has pledged to match your new or increased gifts to the Animal Hospital one dollar for every two. That means that every $100 you contribute is worth $150. So please send your check today; it will do that much more good, contribute to long-term wildlife breeding programs and help save many imperiled animals from extinction.

A reply envelope has been enclosed for your convenience. We hope you'll be as generous as you can.

Sincerely,

William Conway
General Director

Caring for 3,500 wild animals is all part of a day's work

for Dr. Emil P. Dolensek, chief veterinarian for the New York Zoological Society. He is responsible for the health and well-being of some 570 species of mammals, birds, reptiles and amphibians at the Bronx Zoo and New York Aquarium – 94 of them extinct in the wild or threatened with extinction.

Say "Ah-h-h."

Animals have many of the same medical problems we do – cataracts, tumors, broken bones, respiratory and intestinal disorders, bacterial infections – along with a host of exotic animal diseases. About 600 animals are examined or treated each year in the Zoo's Animal Hospital – the first ever built in the world – where they can be isolated or undergo surgery or be x-rayed.

Other animals are cared for in their habitats on the Zoo grounds, when Dr. Dolensek and his hospital staff make their daily rounds, stopping to administer an antibiotic, take a blood sample, give an elephant a pedicure or check on the progress of a newborn nyala antelope.

New York Zoological Society
Bronx,
N.Y. 10460

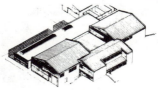

from the nest as it is laid. Chicks can then be hand-reared, as our work with the Andean condors has shown, and fed by keepers wearing adult condor-head hand puppets to prevent dependence on human contact. When our fledgling Andean condors were old enough to fly, they were successfully set free in the Peruvian wilds – a model to replenish diminishing local stocks.

Your support is needed

The new hospital complex will cost $4.9 million to build and equip. The City has pledged $3.3 million, but the rest must come from foundations, corporations and individual animal lovers who care about the well-being of all of God's creatures – from polar bears . . . to penguins . . . to pythons.

Your gift of $5,000, $1,000, $500, $250, $100 or $25, will help ensure the finest veterinary care for all the animals in our City's zoos, and at the same time increase the survival chances for hundreds of magnificent and threatened species in the wild.

For these reasons, and for reasons special to you, we hope you'll be generous. Donors of $1,000 or more will be honored with individually inscribed bronze medallions located at the Hospital; donors of $250 and above will have their names inscribed on a bronze plaque in the Hospital entrance; donors of $100 will be invited to the dedication ceremony in 1984, and also receive a beautiful memento of the occasion; and names of $25 donors will be entered in our Book of Health on permanent display in the reception area. There are also opportunities to memorialize someone special by underwriting the cost of one of our laboratories or animal care chambers. For further information, please contact James Meeuwsen, Director of Public Affairs (212-220-5090).

Please be generous. Your gift today will make a life and death difference to animals in the wild and in zoos – animals that belong to us all, that are our natural heritage and our legacy to our children and grandchildren.

Contributions are tax-deductible to the extent provided by law. A copy of the Society's annual report is available from the New York Department of State, Albany, NY 12231, or from our office.

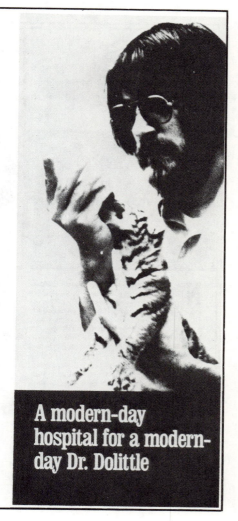

A modern-day hospital for a modern-day Dr. Dolittle

193

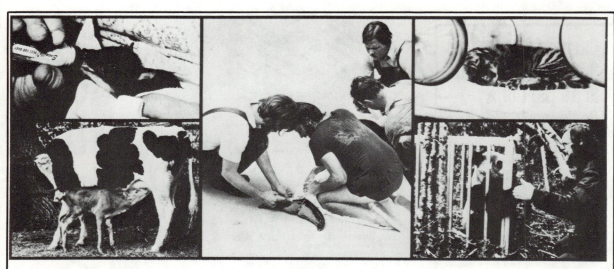

Now the Animal Hospital – in continuous use since 1916 – can no longer keep up with the demands being placed on it. There simply is not enough space to quarantine new animals, provide adequate medical and surgical care to the changing Zoo population, continue vital graduate and postgraduate training in zoological medicine and conduct the basic and applied research that may hold the promise of survival for our most endangered wildlife.

And in just a few years, when New York City's zoos in Central Park, Prospect Park and Flushing Meadows Park, which are scheduled to be rebuilt, come under the supervision of the New York Zoological Society, the Animal Hospital's limited capabilities will be stretched past the breaking point.

As an animal lover you'll be happy to know that no delicate new baby or sick animal will want for care. A brand new hospital is scheduled to open in 1984. With 18,000 square feet of space, it will be seven times larger than the present cramped one-story building – a modern hospital for a modern-day Dr. Dolittle.

All creatures, great and small

The new facility, which will be located on the western perimeter of the Zoo, will have separate areas for animal care, surgery, research, pathology and administration. Special elephant-sized doors and an overhead track system will enable the Hospital's staff to care for large animals with less need for tranquilizing drugs. Closed-circuit TV, environmentally controlled chambers, the most up-to-date x-ray equipment, modern research labs for microbiology, virology, cytogenetics and reproductive biology will make it in many respects the most advanced zoological hospital in the world.

Here new methods of diagnosing and treating disease can be developed, and nutritional deficiencies which lead to illness and death can be detected. Here a proboscis monkey can have a gallstone removed, a Siberian tiger can have a tooth filled, an anorexic anteater can be fed intravenously, and a newborn snow leopard can be hand-reared safely.

And here, revolutionary work in reproductive biology can be continued – work that recently resulted in the birth of a rare wild gaur to a Holstein dairy cow – the first successful issue of an embryo transfer from a wild endangered species.

Safety and survival

Captive breeding programs such as this have become increasingly important to save about 1,000 endangered animal species before they vanish from the earth. Zoos like ours have become Noah's Arks – places of safety where imperiled species can live, breed and raise their young through programs that include artificial insemination, embryo transfer and the establishment of frozen sperm banks for use by future generations. The New York Zoological Society is helping ensure that pandas and snow leopards, rhinos and mountain gorillas do not follow the dodo into extinction.

The California condor now has a better chance, thanks to techniques of propagation and rearing pioneered by the New York Zoological Society with its less rare cousin, the Andean condor. Although this species normally breeds every two years, its production of eggs can be accelerated by removing each egg

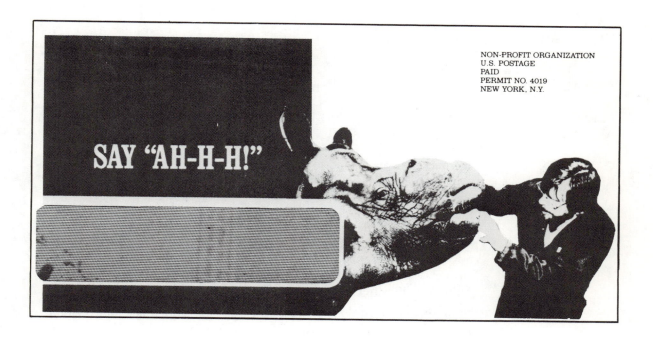

SAY "AH-H-H!"

NON-PROFIT ORGANIZATION
U.S. POSTAGE
PAID
PERMIT NO. 4019
NEW YORK, N.Y.

Yes, I care
about the health and well-being of the thousands of animals in zoos and in the wild, from polar bears . . . to penguins . . . to pythons. Enclosed is my tax-deductible gift to help the New York Zoological Society build its modern Animal Hospital:

- ☐ $5000
- ☐ $1000
- ☐ $500
- ☐ $250
- ☐ $100
- ☐ $25
- Other $_____

I understand that every dollar of my new or increased giving will be matched with half that amount by a generous friend of the Society.

Please make your check payable to the New York Zoological Society
A copy of the Society's annual report is available from the New York Department of State, Albany, NY 12231, or from our office.

New York Zoological Society
BRONX ZOO, BRONX, NY 10460

ORGANIZATION REPRESENTED:	Planned Parenthood Federation of America, Inc. New York, New York
DESIGNED/ PRODUCED BY:	Craver, Mathews, Smith & Company Falls Church, Virginia
DATE OF 1st APPEAL:	1982
TYPE OF APPEAL:	Acquisition
PURPOSE OF APPEAL:	To enlist new contributors to Planned Parenthood.
CAMPAIGN RESULTS:	This package was mailed to more than 15 million prospects. It produced more than 170,000 new donors for Planned Parenthood and nearly $5 million in income.
COMMENTS:	This direct mail "classic" has become one of the best known direct mail packages using a celebrity signer. As Katharine Hepburn's mother was a co-founder of Planned Parenthood, credibility of the signer is insured. Further, Ms. Hepburn's reputation for being independent and outspoken further qualifies her to write on the controversial issue of abortion.
	Other effective techniques used in the appeal include use of a live stamp and a personalized order card. The smaller size and linen-like finish of the envelope and stationery give the package an exceptionally personal look.

Katharine Hepburn

Dear Friend,

    Normally, I don't get involved in public controversy. But reproductive freedom is a basic, _personal_ issue, and one that I feel very strongly about for personal reasons.

    Over 50 years ago, my mother helped Margaret Sanger found a new, controversial organization called the American Birth Control League. That organization later became Planned Parenthood, and since then has been in the forefront of providing family planning services to millions of Americans.

    Now, I have joined Planned Parenthood in carrying on my mother's struggle so many years later because there are two proposals that will be considered by the next Congress that could destroy completely all of her tireless work.

    The _Human Life Statute_, sponsored by Senator Jesse Helms, would impose a permanent ban on all federal funding of abortions for poor women and would encourage quick court review of _Roe_ v. _Wade_, the historic 1973 Supreme Court decision that guaranteed women the right to make a personal choice about abortion.

    The _Human Life Federalism Amendment_, sponsored by New Right Senator Orrin Hatch, (the Hatch Amendment) would give both Congress and the states concurrent power to outlaw all abortions.

    I'm writing you because one of these frightening proposals could very well pass the Congress of the United States in the next several months.

    Even our recent pro-choice victory in the U.S. Senate has not deterred the New Right.

    In the closing days of the 97th Congress, Senator Helms's Human Life Statute was tabled by a vote of 47-46 in the Senate. Orrin Hatch's anti-abortion constitutional amendment was withdrawn for lack of support.

    These were critical battles. But not conclusive ones. You and I won by just _one_ vote. _The_ _fight_ _is_ _far_ _from_ _over_.

    Senators Hatch and Helms, and their New Right allies around the country, have vowed to renew their fight, stronger than ever.

                            (over, please)

Planned Parenthood® 810 Seventh Avenue New York, New York 10019

Next time they could succeed.

If that happens, you and I will lose one of our most fundamental individual rights.

There is only <u>one</u> way to stop this from happening.

The American people must be shown <u>quickly</u> that the threat is real, that tragedy will follow for millions of innocent women, men, and children, and that our Constitution was not intended to be used by the Moral Majority or any other group to foist its particular religious beliefs on the rest of us.

Most politicians will not stick their necks out unless they sense the support of the American people.

But, so far, the loudest voices have been those of the militant anti-abortionists who have screamed loudest with such hostile slogans as "Stop the Baby Killers."

There are people who hold deep religious beliefs which forbid abortion. But they conduct their own lives according to their own beliefs and do not attempt to impose those beliefs on the rest of us. Those are not the people who pose a danger to individual rights.

What deeply troubles me, however, is that a minority is using whatever political power they can muster to force their point of view on you and me.

We must oppose them. If we remain passive, they will surely win.

Right now Planned Parenthood, the oldest and most respected family planning organization in America, is conducting an emergency national campaign to educate the public on this vital issue.

This campaign, which will cost $3.6 million, is part of a massive educational effort -- called the <u>Public</u> <u>Impact</u> <u>Program</u> -- designed to provide leadership in the fight to preserve the most basic of human rights: the right to decide when or if to bear children. The program includes radio, TV, and newspaper ads, grassroot organizing, and lobbying efforts in Washington. Also, through its 190 affiliates and 711 community-based clinics, Planned Parenthood is providing counseling and medical services to millions of Americans who otherwise may be unable to afford such services.

(next page, please)

As this campaign is carried to the people, millions of Americans will be learning that passage of legislation or a constitutional amendment banning abortions would:

** Prevent an abortion for a woman who has been exposed to X-ray treatments or proven dangerous drugs and whose doctor expects brain damage or deformity to the fetus.

** Prevent the use of the IUD and some other effective and safe birth control methods because they might technically "abort" the pregnancy during the first days after fertilization.

** Prevent an abortion for a 14-year-old girl impregnated by her father.

** Prevent an abortion for a woman who already has several children and whose husband is guilty of family brutality, causing the woman serious emotional problems.

** Prevent an abortion for a 16-year-old high school student who has no prospect for a stable home and whose pregnancy will end her chance for an education.

** Cause medically safe abortions to be replaced by back-alley butchery, and self-induced procedures of desperate women, many on the verge of nervous breakdown, or even suicide.

** Substitute cold constitutional prohibitions for individual choice based on sound advice from a woman's personal physician.

** Like the Prohibition Amendment, a constitutional amendment banning abortion would give crime another lucrative market in illegal abortions and black market adoptions.

Most reasonable people, learning these _uncontested_ _facts_, would agree that abortions certainly should be available to women like these, and those in many more similar situations.

Most reasonable people agree that the decision for an abortion should be left to the woman and her physician ... as are other medical procedures.

(over, please)

The Moral Majority cannot counter these uncontested facts except to preach that "abortion is a sin" and that any suffering is the "price the woman must pay" for getting pregnant.

Once the American people know the facts, they won't buy these simple outdated platitudes of television preachers.

That's why I am helping Planned Parenthood raise $3.6 million immediately -- for a national media campaign, for organizing citizens to stand up against repressive legislation that would limit individual rights, and most important, so that Planned Parenthood's affiliates and clinics can continue providing medical and educational services to millions of Americans each year, many of whom have no other way to pay for their reproductive health care.

Your help is vital.

Most people really haven't taken a firm stand on abortion. This battle is like a political campaign, and will be won by the side which does the best job of presenting the issues. The use of television and other media is the only way to quickly educate the public. The Right Wing taught us this lesson.

The time is now. We must buy radio, TV, and newspaper ads immediately, before Congress decides on this issue. We don't have a minute to lose.

Planned Parenthood has never lost sight of Margaret Sanger's and my mother's original goal: to give all people the right and the ability to determine for themselves whether and when to bear children.

These brave women knew even then that no woman, black or white, rich or poor, can ever truly be free without the right to personal control over her own reproductive life.

You now have an unique opportunity to become part of this historic debate. Neither you nor I should expect "someone else" to take our responsibility. Everyone's help is desperately needed.

Please send as much as you can today.

Sincerely,

Katharine Hepburn
for Planned Parenthood

Response Card and Carrier Envelope

Dear Katharine Hepburn . . .

I want to join you and Planned Parenthood in the battle to protect a woman's right to reproductive freedom.

To help you and Planned Parenthood conduct the emergency national newspaper and television campaign, and to help Planned Parenthood's affiliates and clinics continue providing vital medical and educational services, I am enclosing my tax-deductible contribution of:

☐ $20   ☐ $25   ☐ $35   ☐ $50   ☐ $100   ☐ $250   ☐ Other $_____

Please make your tax-deductible check payable to Planned Parenthood Federation of America, Inc. *and return along with this form to* 810 Seventh Avenue, Box 5687, New York, New York 10249.

```
S. E. Rinkle
4312 Azale Drive
Raleigh, NC  27612
```

7229

A copy of the last financial report filed with the New York Department of State may be obtained by writing to: New York Department of State, Office of Charities Registration, Albany, New York 12231, or to Planned Parenthood.

Katharine Hepburn

ORGANIZATION REPRESENTED:	Save the Children Westport, Connecticut
DESIGNED/ PRODUCED BY:	Epsilon Burlington, Massachusetts
DATE OF APPEAL:	1983
TYPE OF APPEAL:	Renewal
PURPOSE OF APPEAL:	This renewal appeal was designed to motivate past donors to make a contribution to Save the Children during the holiday season.
CAMPAIGN RESULTS:	The objective was to raise $175,000 from Save the Children's house file of contributors. The strategy employed was a two-part mailing series. The first mailing produced a 9 percent response and $215,000 gross income. The second mailing was a reminder which produced a 5 percent response and $98,000 gross income. Together the two mailings generated $313,000 in gross income for Save the Children.
COMMENTS:	Both the first appeal and the follow-up use simple but effective packages thanking donors for past support, encouraging them to give again, and reminding them of the work done at Save the Children.

The first mailing was a one-page personalized letter with holiday graphics. The letter mentions suggested contributions based on the donor's past level of giving. The general theme of the organization is succinctly stated and brought home by the picture of the smiling child used on both carrier envelope and response card.

The second mailing was a personalized slip with a free-standing Christmas card. Personalization is enhanced by mention of the donor's hometown. The picture of the children on the card, together with a brief note from Save the Children's President on the back, is a wonderful way to say thank-you for past support—and make the donor feel motivated to contribute again.

 Save the Children

52 Wilton Road
Westport, Conn. 06880 USA
(203) 226-7272

November 17, 1983

Mr. John D. Sample
Epsilon Data Management
24 New England Executive Park
Burlington, Massachusetts 01803

Dear Mr. Sample:

It's not easy for me to write you, just before the holidays, and ask you to do even more than you already have.

You are one of Save the Children's most valued supporters. As a sponsor and a contributor, you've provided medical care for children in war-torn Lebanon. You've brought clean drinking water to families in Nepal. And a little girl in Mexico can see better today because you made her eye operation possible.

Yet so very much remains to be done. While excited boys and girls in Burlington are opening holiday gifts, many children around the world need warm clothing and medical treatment.

Refugee camps are overcrowded in Sri Lanka and Somalia. Children need vaccinations in Greece and Mexico. Drought and hunger plague Upper Volta.

A New Year will soon be here. With your help, we can bring hope, and health, and happiness to suffering children around the globe. There's much to be done. As you know, there are thousands of reasons to support Save the Children, and each of these is a little child.

In the spirit of the holidays ahead, please do what you can by sending $100, $150 or more to Save the Children now. Your contribution means food, and medicine, and crops and schools...and hope.

With every good holiday wish,

David L. Guyer
President

DLG/km

Initial Appeal

Save the Children.

52 Wilton Road
Westport, Conn. 06880

ADDRESS CORRECTION REQUESTED

Save the Children.

52 Wilton Road
Westport, Conn. 06880 USA
(203) 226-7272

Dear Mr. Guyer:

I wish to share my good fortune with
little children in need. Enclosed is a
special Holiday contribution of:

( ) Other $....   ( ) $150   ( ) $100

Holiday Reply

1417

Please return this slip with your check made payable to Save the Children
Thank you. *Remember, your gift is fully tax-deductible.*

Follow-up

Seasons Greetings from the children

Dear Mr. Sample:

     If your Holiday contribution isn't in the mail, please send it today. Reflect on all that you have in Burlington. Won't you share some of it this Holiday Season with little boys and girls who have much less? Thank you.   -- David L. Guyer

Save the Children

( )Other $.....   ( )$100   ( )$93

Mr. John D. Sample
Epsilon Data Management
24 New England Executive Park
Burlington, Massachusetts 01803

Special Holiday Reply Form

52 Wilton Road
Westport, Conn. 06880 USA

01721WARH736

1412

Please return this slip with your check made payable to Save the Children. *Remember, your gift is fully tax-deductible.*

CHAPTER **8**

From Production to Post Office

WORKING WITH GRAPHIC ARTISTS

Not every graphic artist can bring the right look to your direct mail campaign. Many artists cannot resist imposing sophisticated, innovative design ideas on your package—and that may be exactly what you do not want.

To get the right image for your package, engage an artist who has experience in direct mail. If you don't know such an artist, call a direct mail consultant or a nonprofit organization whose packages you admire. Ask whether the packages were successful, the artist was easy to work with, and deadlines were kept. And don't forget to ask about cost. If you get all the right answers, you now know of an artist who may transform your copy into a dynamite package.

When you meet with the artist, be prepared to provide the following information and materials:

1. The number of components in the package.
2. The details and sizes of each component (i.e., two- or four-page letter, single or double response card, etc.).
3. Photographs, logos, or other art you wish to use.
4. Your timetable. (Don't expect miracles. The artist generally needs a week to produce a rough sketch and another week to set type and provide finished art.)
5. The likes and dislikes of your president or executive director (or whoever has to give final approval). For example, if your boss hates the color green, say so *now*. If he insists that your organization's ugly logo be used, don't give the artist the impression that she can reduce it to the size of the period at the end of this sentence.
6. The written text for your package. Not only is this necessary for figuring size and type, but a good artist will want to read the copy. The message and the feeling the copy evokes will provide a base for appropriate design.
7. Any rough sketches you may have developed which could help the artist visualize what you want the final piece to look like.

This last point is very important. If you have ideas about how the package should look, don't hesitate to give the artist your own rough sketch. If your ideas are good, the artist will incorporate the best of them into the design and present a final sketch that—had you the talent—is exactly what you would have drawn.

A case in point. Below (see Figure 8-1) is a sample sketch of a response device we gave to the Washington, D.C., designers, Barbieri and Green. You may laugh at the roughness of the sketch, but they didn't. In fact, we were delighted with the way they executed our instructions. Moreover, the campaign was highly successful.

Figure 8-1. Oram Sketch for Center for Environmental
Education Carrier Envelope

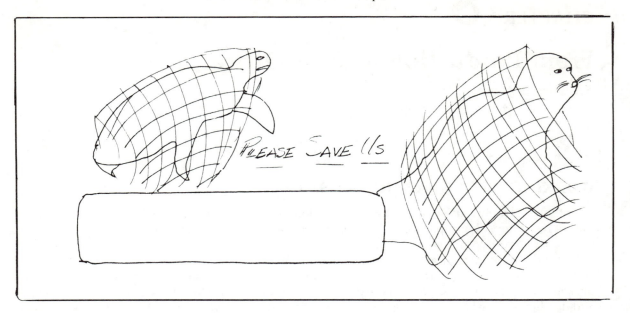

Figure 8-2. Artist's Rendition of Center for Environmental
Education Carrier Envelope

In discussing package design with your artist, be sure to emphasize the importance of the following:

1. *Size of type face.* Body copy for a response card or brochure set in less than 10 point type is too small. Don't ever let an artist convince you otherwise if you want your copy read. Twelve point type is often better.

2. *Reverse-out type.* While the look of white text reversing out of a strong color can be graphically striking, it is extremely difficult to read. If you want to reverse out a small section of your brochure for effect, go ahead. But make sure that this information isn't critical and that the type is sufficiently large to read in reverse.

3. *Use of all capitals.* ALL CAPITALS ARE MONOTONOUS AND HENCE DIFFICULT TO READ. AVOID THEIR USE EXCEPT FOR SHORT HEADLINES.

4. *Unusual Typeface.* If the typeface is the first thing you notice in a brochure or letterhead or response card, it's not right for direct mail. The type (and this applies to typewriter type as well) should command you to read the written word, not command you to admire the typeface.

5. *Background design.* Often artists will take a liking to an organization's logo or some other organizational component such as a church steeple or entrance gates—and will use this design in a light background over which your letter is printed. Warning: If you superimpose your letter over *any* design, no matter how light the screen, it will cut down on readability by at least 30 percent. Can you afford to lose 30 percent of your potential donors?

Some direct mail experts claim that professional graphic design has little or no place in direct mail. In fact, they maintain that the entire package should have a completely homemade look. Many practitioners of the homemade look go so far as to type their letters on a manual typewriter rescued from the junk yard, and to deliberately leave in spelling and typographical errors.

In general, we find this practice insulting to the prospective donor. We do agree, however, that direct mail graphics design should not look slick . . . that it should not look expensive . . . that it should not look arty.

The experienced artist will not try to create a package that will win design awards. Rather, he or she understands that the artist's job is to create a background for your appeal, to draw the reader from point to point, to create an image reflective of your organization's image (or desired image), and, most important of all, to make every element of the package highly pleasing to look at and extremely easy to read.

What Will It Cost?

Depending on the area of the country, art for a complete package, consisting of a letter, small brochure, response device, carrier envelope, and business reply envelope, will cost between $500 and $1,500. The cost includes an initial sketch, final layout, typeset, and final "camera-ready" art boards. If your package requires more than a simple design—that is, if you need a new logo or even new letterhead, or if you need one or more complex line drawings, the package will be more expensive. In New York City and Washington, D.C., we typically pay between $600 and $1,200, depending on the job's complexity. To be safe, budget your art at $1,000.

Before you conclude your first meeting with the artist, ask that the quoted price be confirmed in writing. And remember that the best time to make changes is when the artist gives you a rough sketch, not when the final art is presented. Naturally, you *can* make changes at any point, but they will become increasingly costly as you get closer to the finished product.

A word of advice: some artists and almost all photographers base their prices on whether their work is for one-time use only. Be sure to explain that if your package is successful, you plan to reprint it over a prolonged period. Most artists will give you outright ownership of work created for you as long as you don't use it commercially (i.e., convert the work into posters, note cards, etc., which you will sell for a profit). The questions of ownership or multiple use are negotiable.

WORKING WITH PRINTERS

If you don't know a good printer, your artist can help you locate one or you can ask colleagues. It is important for you and the artist to meet with the printer when the rough design has been completed. This will enable you to learn whether your package can be produced within your budget and schedule.

The early meeting with the printer is important for other reasons. Here are a few near disasters from which we have been rescued by conscientious printers.

1. Designing a brochure that because of a fan-fold could not be machine-inserted into the carrier envelope.
2. Designing a carrier envelope where the entire front panel was covered by a dramatic photo. We learned that it would not reproduce well with standard printing and that the cost for lithography printing—which would have looked smashing—was $53 per thousand.
3. Designing a response device that was too narrow for machine-inserting. The salvation of this error would have meant hand-tamping each package—at a price.
4. Designing a folded double response device with the fold at the wrong end. Yes, there is a wrong end because the grippers on the machine inserter must grip a folded edge.
5. Designing a brochure with heavy photo coverage on both sides to be printed on 50 lb. offset paper. The printer pointed out that we could either print on 70 lb. paper or save money by re-designing the brochure.

Getting Bids for Printing Jobs

Obtain three bids for comparison. Be sure to give each printer identical specifications: the type and weight of paper, the exact size of each printed piece, the number of colors, halftones (photographs), and bleeds, etc.

It is important to tell the printer when you need the job. Often, one printer can produce a job in less time than others. This could be because they have exactly the right press facilities for your job; or because business is slow.

Should all your bids come in under or just at budget, you will have to use other criteria to select your printer. Ask for samples of similar work the printer has done for others. And check references to be certain that other clients are happy with the quality of work and the dependability of delivery.

What to Discuss with Your Printer

Be sure you and your printer are clear about these items *prior* to signing a contract for a job.

1. Ask for written price quotations. The quote should break out how much each package item costs per thousand in addition to giving the total cost.

2. Ask the printer about his company's overrun estimates. The industry standard on printing overruns (for which the client is obligated to pay) is 5 percent on quantities of 250,000 or more and 10 percent on quantities of less than 250,000. For our part, we contract with each printer with whom we do business to pay no more than 5 percent regardless of the quantity. (And in fact, the overruns usually amount to only between 2 and 3 percent.) There is no real way to protect yourself from *underruns*. However, the 5 percent allowance on overruns makes the likelihood of an underrun quite unlikely.

3. Agree in advance on delivery dates, allowing some flexibility in your schedule for time to correct errors.
   - Delivery of "bluelines" or "blues" (reproductions of the artwork on blueprint paper, cut and folded to size).
   - Delivery of *advance* samples to you. Samples are taken off the press early and hand-trimmed.
   - Delivery of entire job to the mail house. Be sure to specify how the mail house wants the various items packed.
   Note: Often the printer and the mail house are the same—hence the term "lettershop"—which can save a day or more in transportation.

4. Ask the printer to provide, in advance, samples of the various paper stocks for the job. It is not sufficient to simply order 50 or 60 pound stock, as within these weight specifications, paper quality can vary dramatically.

5. Ask the printer to provide samples of direct mail materials he has produced for other clients. Incidentally, as with graphic artists and mail houses, it is important to call these clients for references. Ask specifically about quality of work and dependability of delivery.

6. Give your printer *specific* instructions in *writing*. Without written instructions, you are without recourse should something go wrong with your job. With written instructions you can usually correct a disaster—i.e., wrong color, wrong size, etc.—at no cost to you. And you can get the price of a barely acceptable job greatly reduced.

Fail-Safe Proofreading

Ask your artist to provide galleys of the typeset pages *before* they are pasted down on the art boards. If typos or other mistakes are found at this stage, they will be less costly to correct. Once they have been pasted down and shipped to the printer, your final opportunity to correct mistakes will not occur until you receive the blueline.

We strongly advise you to proofread the typeset copy *twice*—once for sense and a second time *backwards* to catch spelling and punctuation errors.

Incidentally, if you don't know proofreading symbols, ask your artist or printer to recommend a book. The correct proof marks will enable the typesetter to make the proper corrections the first time around, and will save you time and money.

After you have proofread and approved the second set of galleys, your artist will transfer them to "boards"—so called because the type and art are pasted onto art board in a precise format that is camera-ready. Then, following the artist's instructions, the printer will do all necessary preparatory work and will photograph these boards. This photo, cut and folded to resemble the final product, is called a blueline.

The blueline is your fail-safe opportunity to catch elusive mistakes not discovered earlier. However, the real purpose of the blueline is not for discovering typos. Catching typos at this stage is expensive as the job must be re-routed through the artist and typesetter, and another blueline must be made.

Check your blueline carefully for the following:

- Is the fold correct?
- Is the size correct?
- Are the photographs (and captions) correctly placed?
- Are the pages consecutive (i.e., did the printer accidentally transpose pages 1 and 3)?
- Does any printing on the response card "show through" the window on the carrier envelope? (Was it supposed to?)
- Is the printing quality good? (Too dark? Too light?)
- Are there "hickeys" (unattractive spots often caused by dust on the negative) in the photographs (or anywhere else in the piece?)
- Are the color breaks correct (i.e., are the parts meant to be blue actually blue and not red, etc.)?

If you find it difficult to judge printing quality by looking at a blueline, ask the printer to provide a color key. This will cost a bit more, but because it breaks out all colors on overlay acetate sheets, it can be well worth the additional cost—especially on a complicated job.

We have shown up more than once at a printshop to check color and quality while the job is on the press. This may not endear you to your printer but think how good *you'll* feel when you know your work is being done properly.

WORKING WITH LETTERSHOPS

You have come a long way. You have planned, budgeted, created, conferred with artists, negotiated with printers, and corrected galleys and bluelines. Now you are ready to mail. The choice of a mail house is no less critical than the choice of an artist or printer.

There are big mailing houses and small mailing houses. There are the expensive and the less expensive. There are good and bad. In our experience, we have been unable to relate expensive to good, inexpensive to bad, or any other combination of the above.

Once again, the best way to choose a lettershop is to ask your colleagues in other organizations for referrals. Then, as with printers, obtain three price bids.

A good mail house or lettershop will:

1. Inform you promptly when expected lists do not arrive on time, or when they arrive improperly coded or in an unacceptable format.
2. Open your printed materials on receipt and notify you immediately if there are shortages in quantity or a question about quality.
3. Call promptly if your written instructions are not absolutely clear.
4. Not bump your job for another—perhaps more lucrative—job.
5. Keep you informed of well-founded rumors (e.g., a back-up at the bulk mail center, a potential postal increase, fast- and slow-moving mail in certain periods).
6. Not reverse codes. If you are testing a package, the mail house sets up a fail-safe system to insure that the test elements are mailed correctly.
7. Mail on time—assuming that you and your printer are also on time—and will advise you promptly of any delays. Note: It is useless for a mail house to deceive a customer about the drop date because the post office receipts which will be submitted with your mail house bill will verify the actual date(s) of mailing.

Your Responsibilities to the Mail House

1. Obtain the correct postal permits well in advance or arrange for the mail house to do it for you. How to obtain postal permits is discussed later in this chapter.

2. Send an advance listing, with assigned key codes, of the lists that are expected at your mail house.

3. Send written instructions to the mail house with a sample package, inserted the way you want it. If you do not have advance samples from the printer at this point, photocopy the artwork and send a dummy package to the mail house. Instructions should be typed clearly and should leave no room for guesswork. Most important are the mail date and instructions on how to handle split tests.

4. Send the postage check in advance. Usually, mail houses require the check five working days in advance and most will not start work until it has arrived.

5. Do not relax after you have completed all of the above, expecting that the mail house will call you should problems arise. They might and they might not. Call to make certain your materials have arrived and that work is progressing on schedule. Then call again the day the mail is scheduled to drop just to make sure.

6. Ask the mail house to send you a half dozen "live" samples right off their inserting machine. Unlike the samples from the printer, live samples show you exactly how your mailing looks to recipients.

7. "Seed" yourself in the mailing. Make sure several pieces are addressed to you so that you will know when others receive their mail and when you may expect returns.

How to Cope with Late Mailings

Even if you have done everything humanly possible in working with your list broker, printer, and lettershop, Murphy's Law can still prevail. Let us here forewarn you of potential last minute pitfalls. For example, suppose your lettershop calls at 5 p.m. on Friday to advise that of 20 lists expected, only seven sets of labels have arrived. Your mail date is Monday.

First, call your list broker—who then can begin tracking down the missing lists. This can be a long process, as the broker must call the owner who must call his or her list maintenance bureau. Then, each of these steps must be repeated in reverse. Chances are, when your broker finally gets back to you, you will be advised that some of the lists are definitely en route and that others haven't gone out yet because someone's great uncle died, but are you willing to pay an additional charge for shipping UPS Blue Label?

Doubtless you are willing to pay, but even such special handling won't meet your deadline. You now call your mail house to ask whether it can make a partial drop (i.e., those lists that have arrived.)

The answer depends more on how busy the mail house is than on how good a customer you are although the latter helps. Many mail houses will drop a partial mailing for you and mail the balance on receipt, or as soon thereafter as possible.

But what of the balance? What about the fact that you have contracted for a particular mail date, and that your material is date-timed to coincide with a political or social "event" that will make the mailing many times more effective? We cannot provide you with the right answer for all cases, but let us here give you some alternatives:

- In contracting for a specific date for the use of a list, you have not promised to mail *on* that date, but within that *week*. Thus you have some leeway. And if it is the list owner's fault that the list was not received on time, the broker usually can arrange to have your time extended.

- If your material is dated and critical, you may wish to mail first class.

- If your material is *not* dated and the list broker gives you permission to mail late, you should ask whether a competing organization might be mailing to the same list at the same time. If so, you should ask for a new mail date.

It is important to remember that late delivery of materials can cause the same havoc as late delivery of lists. It is therefore prudent to ask your printer to print and deliver your response devices first if possible. Thus, if any other portion of your printed materials arrive late, a cooperative mail house usually can get a head start affixing the mailing labels to the response devices. This logistical trick has saved many potentially late mailings from disaster.

Further Thoughts on Artists, Printers, and Mail Houses

Because your artist is likely to work nearby, you will be in close and regular contact. But most business with printers and mail houses is conducted over the phone as many are remotely located.

It is a good idea to visit your printing plant and mail house (or lettershop) in the beginning to educate yourself about techniques and to meet the people with whom you will be working. This makes for a far better relationship in the long run. People who know you will be more likely to go the extra mile when a problem arises.

If your mail campaign is at an ongoing stage, and you are happy with the services provided by your artist, printer, and mail house, you might wish to give each a schedule of future mailings. The more they know about your plans, the better they can serve you. For example, your printer may be able to order a preferred paper that he would not have been able to get on short notice. Or, your artist will be able to warn you in advance if he or she expects to be especially busy during a certain time of year. Your mail house can schedule you in their work log. This type of planning pays off for you too, because by planning out the year, you know when you have to write a new package or start ordering lists for the next campaign.

In Chapter 1 we provided a schedule which incorporated working with artists, printers, mail houses, and list brokers. We refer you again to Figure 1-1.

In addition, we are providing a blank Production Specifications and Budget form (see Figure 8-3) for you to copy and use for your own campaign.

WHAT YOU NEED TO KNOW ABOUT POSTAL REGULATIONS

Cost to Mail

Most nonprofit organizations qualify to mail at the nonprofit bulk rate. As of mid-1984, the nonprofit rate stood at $52 per thousand or 5.2¢ per piece. Obviously, this is a major savings from first class postage at $200 per thousand or 20¢ per piece.

Because of this substantial savings, most qualifying organizations elect to mail all prospect appeals and most renewal and special gift appeals at the nonprofit rate.

Permits

Everything you need to know about postal permits and regulations is contained in the *Postal Service Manual* issued by the U.S. Postal Service. An even better guide, in our opinion, is the *Manual of Postal Information* published by the Envelope Manufacturers Association, 1300 North 17th Street, Arlington, VA 22209. Currently out of print, this guide will again be available in January 1985 and may be obtained through envelope manufacturers who are members of the Association.

If you do not have either manual, or if you find the information confusing, the following should be of help.

If you are a 501(c)(3) or a 501(c)(4) organization, it is a simple matter to obtain a bulk rate mailing permit. Submit completed Form 3624 to the local postmaster with proof of status, such as articles of incorporation, bylaws, and certificate of tax exemption. Your application must show that the primary purpose of your organization is religious, educational, scientific, philanthropic, agricultural, labor, veteran, or fraternal, or that it is a qualified political committee. Other types of nonprofit organizations do not qualify for special rate usage. The annual fee for this permit is $40.

Basic Third Class (nonprofit) Mailing Requirements

The mailing requirements for third class (nonprofit) mailings (as of January 1984):

- Mailings must consist of at least 200 pieces or 50 pounds.
- Letters must be presorted by zip codes in packages and sacks to the finest extent possible.
- Each piece must be identical in weight, although textual matter need not be identical.
- All bulk rate mailings must be mailed at the post office from which the permit was issued.
- The authorized permit holder must be identified on the carrier envelope. The name and return address of the authorized permit holder must appear in a prominent location. Pseudonyms of persons or organizations may not be used. If the mailing piece bears any name and return address, it must be that of the authorized permit holder. A well recognized alternative designation or abbreviation such as "The March of Dimes" or the "AFL-CIO" may be used in place of the full name of the organization.
- There are no maximum size standards for a single piece of third class mail. There are, however, maximum standards for third class carrier route presort which are: not more than ¾" thick, not more than 11½" high, and not more than 13½" long.
- As for minimum size standards, all third class mailings must be at least .007" thick, rectangular in shape, at least 3½" high, and 5" long.
- Third class mail may receive deferred service. The Postal Service does not guarantee the delivery of third class mail within a specified time, (as most fund raisers, unfortunately, know all too well).

Figure 8-3. Production Specification and Budget

TYPE OF MAILING _____   DATE _____

QUANTITY _____   MAIL DATE _____

BUDGET _____

( ) Check here if testing is involved, indicate nature of test and use additional form to cost out.

ITEM	SPECS (color, size, etc.)	BEST BID (per M)	VENDOR
I. CAMERA READY ART			
II. PRINTING			
Carrier Envelope			
BRE			
Letter			
Response Device			
Lift Note			
Other (specify)			

SUBTOTAL (per M) $_____   (job total) $_____

ITEM	SPECS	BEST BID	VENDOR
III. LETTERSHOP			
Label, insert, sort, tie, bag and mail			
Meter or affix live stamp			
Merge/Purge			
Laser or computer			
Other (specify)			

TOTAL (per M) $_____   (job total) $_____

ITEM	SPECS	BEST BID	VENDOR
IV. OTHER			
Postage			
Lists			
Other			

GRAND TOTAL (per M) $_____   (job total) $_____

Posting Your Mail

There are three ways to affix nonprofit postage.

1. *By pre-printing an indicia on your carrier envelope.* We consider this the least desirable look for an appeal. If you choose this method, the permit must be prepared in one of the following formats.

   Note: For carrier route presorted nonprofit mailings the words, "Carrier Route Presort" or "Car-rt-sort" (explained below), must be included in the permit imprint (as shown below) or imprinted on the mailing piece within two lines directly above the address.

Figure 8-4. Pre-printed Nonprofit Indicia

2. *By metering each piece of mail at the lettershop.* Even though postal regulations require you to omit the month, date, and year, and to substitute the words "Non Profit Org" for the phrase "Bulk Rate," this type of postage is far more personal looking than the indicia above.

Figure 8-5. Metered Nonprofit Postage

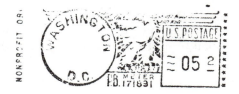

3. *By affixing a "live" pre-cancelled nonprofit stamp.* Of the three ways of affixing nonprofit postage, this is the most expensive. But it certainly comes the closest to looking like first class mail. If fact, many mailers have observed that such mail sometimes moves through the postal system as quickly as first class mail.

Figure 8-6. Live Nonprofit Stamp

217

As stated earlier, we try to avoid the distinctly third class look of the pre-printed indicia with one exception noted below. There is some cost savings in using the pre-printed indicia, but usually not enough to offset results from using metered or stamped mail.

Depending on quantity, the average cost of metering your mail is between $1.25 and $1.75 per thousand and for affixing a live nonprofit stamp, the average cost is between $2.50 and $3.75 per thousand (1984 rates).

Many postage tests have been conducted to ascertain whether the stamp outpulls the meter or the meter the indicia. The results? In *most* cases, both meter and stamp outpull the indicia and in some cases, the stamp does better than the meter. *But not always.* We have found that the simpler the envelope, the more important the look of the postage. Thus a commercial looking envelope with a great deal of illustration and text might do just as well with an indicia, while a simple, dignified envelope might benefit from a live stamp.

The tests we have conducted vary so widely from client to client that our best advice is to test this for yourself. If in doubt, however, *you will not go wrong by metering your mail!*

Business Reply Mail

Whether you elect to receive your contributions in-house or through a bank lock box, it is usually economical to open a Business Reply Account at your local post office. The annual fee of $75 will be amortized quickly if your mailing returns number just 300 or more for the year.

Here is how it works. Without such an account, your postage-due mail will be delivered to your office where you must pay in cash, each day, at 38¢ per piece. However, if you have a Business Reply Account, you deposit money into that account equal to your anticipated returns (plus the $75 of course) and your account is then charged at the rate of only 25¢ for each piece received. When your account runs low, you deposit more money. If it runs out, the post office will stop delivering your postage-due mail and within a few days you are certain to notice that another deposit is required.

Everything you need to know about first class business reply mail can be found in the two postal service manuals mentioned earlier. To make life simpler for you, however, we include here the information on business reply mail from the *Manual of Postal Information.**

BUSINESS REPLY MAIL

Persons who wish to distribute and receive business reply mail must apply to the post office for a permit. An annual fee is required. The fee is for the calendar year, January 1 - December 31. . . . Any user of the business reply service may establish a business reply account. When business reply postage and fees are paid from a business reply account, a lower business reply piece charge is applicable. An annual accounting fee is required to establish a business reply account. . . . Business reply mail pieces may be distributed in any quantity desired. The permit holder guarantees payment on delivery of postage and fees on returned business reply mail.

Business reply mail pieces will be accepted for return mailing at all post offices in the United States and its possessions including military post offices overseas, except the Canal Zone. They should not be sent to any foreign countries, including Canada, Cuba, Mexico, Philippine Islands and the Republic of Panama, as they cannot be returned from any foreign country without prepayment of postage. . . .

---

*Reprinted with permission of the Envelope Manufacturers Association from *Manual of Postal Information* © 1982 by the Envelope Manufacturers Association.

PRINTING REGULATIONS

Any photographic, mechanical or electrical process or any combination of such processes other than handwriting, typewriting or handstamping may be used to prepare the address side of business reply mail.

The background of business reply mail pieces may be any light color that allows the address, postmark and other required endorsements to be readily discerned. Brilliant colors may not be used. Green diamond borders or other borders are not authorized for business reply labels, cartons and envelopes larger than 6 × 11 inches. . . .

Figure 8-7. Post Office Specifications for Business Reply Envelope

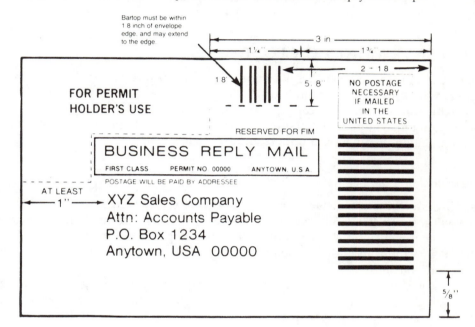

REQUIRED FORMAT ELEMENTS

All of the pre-printed endorsements and markings shown in the illustration [above] are required. They include:

1. "NO POSTAGE NECESSARY IF MAILED IN THE UNITED STATES", in upper right hand corner, no further than 1¾ inches from the right edge.
2. The appropriate "Business Reply" legend in capital letters at least ³⁄₁₆ inch in height.

Authorized legends are:

Legend	For use on
BUSINESS REPLY MAIL	Letters, cartons, and cards at letter rate.
BUSINESS REPLY CARD	Cards qualifying for post card rate. (The legend "Business Reply Card" must be used to be eligible for the lower card rate. . . .)
BUSINESS REPLY LABEL	Labels. (Business reply envelopes and cards may not be used as labels to return matter to the permit holder. However, the permit holder of a business reply label guarantees payment of first-class postage upon the return of any mailable matter having his business reply label affixed).

HOW TO SAVE MONEY ON POSTAGE

If your mailing is (a) national, with a minimum of 200,000 pieces, or (b) local (within a large metropolitan area), with a minimum of 75,000 pieces, you probably qualify for a Five Digit Pre-Sort, which means that you can mail at 4.3¢, a savings of .9¢ for each piece.

Although your mail house or lettershop will handle the tedious job of sorting the mail according to postal regulations, you should understand the basics.

Why Pre-sort?

Pre-sorting is a way to cut postage expense. For example, a nonprofit mailing of 200,000 pieces at 5.2¢ each will cost $10,400, while the same mailing—where 50 percent qualifies for pre-sort—will save you $900 in postage. The computer and lettershop charges to effect this saving are only about $2.50 per thousand—still a net savings of $650. Naturally, prices—and savings—vary from company to company.

It is necessary to merge/purge prior to pre-sort. Organizations planning a merge/purge for other reasons and mailing sufficient numbers in one zip string (and who are *not* testing packages) should take advantage of the potential savings.

If it is important for you to test packages and you still want to pre-sort, your national mailing must be at least 500,000 pieces or larger (i.e., each zip string must be 200,000 pieces); less for local mailings. Your computer bureau can advise you on the exact numbers.

Carrier Route Pre-sort

This is much the same as five digit pre-sort except that you must sort your mail down to even smaller areas (carrier routes). Thus it is necessary to start with a mailing of no fewer than 500,000 pieces to make it economically worthwhile.

If you qualify, however, the savings will be even greater. Assuming that you qualify for at least half of your 500,000-piece mailing, you can mail the qualified portion at 3.3¢—a 1.9¢ savings per piece. You will save $4,750 in postage. Estimating increased computer and lettershop costs of $1,250 to do the sort, you still save a comfortable $3,500. And just think of all the creative things you can do with $3,500 that might have been spent unnecessarily on postage.

Address Correction Services

At least once a year (ideally more often) you will want to clean your list. The most efficient and economical way to clean your list is to mail a house appeal with the words

ADDRESS CORRECTION REQUESTED
RETURN POSTAGE GUARANTEED

printed on the face of the carrier envelope. If your appeal is undeliverable to the addressee, the post office will return your letter together with a new address if one is known. The fee for this service is 25¢ per letter returned to you—a modest investment when you consider that otherwise you would have continued sending non-forwardable third class mail at a cost of 15¢ to 25¢ each time you made an appeal.

SIXTEEN MONEY-SAVING PRODUCTION AND MAILING TIPS

1. Obtain several printing bids for the best price.
2. Ask your printer about the most economical size for each component of the package.
3. Order envelopes from envelope manufacturers as opposed to buying them ready made off-the-shelf.
4. Use standard left-hand window envelopes (as opposed to more expensive center or right-hand windows).
5. If you are a large mailer, order envelopes in large lots, especially the Business Reply Envelopes which rarely change. As for carrier envelopes with name and address printing, you can always overprint teaser copy later.
6. Confine use of two colors to the first page of your letter; no need to pay for extra color just to have a blue signature on page 2 or 4.
7. When using personalization, try ink jet or impact printing instead of computer fill.
8. Test partial personalization (i.e., personalize only the response card and test it against a fully personalized package).
9. On house file mailings, test regular reply envelopes where the donor affixes his own stamp against business reply envelopes (where *you* pay).
10. If Number 9 frightens you, print the legend "your stamp is an extra donation" on all of your business reply envelopes.
11. If your mailing is sufficiently large, use Five Digit Pre-Sort or even Carrier Route Pre-sort.
12. Proof carefully at all stages of package development and avoid costly changes at the blueline stage.
13. Weigh all package components *before* printing to avoid unexpected additional postage costs. (This is especially important if you are mailing first class.)
14. Know how many printer's overruns you are required to pay for.
15. Purchasing stock photos is expensive. Build up your own photo library.
16. Keep your list clean by doing a special "Address Correction Requested" mailing at least once a year. Nothing is more costly than mailing to constituents who are unable to respond to your appeal.

TRACK IV
Getting Sophisticated

CHAPTER 9

Testing Techniques

ELEMENTS TO TEST

We once had a client for whom we developed a strong fund-raising package, including a four-page letter. The package worked well for the organization, earning a .9 to 1 percent return and a $22 average gift on the pilot and the two succeeding roll-outs. The client was reluctant to allow us to change the basic letter, but in the course of two years of prospecting we managed to test the following elements:

1. *Teaser copy.* The original envelope was a plain corner card. We tested one with dramatic teaser copy.
2. *Endorsement letter.* The original letter was signed by the organization's president. We tested the addition of a short letter of endorsement from a person who had benefited from the program.
3. *Special enclosure.* A leading newsletter featured a glowing story on the organization. We reprinted the article and tested it.
4. *Postage.* We conducted a three-way test, metered nonprofit postage (the control) vs. a live nonprofit stamp vs. a live first class stamp.
5. *Premium.* We tested offering an inexpensive book (of which there was a surplus) for contributions of $50 or more.

Here are the results of the tests:

1. The teaser copy on the test envelope (at a 1.1 percent return) outpulled the plain envelope, which elicited a .9 percent return.
2. The package that included the letter of endorsement (mailed in the plain envelope so as not to skew the test) received a 1.3 percent return, compared to a .98 percent return.
3. The package that included the reprint (again mailed in the plain envelope) earned a 1.6 percent return, compared to a 1 percent return for the control package.
4. In the postage test, the live first class stamp produced a higher average gift ($25, compared to $22). The live nonprofit stamp produced a virtually identical result ($24).

5. The portion of the mailing that offered a premium for joining increased the return from .80 to .95 percent.

What can we learn from the results of these tests?

Teaser Copy

Does the fact that the envelope teaser won over the plain envelope mean that plain envelopes are *passé*? Envelope teasers and art are used to make an envelope stand out. However, you have noticed that when all envelopes in your mailbox use teasers, they all begin to look alike. Therefore, unless your teaser or art is so unique or commanding that it stands apart from the mass, it probably will not work. In fact, an argument could be made that we have reached a point where the *only* envelope that stands out is the plain envelope. Perhaps. But before you throw out the idea you have on the drawing board, picture yourself in a bookstore surrounded by thousands of book jackets. Each book jacket is different, employing a variety of typefaces, photographs, drawings, colors, copy teasers, and endorsements. Does this make you leave without a purchase? Of course not. And as you browse through the shelves, aren't you frequently attracted to a cover that catches your fancy?

It's the same with envelope teasers. The teaser copy used in the test just cited won because it was good. When teasers are mediocre they usually fail. Making the judgment as to what is and what is not a good teaser is difficult. If you feel incapable of making that judgment, either use a plain envelope or test the teaser against a plain envelope.

Special Enclosures

Does the success of the endorsement letter and the reprint tell us that they should become standard inserts? If endorsement letters and news reprints become standard in all direct mail packages, they will quickly lose the special punch they now provide. Still, of all the inexpensive ways to jazz up a package, the inclusion of a really good newspaper or magazine article from a prestigious publication or a *relevant* endorsement letter from a credible signer remain two of the best ways to increase results. Test for yourself.

Postage

Do the results of the first class postage test mean that first class postage should be used on prospect mail? The postage test cited did elicit a higher average gift. But when the additional cost of the first class postage was subtracted from the additional income in this test, there was a significant loss of net income. On the other hand, the nonprofit live stamp part of the test that brought almost the same results was cost effective. This does not mean that first class should never be used on prospect mail. However, it should be reserved for small mailings to very select lists where there is very good reason to believe that a good percent return and high dollar gift will ensue.

Premium

Does the better return on the premium offer mean that one should make it a rule to offer such incentives to gift giving? The mailing that produced a respectable increase by offering a book as a premium would seem to indicate that premiums are profitable. But before you rush out to order bumper stickers, books, and decals, let us share the analysis done 14 months after the test mailing. When renewals were sent the following year, only 40 percent of the new members who responded to the original premium offer renewed their memberships, while 60 percent of those who had joined without benefit of a premium renewed. Thus, great caution should be used before deciding to offer them year after year. Premiums can be an effective inducement, however, to renew lapsed members or to upgrade members to a higher category of giving.

For every test that proves a point, an almost identical test performed for another organization can have startlingly different results. Newspaper reprints and endorsement letters do not always work better. Some organizations offering premiums to join have no difficulty renewing their members. Plain envelopes frequently win the test. But when it comes to first class postage on prospect mailings, these rarely are economical for *any* organization.

Good ideas are worth testing. The worst mistake you can make as a direct mail professional is not to test and test and test until you come up with one or more winning combinations.

With so many testing possibilities, let us list those that are the most worthwhile.

TESTS	EXAMPLES
Letter length	Two pages vs. four or six pages.
Letter signer	A celebrity signer vs. your president, or one celebrity vs. another.
Envelope art and teasers	No message vs. a "grabber" teaser copy or art.
Postage	Meter vs. indicia vs. live stamp.
Premiums	No premium vs. premium, or test two premiums against each other.
Petition	Petition must be relevant to your goal.
Questionnaire	You may learn something of value.
Package format and size	Test a smaller (or, in some cases, larger) envelope.
Additional descriptive brochure	Try restating membership benefits illustrated with photographs.
Bold new graphics and color on old package	If you have tested new packages and "old faithful" still outpulls them, jazz up "old faithful" and test it against its former self.
Special enclosures	Decals, bumper stickers, etc.
Personalization	Computer or laser letters or response devices.

Ensuring Valid Tests of Individual Elements

In testing the package elements listed above, take care that you design a valid test. This requires that the next test package maintain as much sameness with the control package as possible—except for the variable you are testing.

If you are testing a long vs. a short letter, for example, make sure you are testing the length of the letter and not the message. If your control package is the short letter, be sure to open the long letter with the same (or very similar) first paragraph and include all of the thoughts and ideas from the control letter intact. If a brochure accompanied the original short letter, extrapolate the information from the brochure and incorporate it into your long letter. This has two advantages. It helps to lengthen your letter painlessly and you won't inadvertently omit information that might have contributed to the success of the control package.

Additional tips:

- Use the same signer.
- Use the same photographs and art.
- Use everything else exactly the same.

Testing letter signers can be difficult as the signers' personalities may vary. Nevertheless, the two letters should be as similar as possible. You may not be able to control every word, but you can control the basic message, tone, length of letter, art, and so on. If you don't, you will never know whether that movie star's signature made his package win or whether it was those inspired opening and closing paragraphs you gave him (and not the president of your organization) to say.

In short, in testing any component of a package, make every effort to leave the rest of the package as it was, including premium offers, postage, graphics, envelopes—everything.

TESTING A NEW MESSAGE

A crisis or a news story or a new program often can be the inspiration for an exciting new appeal for your organization. Naturally, you will not risk discarding your control package in favor of a new idea, but you will want to test the new concept. To be fair to both old and new packages, be certain that the new package maintains as much sameness with the control package as possible.

Following are elements that usually can remain the same.

- Length of letter
- Size and format
- Colors
- Postage
- Premiums or other special offer
- Size of gift requested
- Mail date
- Lists

It will be difficult, and often impossible, to have the following components remain the same.

- *Letter signer*. The test would be purer if the same person signed both letters. However, the very fact that you are writing on a different subject may call for a different signer—one with special credibility in the subject area. If not, go with your original signer.
- *Art*. If you have a new subject to describe, you are going to need new photographs.

228

But, you protest, if I keep all those things the same, how can I create a new package?

A truly new package does not come out of the process of testing technical elements of the package. Rather, it should take an entirely new approach and content. For example:

1. An environmental organization might develop a series of packages stressing different issues such as wildlife, acid rain, federal government budget abuse, and so on.
2. A wildlife organization or a zoo could feature a different endangered species, testing each animal's relative appeal.
3. An international health organization could test a package emphasizing services to third world countries against one that concentrated on services to U.S. families.

Let us illustrate our premise with the following story, told by our good friend, the late Sanky Perlowin, an Oram executive for some 20 years, and head of her own New York consulting firm until her death in 1984.

"People are always asking me how Planned Parenthood has managed to do so well over the years. They point out that their own direct mail results fluctuate depending on causes that are 'in'—or 'out' at any given time.

"But often there is a way to get around this. Let's look at Planned Parenthood's history.

"In the early days, the fund-raising appeals promoted the Margaret Sanger birth control clinics. In the '60s, when the environment became the 'in' cause, Planned Parenthood became an environmental cause. After all, overpopulation is at the very core of our environmental problems.

"When civil rights was the *cause célèbre*, Planned Parenthood became a civil rights organization. After all, we were primarily serving minorities.

"As the women's movement flourished, we re-cast Planned Parenthood as a feminist organization. And certainly THAT was true enough!"

As Sanky put it so well, an organization cannot—if it is to survive the whims of charitable giving—afford to look at itself in a narrow context.

So in planning your next all new package, see whether you can't come up with some innovative hook to a burning issue of the day on which you can build a different—yet completely honest—portrait of your organization and those it serves.

WHAT TESTING ISN'T

A former client develops several entirely new packages each year and tests them to see which is best. When he showed us letters sent over the previous several years, we were surprised by those he declared to be the winners. To us, they seemed weaker than the letters he had judged to have lost on his tests.

Unfortunately, this client's faulty methods of testing and interpreting the results of his tests are not uncommon among nonprofit organizations. Here's how we saw it:

His hypothesis: Last summer's mailings were disappointing, our client thought, so he developed a new package for a January mailing. An analysis of the January mailing "proved" to him that the new package was superior to the old one by a margin of three to one. On this basis, he decided to use the new package in a major roll-out.

Facts: Our client had ignored some very important factors. First, the package he'd used in the summer was not tested against his new one. Further, he mailed to different lists in January—only mailing to two of the 16 lists he had tried in the summer. Also, the January mailing was sent with a live nonprofit stamp, while the summer mailing had used a pre-printed indicia. And, obviously, the two packages had not been tested at the same time of year.

229

Our analysis: January is the very best month for direct mail, and summer months are usually the worst. The improved results might be attributed as easily to the month of mailing as to the new package. Further, a list-by-list analysis of the returns showed that it was the new lists that had carried the January mailing. The new package had only pulled a little better than the original package did on the same lists.

Our recommendations: We advised the client (who still had a supply of 40,000 of the old package, as well as 40,000 of the new) to conduct a *real* test before he plunged into his next roll-out. Here is how we structured his test for a March 15 mailing. Lists selected to re-test included four lists of 10,000 each (previously used only in the summer mailing) and four of the best lists of 10,000 each (previously used only in the January mailing). The total mailing was 80,000.

		CONTROL PACKAGE	TEST PACKAGE
List A	10M	2500 Live Stamp 2500 Metered	2500 Live Stamp 2500 Metered
List B	10M	2500 Live Stamp 2500 Metered	2500 Live Stamp 2500 Metered
List C	10M	2500 Live Stamp 2500 Metered	2500 Live Stamp 2500 Metered
List D	10M	2500 Live Stamp 2500 Metered	2500 Live Stamp 2500 Metered
List E	10M	2500 Live Stamp 2500 Metered	2500 Live Stamp 2500 Metered
List F	10M	2500 Live Stamp 2500 Metered	2500 Live Stamp 2500 Metered
List G	10M	2500 Live Stamp 2500 Metered	2500 Live Stamp 2500 Metered
List H	10M	2500 Live Stamp 2500 Metered	2500 Live Stamp 2500 Metered
Mailing	80M	40,000 Control 20,000 Control Stamp 20,000 Control Metered	40,000 Test 20,000 Test Stamp 20,000 Test Metered

Since the lists were all repeat uses of proven lists, they were ordered in quantities of 10,000 instead of the usual 5,000 for a first-time list use. This larger quantity allowed each list to be split into four 2,500 parts, which would be the minimum quantity required for a valid test. The four parts to each list then were used to test both the two different packages and the stamped vs. metered postage.

The results of our by-the-book test were eye opening for our client. Overall, the package that brought in the largest average gift was the control package, both with and without the live stamp. (The control pulled an average of $23 vs. $19.50 for the new package.) It should be noted that on almost half of the lists, the live stamp did somewhat better.

Significantly, the lists used in the summer mailing did not perform, as a group, as well as those chosen for the January mailing—i.e., a .84 percent return vs. a .98 percent return.

What We Learned

Our client had been much too quick to blame disappointing results on the package. This much was proved by our re-test in which the control package elicited substantially larger gifts.

When the mailer saw the results of the January package, he assumed that because they were better, it meant that the package was better. In fact, the factors that conspired to make the second package *look* so much better were: (1) the excellent month in which it was mailed, and (2) the improved list selection (remember that even the original package performed better on the new lists). Another thing we learned was for this organization at least, live stamps seem worthwhile.

RULES FOR TESTING

Following are six rules to follow in testing:

1. All tests should have as their goal a measurable increased percent return and/or average gift. Test results showing a difference of less than .1 percent return are meaningless, unless, of course, the winning package was vastly cheaper to produce, in which case you can apply the savings against the revenue. Similarly, 50¢ or $1 increases in average gifts are not significant enough to prove conclusively the winner in a test. If your average gift is between $5 and $15, look for an increase of between $2 and $3. If your average gift is between $20 and $30, look for an increase of between $3 and $6.
2. To be accurate, test only one thing at a time. (This rule excludes lists, which you are *always* testing.)
3. Mail test packages within the same week.
4. Mail test packages at the same postal rate, unless it is postage you are testing.
5. Mail test packages to the same lists and split your list for testing on an nth (or random sample) select. In other words, a test where half of the mailing goes to a different zip selection than the other half is not a valid test.
6. Any test conducted using fewer than five lists of 2,500 names each is rarely valid. Ten lists of 5,000 names each is preferable.

FORMATS TO TEST

Letters are not the only vehicles used to raise funds through the mail. We have also tested the use of:

- Self-mailers
- Greeting cards
- Telegrams
- Pseudo-telegrams
- Partially computerized letters
- Fully computerized letters

Self-mailers

Although self-mailers serve other purposes, such as advertising, we do not like them for fund raising because no matter how attractive, they do not convey the impression that they contain important material. Important material comes in envelopes with four closed sides—period. Self-mailers are perceived to be more third class than most third class-looking sweepstakes giveaways. And if this isn't reason enough, consider this: self-mailers for most organizations produce unusually low average gifts.

Greeting Cards

Until we took on a client that earned substantial net income through sending seasonal greeting cards, we would have scoffed at the idea. Hundreds of thousands of dollars later, however, we no longer scoff.

The ASPCA of New York City traditionally sends Christmas, Valentine, and Easter cards to its members and donors with a business reply envelope. There is no direct request for a contribution. These mailings generally produce a 10 to 20 percent return. On Valentine's Day, 1984, we tested a simple valentine card against a valentine card with a computer letter that asked in a straight-forward manner, for contributions. This valentine mailing pulled over 50 percent more gifts than the previous valentine and 40 percent more income.

These returns reinforced the basic tenet that letters that ask straightforwardly for gifts should be included in all fund-raising packages. However, we will continue to test these methods in future holiday mailings for the client.

Telegrams

Real telegrams are expensive and often frightening. They therefore should be used only when your organization has a real emergency that will compensate for the cost as well as the anxiety elicited in your recipient.

Pseudo-telegrams

There are many "look-alike" telegrams. One organization called TELEPOST offers a particularly good service. All you do is provide the text for the message (one page is all that we recommend for this kind of a message, although it can be as long as you wish), the appropriate number of business reply envelopes, a check to cover first class postage, and a magnetic tape of your list. TELEPOST does the rest—and quickly too. From the time you give them your copy until your mailing goes out is only 48 hours.

You also can achieve the emergency look of a telegram without hiring a firm specializing in such formats. We have produced some very compelling appeals with the help of an artist who uses dramatic type and color. The best color combinations to achieve the desired effect are yellow and black and red and white.

Of course, few people are fooled into thinking that they have received a real telegram when they receive a TELEPOST letter or your own home-made version. The point is made, however, that yours is an emergency situation. So whatever you do, don't squander your "telegram" by delivering an ordinary message. Save your money for a real crisis or you'll soon be known as the organization that always cries wolf.

Computer Letters

Computer letters can make your direct mail appeals look like a personal letter to your mother. Well—almost.

There are many things we love about computer letters and several things we hate. At the top of our hate list is the computer letter that inserts your name not only on the address and salutation, but too frequently throughout the body of the letter. Fund raisers who succumb to this technique never learned the first rule of letter writing: Write your letter as though you were writing a real letter from one person to another. When was the last time you wrote to a friend and inserted your friend's name five times in the body of the letter?

The other thing we don't like about computer letters is that too many of them *look* like they came off a computer rather than a typewriter. But as technology progresses, more and more computer bureaus are able to turn out computer letters that look *almost* like the real thing.

There's no getting around it. Computer letters (and laser letters) are more expensive than a printed letter. As a consequence they are rarely cost-effective in direct mail prospecting. But there are exceptions even to this.

Computer letters are invaluable when it comes to special handling of your member or donor file. Before you send a computer letter to your entire house file, however, we recommend that you test it against your usual format. And when you do, follow the rules cited earlier.

- Use the identical letter.
- Use the same signer.
- Use the same postage.
- Use the same list.
- Mail at the same time.
- Do everything else exactly the same.

CHAPTER 10

Making Friends with the Computer

Don't be afraid; come on in.

The computer over there in the corner won't hurt you. It won't make you feel like an idiot, try to get your job, or make your job a nightmare.

The computer is your friend. As a matter of fact, it can be your *best* friend in successful direct mail fund raising.

What's more, in order to become friends with the computer, you don't have to become a computer expert. In fact, you don't have to know how to turn it on or off. It isn't even necessary to buy one of your own (although for some organizations this is worth considering).

When you realize all the things you can do with a computer, you will wonder how you ever managed without one.

THE PERSONAL TOUCH

Haven't you dreamed of being able to address a donor, "Dear Mr. Simms" or, in some cases, "Dear Bob"? Haven't you longed to tell Mr. Simms the date and exact amount of his most recent gift so that you can ask him to match—or even increase—it? Haven't you envied others who personalize their appeals by referring to the city and state in which their donor lives? And don't you wish you could send Mr. Simms a thank you letter telling him that he has been a supporter for the past five years? (And don't you think Mr. Simms would be impressed by your knowledge and appreciation of his loyalty?)

In other words, wouldn't you like to send out personal letters similar to those portrayed in Figures 10-1 and 10-2?

Well, as soon as you get your list on computer—that is, if it is done right—you will be able to do all these things and more!

The sample computer letters portrayed in Figures 10-1 and 10-2 were both highly successful in quite different campaigns.

The first (Figure 10-1), for the American Society for the Prevention of Cruelty of Animals (ASPCA), was a personalized Valentine sent to the Society's members and donors in 1984. (We just wish you could see it in all its red, pink, and white glory.)

Compared to non-computerized Valentines sent by ASPCA in past years, this appeal experienced a 45 percent increase in the rate of return and earned substantially more income for the organization.

Figure 10-1. ASPCA Computer-Personalized Letter

HAPPY VALENTINE'S DAY!

Mildred Stanley

ASPCA
The American Society for the
Prevention of Cruelty to Animals
441 East 92nd St., New York, N.Y. 10128

Your kindness and generosity keep us optimistic in times of trouble. We count on the tenderness of your heart, and love you for it.

Naturally, all of us here at the ASPCA would like to be adopted -- to have homes and families to call our own. Happily, many ASPCA foundlings were adopted this past holiday season.

ASPCA adoptions have a high success rate. This is largely because the adoption staff will not knowingly release one of us if we are to be given to someone as a surprise gift. And the staff protects us from people not fully committed to responsible pet care. You can guess the reason why! Most of us are here in the first place because we were never truly wanted.

Boots and Timmy, for example, represent the hundreds of unwanted 1983 Christmas gifts turned over to the ASPCA by surprised new "owners" who were unable -- or unwilling -- to care for them.

The ASPCA spends an average of $50 on each pet it prepares for adoption. This includes a medical exam, medication, shots and grooming as appropriate, and a spay or neutering operation at an ASPCA veterinary center.

Your gift of $50 will sponsor one of us for adoption. And a gift of $20 -- or whatever you can send -- will help care for many of our other needs.

So please, don't let us spend this holiday without a Valentine from you! By giving now, you can fill our hearts -- and those of our new families -- with the special love of a happy home.   HAPPY VALENTINE'S DAY --
                                  FROM YOUR MANY FRIENDS AT THE ASPCA!

- -

Yes! I want to be Timmy's and Boots' Valentine!

Enclosed is my tax-deductible gift of:
- ☐ $20
- ☐ $500
- ☐ $50
- ☐ $1000
- ☐ $100
- ☐ Other $_____

ASPCA
The American Society for the
Prevention of Cruelty to Animals
441 East 92nd St., New York, N.Y. 10128

V4L

Mildred Stanley
2129 Aline Ave.
Viego, CA 91402

☐ I am giving $_____
  to the ASPCA
  ☐ to honor ☐ in memory of :

☐ I want to give an
  ASPCA membership
  ($20 minimum) to:

_____
_____
_____

Please detach this coupon and return it in the enclosed envelope. Your postage stamp will help us feed another orphan. Please use your cancelled check as your receipt.

000601000762632145440101040 6504431515 199990

Figure 10-1. ASPCA Computer-Personalized Letter (Continued)

237

The second example of a computer-personalized appeal (Figure 10-2) was done for the Zoological Society of Philadelphia in 1983. It was the fourth of a series of special prospect mailings begun in 1980, simultaneously inviting area residents to join the zoo and to attend the annual spring membership event.

The mailing shown was sent almost two months prior to the May 14th party and was backed up by an intensive public relations campaign. And because the "Family Reunion" party was for members only, an additional impetus was placed on the prospective member to join prior to the event.

This "membership-public relations-special event" format, which has enlisted thousands of new members in the Philadelphia Zoo, is one that certain other membership organizations (not necessarily zoos) can successfully imitate.

If you are interested in becoming a computer expert, you will do well to read other books on the subject. But if your primary interest is in streamlining your donor file and raising more money through your direct mail program, this chapter will help.

Computers are ideally suited for direct mail because of their ability to store large amounts of information accurately. They also can be used to process the stored information and output different parts of that information for many different tasks.

Thus the computer not only enables you to send personalized letters, it also updates your membership records and provides reports about the types of donors you have. Do you want to know where your donors live? How many donors renewed last year? How many donors gave more than once last year? How many donors increased the amount of their gift? Ask the computer. If your computer has been programmed correctly, it will be able to answer your questions.

ANALYZING YOUR NEEDS

To make certain that you get the right system, your first task is to analyze your file and your needs. If you do not analyze these needs critically, you will pay dearly later. Following are suggested potential needs. Note those you think you will require and then discuss them with several service bureaus.

IS THIS YOU?

If you are still maintaining your valuable list of donors on 3″ × 5″ cards, you know how tedious and time-consuming the process is of updating giving history, correcting addresses, and so on. If you are like most organizations still maintaining records on cards, you probably also keep a corresponding file at a mailing house or lettershop to print mail labels. This file is made up of paper or metal plates, the most common being "Speed-A-Mat" plates that are inked for addressing. (The only information on the plate is the name and address; all donor information is recorded on the 3″ × 5″ card.) When records are updated, *both* the card and the plate must be handled. This means that someone must hand record new giving information on the card and physically move the plate to a section of the file indicating that the donor has renewed his gift.

If only the card is updated you will have internal knowledge of a new gift, change of address, or a death. But when your next mailing goes out if a new metal plate has not been made, or the old one deleted, your recently renewed donor will be annoyed . . . the widow of your decreased donor (who remembered you in his will) will be angered, and your mail will never reach the faithful donor who has moved. Think about it! If all of this sounds complicated, consider that some organizations maintain *only* cards and send their irreplaceable donor records out to a mail house for addressing each time they mail.

If you are maintaining your list in this manner because you have always believed computer maintenance to be too expensive, you owe it to yourself to check it out. Nothing is more costly than losing a donor—either by accidentally losing his giving record or by losing him because your system did not allow the flexibility and speed necessary to compete in today's highly competitive marketplace.

What is more, as you will learn in this chapter, maintaining your donor list is just the beginning of what the computer can do for you.

Figure 10-2. Zoological Society of Philadelphia
Computer-Personalized Letter

the
Zoological
Society of
Philadelphia

34th St. & Girard Ave., Philadelphia, PA. 19104 (215) 243-1100

**CR 33

Ms. Pat Calhoun
10 Cherry
Cherry Hill, NJ 08002

Dear Ms. Calhoun,

    You are personally invited to join our family ... and at The Philadelphia Zoo, our family comes first!

    We take great care of our amazing animal collection because our membership family takes great care of us! They're the reason we're not only America's First Zoo, we're one of the finest.

    Did you know that families have been fascinated by our ferocious lions, playful penguins and mimicking monkeys for over 100 years? Last year alone, we enjoyed over 80,000 visits from our members -- a record high! We're glad they love the Zoo so much -- and we want to show our appreciation ... by having the biggest, best Philadelphia-style Family Reunion ever!

    That's right -- a Family Reunion with all the trimmings ... and we are inviting the Calhoun Family to join our fun -- by joining our family. On May 14th, from 4:00 p.m. to 8:00 p.m., we're going to open our famous Victorian gates for your family to visit the Zoo like never before! It'll be the beginning of a full year of happenings for you and yours!

    Our Zoological Garden will be filled with dancing clowns, spell-binding magic and marvelous movies ... plus games and prizes -- and free surprises! We'll have exclusive behind-the-scenes tours of your favorite exhibits, and "special guests" to help us make our Family Reunion a big success!

    Bring the family picnic basket and relax on green lawns, surrounded by blooming azaleas, magnolias and cherry trees.... Take a stroll through Penn's Woodland Trail, our newest exhibit -- a wonderfully serene oasis of animal life in the Delaware Valley.

    See elephants and tiny tree shrews, hippos and Siberian tigers, pink flamingoes and proud peacocks -- bring your

camera and see what wild game you can capture! You'll even
have a chance to preview the newest members of our Zoo
family before the public sees them -- the rare and wonderful
Lesser Pandas (not the large black and white Panda Bears)
and the strikingly beautiful Golden Lion Tamarins! There's
so much to do and see at the Zoo -- and it's all yours for
free when you become a member of our family! For only $35,
your family will receive:

* Free admission to the Zoo for one full year;
* Five free guest passes;
* A free subscription to the Zoo's spectacular
  full-color wildlife magazine, ZooOne;
* The special members-only newsletter, ZooToo;
* Free or discounted admission to special members-only
  programs, lectures and film series;
* VIP invitations to explore the wilds of Africa, the
  Orient's mysteries, and other exotic habitats;
* And many other exclusive, year-round privileges!

Just look over the member benefits displayed and pick
the category that best suits you. Fill out your member
acceptance card, and return it to us today so we can rush
you your official Zoo membership card and name tags in time
for the Family Reunion.

And please don't forget that it is only through the
financial help of loyal friends like you that the Zoo is
able to maintain its international reputation for excellence
in animal care, exhibit presentation, research and conservation. There have been many exciting developments at your
Zoo over the last few years. But we need your support to
continue as an historical, cultural and recreational institution of which we can all be proud.

So gather the family and come to the Zoo May 14th for
the time of your life. This is one Family Reunion you
won't want to miss!

Best regards,

William V. Donaldson
President

P.S. Send your $35 check (or more for additional benefits!)
today and you'll receive a free poster of a rare and very
special member of our animal family -- our new Lesser Panda!
This beautiful poster is just one in our new series of
collectible posters available to Zoo members, and will be
given to you when you come to our first Family Reunion
celebration on May 14th! See you there.

1. How do you wish to segment your file (by donors, members, prospects, PR lists, other)?
2. How much information do you wish to store on each record? (Following is a list to use as a guideline.)

   Donor Information

   - Name
   - Address (two, three, or four lines)
   - Prefix (Mr., Mrs., Ms., Miss, Dr., etc.)
   - Suffix (M.D., Ph.D., Jr., Sr., Esq., etc.)
   - Company name or "in care of" if applicable
   - Telephone area code and number
   - Country (if your file includes foreign names)
   - Source code (mailing list code, board member contact, alumni, etc.)
   - Sub-source or secondary code (year of graduation, committees, etc.)
   - Contact code (i.e., technique/approach preferred/solicitation code, including "Do Not Mail.")

   Gift Information (for each contribution)

   - Date of gift (day, month, year)
   - Amount of gift
   - Source code (same as on donor information)
   - Reason code
   - Use of fund restriction code (optional)
   - Form of payment code (outright gift, stock, real estate, EFT, pledge, gift-in-kind, etc.—also optional.)

   Pledge Information
   If you plan to form a "special gifts club" or to accept pledge payments, you will need the following information:

   - Date of original pledge
   - Amount of original pledge
   - Payments against original pledge

   The computer also should be programmed to calculate the following:

   - Balance due
   - Upcoming payment due dates and amounts
   - Pledge expiration date

3. How many gifts will you want to record separately? (Remember, some donors give more than once a year.)
4. At what point do you want to stop recording separate gifts and show past gifts as a cumulative total?
5. What method does the bureau require for submitting input data (forms, response cards, etc.)?

6. How much clerical assistance will you need to do internal coordination and to interact with service bureau, submitting requests, source information, etc.? (Does the bureau provide training for your personnel?)
7. How frequently will you require updates to your file (posting additions, changes, etc.)?
8. How frequently will you require reports, and how long do they take to produce?
9. What types of reports will you need? (Following is a list of reports required by most membership/donor organizations; however, you may need others.)

   - Print-out (also called a master list or galley) of the entire file, including all giving information.
   - Source Key Report (critical in direct mail because you will use this report to determine which lists were profitable and which were not).
   - Donor Upgrade Report by Category
   - Donor Upgrade Report by Average Gift
   - Member/Contributor Report on active and lapsed donors.
   - Galley of suspect duplications (should be run at least once a year to check for potential duplications).
   - Geographic Report (breakout of donors by state, zip, and section center). Note: This report can be obtained with numbers only or with member/donors in each category.
   - Frequency Analysis (if you are like most organizations, one-fourth of your donors give up to three-fourths of your income. This analysis can track the giving pattern of your donors).
   - Renewal Cycle Analysis (critical for the true membership organization).

10. What output (other than reports) will you require (i.e., Cheshire or other types of labels, cards, lists, etc.)?

In addition to analyzing the reports listed above, you will want to discuss the following with the service bureau:

1. Print options (for labels, etc.)—ID number, codes, mail code, or key code, etc.
2. Sort options—alphabetical, zip, ID number, etc.
3. Selection options—codes, zip, date(s) of gifts, amount(s) of gift, code(s) of gifts, total giving, etc.
4. Use of upper/lower case vs. all capital letters.
5. Use of unique identification number vs. name/address match code.

PURCHASING YOUR OWN VS. CONTRACTING WITH A SERVICE BUREAU

Now that your needs are established, you must decide whether it is more practical and economical to contract with a computer service bureau or to purchase or lease your own computer. How do you know which route is best? The answer depends on many things including the size of your file, the amount of processing you will need, and how much you can afford to spend for your own system, including training and employing the operators. In most instances, unless you have a very large file (100,000 or more), you will be better off with an outside service bureau.

If you decide to purchase your own system, you will require the services of a systems consultant, as the type of specialized instruction you will require is beyond the scope of this text. Incidentally, a systems consultant can be of help even if you plan to use a service bureau.

You can use a consultant recommended by a colleague, you can find them listed in the yellow pages, or you can turn to a local university or hospital that has a sophisticated computer operation.

You and your consultant will sit down together and lay out your specific needs and the capabilities that your computer system should have. (You often will find that if you modify your needs *just a little* many service bureaus will have a standard program ideal for you, for which you will not have to pay additional programming charges.)

After you have thought through all your needs, you will want to interview between two and four computer service bureaus.

HOW TO HIRE A SERVICE BUREAU

Following are the most important questions to ask when considering a service bureau:

1. How long has the company been in business?
2. How modern is their system?
3. How much flexibility does their software have?
4. Do they have an in-house programmer? If not, do they have a long standing "on call" relationship with one or more programmers (expert in the system you will be using)?
5. Do they handle accounts similar to yours? How many? For how long?
6. What is their track record on delivery (turn-around time)? On accuracy? On specialized applications? On client (novice) assistance?
7. Will they assign a specific operations person to your account?
8. How often is their equipment down (not functioning)? For how long?
9. Will they allow you to call their maintenance company to get some insight into the reliability of their equipment?
10. Will they show you a sample contract in advance?
11. Does the contract clearly state that you, and only you, own the file?
12. Do they have off-site backup storage?
13. What is their cost structure? (Look for hidden costs and ask hard, specific questions.)
14. Will they supply you with a list of references?

After your questions have been answered to your satisfaction, look carefully at their client list. An impressive list can be persuasive, especially if the salesperson is good. But do not enter into an arrangement based solely on charisma. Call at least four of the service bureau's clients—especially those in the nonprofit area. Ask them hard questions too, especially numbers 6, 7, and 8 above.

HOW THE COMPUTER MAINTAINS YOUR LIST

Now that you have your information in the computer, your file can be sorted or updated at any time. No more 3" × 5" cards—just send the response cards from your prospect or renewal mailings to the service bureau. On a pre-determined schedule, the service bureau will update your file. Updating, simply translated, means changing out-of-date addresses, removing contributors who are deceased or otherwise lost to you, and recording the latest giving information on the donor's record.

Following the update, you will receive reports on your file. Because reports come in various formats, it is critical that you see samples of the reports that will be provided by your service bureau before you contract with them.

A comprehensive report will tell you, in addition to any other information you may request, the number of donors and the dollar values you have in pre-designated gift categories such as $0 to $10, $10.01 to $24.99, $25 to $49.99, $50 to $99.99 and $100 and over. If you regularly receive gifts of $100 and over you will want the reports to break these out as well, i.e., $100 to $249.99, $250 to $499, $500 to $999, and $1,000 and over.

HOW THE COMPUTER ANALYZES YOUR MAILINGS

When you thought about a computer's ability to do the tedious business of posting and sorting, the idea that excited you most was being able to have the computer track your gifts and prepare your mailing analysis. We don't blame you. Manually analyzing large mailings in which many lists and test packages are used is exhausting and often inaccurate.

A computer, however, can provide you with a report that will tell you, on any particular mailing, how much money you received, how many gifts were involved, the average gift, the percent return, the net income, and the profitability factor (i.e., cost to raise a dollar).

And it will look something like the report portrayed in Figure 10-3.

HOW THE COMPUTER HELPS MAKE PERSONAL CONTACT WITH YOUR DONORS

Thus far you have seen how a computer can help maintain and update your list and analyze your mailings. This in itself is sufficient reason to consider computerizing your list, but it is far from all the computer will help you do.

Earlier we alluded to the computer's ability to help you send personalized letters to your top donors (or to your smaller donors in an upgrade campaign). Whatever the reason for personalization, the computer can help you speak personally to your donors when asking for a gift and thank the donors when they respond.

If you have had your list programmed to allow donor segmentation (and we certainly hope that you have), a whole new world is open to you. For example, in a particular campaign, you can mail a telegram to your $100 and over donors, a computer letter to your $25 to $99.99 donors, and a printed letter with a computerized response form to the balance of your file. As the cost of each of these processes varies, you can spend the most money on the technique from which you will receive the most money.

Acknowledgments

When it comes to thanking donors for their gifts, the computer can do the same type of file segmenting. It can generate a tape for a "robotyped" letter to donors of smaller gifts which you still may want to acknowledge. As with the appeal letter, the computer can insert personal messages into the text such as the amount of the gift (or anything else) as long as the necessary information is on file and the computer is correctly programmed.

244

Figure 10-3. Summary Analysis for Campaign A
Analysis Date: 4/12/84

Date Mailed	Mail Code	# Mailed	Cost Per M	Total Cost	# Ret'd	$ Ret'd	% Return	$ Aver	Income/ Cost %	$ Net Income
2/03/84	A001	20,000	210	4,200	240	5,280	1.20	22.00	125.71	1,080
2/03/84	A002	15,000	170	2,550	90	1,530	.60	17.00	60.00	−1,020
2/06/84	A003	30,000	205	6,150	630	14,490	2.10	23.00	235.61	8,340
2/06/84	A004	18,000	185	3,330	144	2,736	.80	19.00	82.16	−594
2/06/84	A005	22,000	190	4,180	242	3,388	1.10	14.00	81.05	−792
2/07/84	A006	37,000	210	7,770	444	8,880	1.20	20.00	114.29	1,110
2/07/84	A007	13,000	180	2,340	117	2,106	.90	18.00	90.00	−234
2/08/84	A008	14,000	165	2,310	56	560	.40	10.00	24.24	−1,750
2/08/84	A009	6,000	170	1,020	41	451	.68	11.00	44.22	−569
2/09/84	A010	10,000	190	1,900	100	1,300	1.00	13.00	68.42	−600
2/09/84	A011	33,000	195	6,435	396	9,504	1.20	24.00	147.69	3,069
TOTALS		218,000	193	42,185	2,500	50,225	1.15	20.09	119.06	8,040

HOW THE COMPUTER MERGES AND PURGES

A merge/purge is the process which allows you to eliminate duplicate names from the prospect lists to which you are mailing. It also enables you to eliminate duplicate names between your own donor or membership file and the prospect lists. This is done by combining many names and addresses from a variety of lists (MERGE) and deleting the duplicate names (PURGE). There are several reasons for doing this.

1. To obtain accurate information on the performance of each prospect list you use, you must remove your house names *which will only serve to inflate your returns artificially.*
2. You can save money by not mailing multiple pieces of mail to the same person. If you have a mailing of 250,000 pieces and a duplication rate of 20 percent (a realistic rate in many cases) you can avoid mailing 50,000 pieces of duplicate mail. At a cost of $200 per thousand, this will result in a savings of $8,500 after paying approximately $6 per M or $1,500 for the merge/purge. Note: It is rarely cost-effective to conduct a merge/purge on a mailing of fewer than 75,000 pieces. Generally we advise a merge/purge on mailings of 125,000 or more.
3. Many donors become understandably annoyed when they receive several identical appeals within a short period of time. Such annoyance can cause you much grief when the annoyed donor happens to be a member of your organization's board and/or one of your major contributors.

Because the execution of a merge/purge requires sophisticated processing, it is a good idea to check out the service bureau that will be conducting yours. Talk to several bureaus about costs as well as their criteria to determine duplications. Obtain samples of what their system will (or won't) be able to detect as a duplicate.

For example, the following duplication is one that a merge/purge program would pick up, thereby deleting the duplicate:

A.   Mrs. Kay P. Lautman   K. P. Lautman
     The Oram Group   President
     1730 Rhode Island Ave., N.W.   Oram Group Marketing
     Washington, D.C. 20036   1730 Rhode Island Ave., N.W.
                                                  Washington, D.C. 20036

It would not, however, pick up the following as a duplicate:

B.   Kay P. Lautman, President   Kay P. Lautman, President
     Oram Group Marketing   Oram Group Marketing
     1730 Rhode Island Ave., N.W.   275 Madison Avenue
     Washington, D.C. 20036   New York, N.Y. 10016

The reason that the computer caught the first and not the second is because the computer reads backwards from the zip. Thus, in example A it would find the first two addresses identical, the last name identical, and the first initial of the name identical.

In the second example, however, although all information on the first two lines is identical, the computer would not pick it up as a duplicate because it immediately reads a different zip code.

Here are three more examples. Which do you think the computer will pick out as a duplicate?

A.   Hank Goldstein, President   Mr. Henry Goldstein, CFRE
     The Oram Group, Inc.   The Oram Group, Inc.
     275 Madison Avenue   275 Madison Avenue, Suite 900
     New York, N.Y. 10016   New York, New York 10016

B.   Mr. Henry Goldstein, President   Mr. Henry Goldstein, President
     Room 900, 275 Madison Avenue   275 Madison Avenue, Room 900
     New York, N.Y. 10016   New York, New York 10016

C.   Mr. Goldstein   Mr. H. Goldstein
     275 Madison Avenue   275 Madison Avenue
     New York, N.Y. 10016   New York, N.Y. 10016

Of the three examples, the only name that most merge/purge programs would kick out as a duplicate is the first. Again, this is because the computer reads backwards and is instructed to disregard all prefixes (such as Mr.) and to read only the first initial of the first name.

In example B, the computer would read Room 900 before reading the address and would assume that the two were different people.

In example C, the computer would get all the way to the name field before deciding that the two people were different because there is not even an initial to identify Mr. Goldstein as Henry or Hank.

By looking at the types of duplications a computer suspects, you will be able to determine whether you would have challenged the name yourself (as a duplicate) and if, perhaps, there are others you might have checked were you looking at the files yourself. This is important as most merge/purge systems allow for a certain amount of flexibility in the determination of duplicate names. By giving a higher priority to one factor, such as a matching street address, and a lesser priority to the first name or initial, the computer can identify duplicate names even if the names on the input lists are misspelled. By discussing the various options with your representative you can tailor the merge/purge to your own organization's needs.

Bear in mind that you do not have to use the same computer house that maintains your file to do your merge/purge. Many service bureaus specialize in merge/purge and unless your own bureau is an expert at this process, you may wish to have a different company handle these two tasks.

You will do well to hire a firm that has handled your type of merge/purge needs before so that it can alert you to difficulties that may arise.

Once you have selected the service bureau to run your merge/purge, you must arrange for your rented prospect lists to be delivered on magnetic tape instead of labels. The service bureau will advise you of the necessary format required. IBM format EBCDIC is the industry standard.

Be sure to discuss scheduling. Most merge/purges take two to three weeks after all tapes have arrived (though some companies can do it in a week). It is best to provide yourself a cushion of extra time to allow for late or missing tapes. And there is virtually never a merge/purge without at least one missing tape!

Once all the tapes have arrived (if they haven't you may decide to proceed without one or two in the interest of meeting your deadline), the service bureau will load the tapes into the computer and—presto—suppress the duplicate names from list to list including your own. What you then receive is a list made up of unique names (i.e., one mail label per individual).

Once the computer determines that a name is on two or more lists, it pulls the name as a duplicate. You want to eliminate multiple usage of the duplicate name, but you still want to mail to it at least once. To do this, you have to decide to which of the original lists the name will be assigned.

There are several methods of doing this. Because the duplicate names will perform between 20 and 50 percent better than the rest of the mailing, each of these techniques will have a different effect on your mailing.

Random Assignment. This method takes the duplicate names and reassigns them to all of the lists at random. Since all of the lists have the same number of duplicates, no one list has the advantage of having more duplicate names than another.

Proportionate Assignment. This method assigns the names to the lists in the proportion in which the duplicates were pulled out. If a list had a high percentage of duplicates, it will get the same high percentage of reassigned names. If a list had a low percentage of duplicates, it will get a low number of reassigned names. This method keeps the relative strength of the lists close to what they were before the merge (i.e., the lists with the most duplicates will still have the most duplicates, etc.)

Priority Assignment. This method allows you to decide beforehand which of the lists will receive a larger proportion of duplicate names and which of the lists will receive a smaller proportion. This is most often done in the case of new test lists, about which you have no return information. The theory is that the multi-names are a part of the new list and are necessary to compare that list's returns with the roll-out lists on which you already have results. However, this will distort the performance of the lists that receive the larger proportion of duplicate names. We therefore do not recommend this method, unless you have some other reason to offset the loss of valid list returns.

In all of these methods, the duplicate names being reassigned are the names that are duplicated from list to list *only*. You would not want to reassign the names that are matched to your house file as the elimination of those names from your mailing is one of the primary reasons for conducting the merge/purge.

THE ADVANTAGES OF MERGE/PURGE

There are other advantages to be realized from a merge/purge, including:

1. Postage can be saved if your merge/purge output is large enough to qualify for a five-digit or carrier route presort (see the section in Chapter 8 on postal regulations).
2. You can segment the file and mail different packages to different parts of the country by having your output split by zip code or sectional center (the first three digits of the zip code).
3. You can conduct multiple package tests by having the service bureau skim off a certain number of names from all of the unique names and split them into several lists. These "created" lists can be used to test different package components or other elements. Since this list is made up of an accurate cross-section of all individual lists, it is an accurate representation of the entire mailing. However, you must take an accurate cross-section of the entire mailing, which would be no less than 10,000 names per individual package test. The process to achieve this is called taking an "nth select" (where a decision is made to select every 10th, 20th, or 30th name and thereby assure a statistically reliable representation as opposed to taking the first 20,000 names on the list, which would all be from the same section of the list).

For example, begin with a total list order of 150,000 names from ten lists of 15,000 each. A duplication rate of 20 percent will suppress 30,000 names and leave a net output of 120,000 names.

Before this list is re-sorted back into the original input lists, have the computer skim off a cross-section of 20,000 names. This leaves 100,000 names in the original input lists and two test panels of 10,000 names each. You can then use these test panels to test various packages against the control.

Following is a step-by-step guideline:

Merge/Purge-Input	10 lists × 15M names each	=	150M
Duplication Rate of 20%	Less 30M duplicate names		30M
Total Merge Net Output			120M

Have the computer skim off 20M names from the remaining 120M and sort them into two lists of 10M each. You then have the remaining names sorted back into their original input lists.

Names in original input lists without duplications	100M
Two lists of 10M each (which represents a cross-section of all of the input lists) without duplications	20M
Total mailing	120M

Mail the control package to the 10 input lists. Mail a different package or test variation to the new cross-section lists. This will allow you to compare the results of several different test packages in one mailing.

Costs of Merge/Purge

Most service bureaus charge additionally for *each* step in the processing. Obtain a price list and discuss the costs with your representative before deciding which tests, if any, you wish to do. Also ask the company to suggest other types of processing done for clients. Chances are they have additional processing procedures that they perform regularly for others which may be just right for you.

But remember, the main savings for a merge/purge comes from:

1. Not mailing unnecessary duplicates
2. Postage discounts for large mailings

Additional processing will drive your costs up and make it harder for the mailing to recover its expenses.

The Merge/Purge Report

The merge/purge report you will receive following the mailing (be sure to ask for it in advance) contains much valuable information. For example, a good indicator of what will prove to be your most successful lists are those which have the highest duplication rate with your own file. Look also for lists having high duplication rates among the prospect lists. Duplication is a good indicator of a strong list. Now check whether your mail file is concentrated in any specific area of the country (specifically small zip clusters). If so, you will want to consider doing geographic test mailings of those zips with the heaviest concentration of duplicate names.

Disposing of the Duplicate Names: Trash or Mail?

While on the subject of mailing lists and merge/purge, we are obligated to discuss a sometimes controversial subject. Many mailers traditionally hold a copy of the list of duplicate names from a merge/purge and mail the duplicates four to eight weeks after the first mailing has gone out.

The strategy is that because these multi-donors (sometimes called multi-buyers) are classic direct mail respondents, this "follow-up" will increase the mailing returns. By mailing to these names twice, you double the chance that a prospect will contribute. The multi-donors can pull as much as 15 to 50 percent better than the original mailing!

Yet while this practice is standard in commercial direct mail (and is becoming increasingly commonplace in the not-for-profit world), there are some brokers and mailers who question the ethics of mailing these multi-donor names.

The question does not arise over cost. Unless you have made a prior (and unusual) arrangement whereby you pay only for the unduplicated names coming out of the merge/purge, you pay for each and every name going in.

Those who question the ethics of mailing to the multi-donors recognize that had you not done a merge/purge, you would have mailed to every single name you paid for. What they object to is the fact that mailing the duplicates at a later date violates the agreement you made to mail during a specific week. And they would remind you that other organizations will be using the lists from which your multi-donor names originally came on the same dates you drop your second mailing.

Now while most mailers would gladly have the broker clear a second (completely clear) mailing date with the various list owners, this is impractical for several reasons. First, since your multi-donor list is a hodgepodge of names from a *variety* of lists, it is impossible for the list owners to know which of the names originally rented to you ended up on your tape of duplicate names.

And there are other considerations as well. How can the list owner or broker or the other mailer absolutely guarantee that these other mailings will go out on time? And what if they go first class? Or what if the post office inexplicably moves them through the mails with extra speed and efficiency or, conversely, at a snail's pace? There is absolutely no way to guarantee when an organization's mail is going to arrive—even with the best of intentions.

What, then, is the answer?

Because we want to give you the very best advice possible, we raised the question privately with a variety of list brokers, list owners, and mailers. Then we raised the question at several public meetings attended by the same mix of people. Of the various views expressed, those who approve of mailing the multi-donor names far outweigh those who do not approve.

If this doesn't satisfy you, we encourage you to discuss the matter with your own broker or brokers. Whatever else they tell you, they will caution you to abide by two (unwritten) rules in mailing the multi-donor names: (1) do not hold the list longer than eight weeks before mailing, and (2) mail only the package (or packages) that were cleared for the original mailing.

We have a tip here. If your original mailing was a package test wherein both packages were cleared by the list owner, tally your results quickly following the first mailing. By doing so you will know within four to five weeks which part of the test won, thus you can mail the winning package to the multi-donor list and improve your chances of increased response that much more.

COMPUTER-ASSISTED DEMOGRAPHIC MAILINGS

One new and particularly useful direct mail process involves the use of demographics to form mailing "clusters" to improve your mail results. Here's how it works. Your file is examined by computer and, through the use of sophisticated processing, a composite is drawn of your average donor. Then this information is used to select mailing "clusters" or zip code areas which contain similar or closely matching individuals to those on your file. Through the use of this method, mailings to these identified clusters should outpull the overall mailing.

This process has shown significant increases in both percent response and average gift. One of its main advantages is its ability to make even marginal lists perform well, thereby increasing your mailing universe.

This type of programming is very complicated and beyond the ability of most computer service bureaus. In order to get the greatest advantage from this technique, make sure you are dealing with a competent bureau and discuss your full mailing strategy with them so that they can determine exactly what processing is required.

SUMMARY

Trouble-free file maintenance, accurate mailing analyses, personalized mailings, elimination of duplication, postage savings, improved acknowledgment system—these are all possible with a computerized system.

The computer can be enormously helpful to virtually every organization regardless of size. And as you grow, the opportunities for computerized direct mail become even more appealing.

Computers are still evolving, and will soon surpass today's sophisticated levels of achievement. It is conceivable that in the near future, mailing without some form of computer assistance will be as obsolete as carbon paper and manual typewriters.

CHAPTER **11**

Telemarketing:
The Next Best Thing to Being There

Among the high tech tools in the fund raiser's kit is that wondrous piece of technology that has been with us throughout the 20th century—the telephone.

At a time when America's mailboxes are stuffed with competing direct mail appeals . . . when person-to-person solicitation becomes more difficult because of a scarcity of volunteers and sheer distance in our mobile society . . . the telephone has come of age. Its capacity to improve response rates, increase the size of average gifts, upgrade donors, and return inactive donors to a more active status is being proven each day by an increasing number of nonprofit groups.

The telephone—like the letter—is but an extension of the individual, the instrument or medium through which an organization's case for support is clearly and effectively stated. Truly, when it comes to direct solicitation and cultivation of donors, the telephone is the next best thing to being there.

SOME COMMON CONCERNS

Before considering the application of the telephone—the fancy term these days is "telemarketing"—to your fund-raising efforts, let's address a few common concerns.

The telephone is intrusive. Its use will anger our donors.

Unlike direct mail, a telephone call does not slip silently through the letter slot. Its presence is announced by a bell, sometimes a persistent ringing bell.

When used properly, however, the telephone fund-raising call is no more intrusive than a friendly call from a neighbor or friend. And that's the trick to making successful use of the telephone.

Here are some suggestions to keep the telephone from being intrusive:

1. *Timing.* Make your calls at reasonable times. The hours of 6:30 p.m. through 9:30 p.m. are the best. Other good times are Saturday and Sunday afternoons. And, for some organizations whose constituencies tend to be at home during the day, the daytime hours are just fine.

2. *Style*. Be polite and friendly. Telemarketing as applied to fund raising often is dismissed without even a test by some fund raisers who mistakenly equate it with those telephone boiler rooms selling underwater real estate. Nothing could be farther from reality.

   A well thought through telephone effort, run by knowledgeable solicitors, is no more intrusive than a personal visit from a volunteer of the organization. It takes far less of the donor's time and far less of the organization's resources.

3. *Audience*. The key to keeping the telephone from being intrusive is to select properly and realistically the audience to be called. Generally, telemarketing for fund raising is best suited to *existing* donors. They are *already* part of the family. You are no stranger to them. And your telephone call does not come to them cloaked in the intrusive garment of a telephone pitchman.

Like a good appeal letter, the well-conceived telephone campaign is designed to (1) thank the donor for previous support, (2) convey information about an immediate and pressing need, (3) ask specifically for a gift, and (4) thank the donor again.

The telephone is an expensive way to raise money. Those long distance charges simply cost too much.

The economic reality is that a properly conducted telemarketing effort is probably the most cost-effective of all the direct response media. Surely uncontrolled and unplanned use of the telephone is wasteful. The same can be said for mail, volunteer solicitation, or television fund raising.

But, when the proper audience is selected and called by trained solicitors using an effective message, the results can produce cost-benefit multiples never heard of in mail.

Most of us initially view the use of the telephone as an expensive medium because we have all been taught since childhood to be watchful of long distance charges. But like the photographer's film or the printer's paper, the long distance phone charge is but a small part of the total cost that makes up a successful effort.

The cost of telephone campaigns should be measured by the same standard as all other fund-raising techniques: the question is not how much you spend to raise money *but* how much money you raise in proportion to the amount you spend. Well run telephone fund-raising efforts generally produce cost/income ratios far superior to those enjoyed by mail alone.

Setting up for telephone fund raising is just too much trouble.

Anyone who has ever organized a college alumni phonathon, trained volunteers, or gone through the logistical problems of a short-term phone effort may be tempted to say, "Never again!"

Although many organizations run their telephone campaigns themselves, there are dozens of professional telemarketing firms that provide a range of fund-raising services. They generally can provide them at a cost lower than the expense incurred by an organization in setting up its own program.

You can receive a list of firms providing telemarketing services for fund raising by writing the Direct Mail Marketing Association, 6 East 43rd Street, New York, New York 10017.

Whether you hire a professional firm or decide to do it yourself here are some applications of telemarketing that we have found particularly beneficial to the organizations we serve.

TELEPHONE ACKNOWLEDGMENTS

It is axiomatic that common courtesy and good fund raising require that gifts be acknowledged promptly and effectively. Often a new donor's impression of the organization will be formed indelibly by that first transaction. The size and frequency of subsequent gifts are often the result of good or bad acknowledgment procedures.

Pick up the phone and thank your donors. You'll enjoy doing it. They'll be amazed and grateful that their gift is so appreciated—that they matter so much to your organization.

The telephone acknowledgment has these advantages: (1) it sets you apart from those organizations who thank their donors only by mail or do not thank them at all, (2) it "bonds" the donor to the organization far more firmly by clearly indicating the importance you assign to that gift, and (3) most important from a long-range development standpoint, the telephone conversation gives you a great opportunity to learn more about the donor.

Because it may be impractical to telephone all donors, segment your list and call only the $50 +, $100 +, $250 + donors—whichever you decide is workable for you.

SETTING YOURSELF APART FROM THE COMPETITION

This book is designed to help you to do things better—to distinguish the fund-raising efforts of your organization, to set you apart from the competition. By coupling use of the telephone with direct mail, you can get a leg up on the competition. More important, you can raise more money for your organization at lower cost.

Each night when millions of Americans toss the day's mail on the kitchen table or the desk, the Great Competition for Attention begins. Your direct mail is in a race with the six, ten, or maybe even a dozen other pieces of mail to get noticed, get opened, get read, and, most important, to get action.

In this book you've seen what the experts do to insure that their mail runs best in this Great Competition. Some will go a step further—they'll pick up the phone.

Pre-Call Your Donors

Test after test, mailing after mailing, have clearly demonstrated that your mail has a better chance of being opened, read, and responded to if you *first* call the recipient alerting him or her to the fact that a mailing is on its way.

We call the technique pre-selling or pre-calling. Its purpose is simple—to pique the attention and interest of the reader even before the mail arrives. To ask the reader to watch for the mailing from a particular organization and to give it preference over other mail.

The results of this technique speak for themselves. An increase in the *net income* from a mailing of between 30 and 50 percent is possible.

The technique and the message are relatively simple: "Hello, Mr. Smith, this is Dan Jones, I'm calling from Jack Frost's office at the Association of Associations. He put a letter in the mail to you tonight and asked that I call and ask you to watch for it.

"You should be receiving it in the next day or so and I think you'll find it of great importance. Please watch for Mr. Jack Frost's letter."

What you have done by using the pre-call or pre-sell technique is to let the prospect know that something out of the ordinary is occurring. They may not know what it is or what the letter is about. And, in many ways that's just fine. Their curiosity is piqued. Your letter will be opened while others lay in anonymity on the kitchen table.

Pre-calling is not for every mailing. In fact it should be used selectively. Generally, *use the technique only for your own house file* and use it only a few times a year. You want to protect the "novelty" of it for it is this novelty that makes it an effective technique.

From a logistical standpoint, pre-calling has the advantage of being able to be done far more quickly than most forms of solicitation *and* it generally does not require as high a level of sophistication where phone solicitors are concerned.

Post-Call Your Donors

Akin to pre-calling is the technique of making the telephone call once the mailing piece has been received. However, there are important differences in the reasons for the use of the post-call.

Unlike the pre-call, which is designed to get the mail opened, a post-call is designed to lift the response rate or the size of the average gift. Or both.

The post-call is far more of a sales approach than the pre-call. Here the prospect already has received the basic message. It is the job of the phone solicitor to come in after the mailing and to *reinforce* the message of the letter—to provide *additional information and urgency* and *negotiate* with the donor over the size of the gift.

Use of the post-call requires careful timing to insure that the donor receives the letter *before* the phone call but not too far ahead of the call that memory of the message is dimmed.

The results of the post-call can be far more spectacular than those of the pre-call particularly where gift size is concerned. Often a donor whose normal gift runs in the $25 range can be upgraded to $100, $300, and sometimes even more. We'll cover this process of substantial upgrading more thoroughly later in this chapter.

The post-call can be made either as part of a carefully orchestrated campaign involving a series of letters and phone calls (we'll deal with that later) or as a one-time follow-up to a specific mailing.

In the case of a one-time mailing and use of the pre-call *vs.* the post-call techniques you may want to do some testing to see which works best for you. There are no universal rules.

Reinstate Your Donors

The economics of direct mail fund raising are such that the most expensive part of the process involves the acquisition of new donors to replace those who have fallen away from active status.

The telephone has proven to be a remarkably cost effective way of reinstating or renewing donors who have failed to renew through direct mail efforts alone. Following a direct mail series of six or seven renewal notices, it is likely that somewhere between 10 and 15 percent of a "lapsed" or "expired" group of donors can be reinstated by telephone.

And . . . they can be reinstated or renewed at *far less cost* than the organization normally would spend to acquire a new donor to replace the donor lost through direct mail attrition.

Just as important is the fact that once reinstated or renewed by telephone, these donors are then able to be put back into the direct mail program. Their performance in future years will be virtually identical to those who never strayed from the direct mail program in the first place.

As a general rule, telephone renewal or reinstatement programs are run at the end of the direct mail renewal cycle. But that should be tested. Response rates and average gifts often can be improved dramatically by putting the telephone solicitation into the renewal process early in the cycle.

As in the case of pre-calling and post-calling, the renewal or reinstatement call revolves around the use of a direct mail piece. Generally, we have found the most effective use of direct mail lies in a mailing which follows the reinstatement phone call.

THE DIRECT MAIL/TELEPHONE CAMPAIGN

Until now we have covered the use of the telephone in generally one-time applications. The one-time use makes the telephone no less effective. But there are other more sophisticated uses.

Let's begin by seeing how the telephone can be used in soliciting generally larger gifts than those which conventional direct mail can attract.

There's no question that in a perfect world any development director or fund raiser would prefer to have trained volunteer solicitors making face-to-face calls on specially selected prospects.

But . . . it's not a perfect world. And from a fund-raising standpoint it's growing even more imperfect. Volunteer solicitors are scarce and growing scarcer. The geographic spread of most organizations' donor constituencies makes organizing expensive and time-consuming.

Enter mail and telephone!

By trying to replicate as nearly as possible the essential dynamics of one-on-one fund raising through the use of direct mail and telephone you can accomplish much.

A campaign built on mail and telephone uses the mail as a cultivation and information device and the phone for the actual solicitation phase. Generally these campaigns consist of two or more letters mailed before the actual telephone solicitation takes place. The purpose of the mailings is to state the case for support, provide a sense of urgency, and to introduce the fact that the prospective donor will be receiving a telephone call.

Following the initial mailings is the all-important phone call or calls. The purpose of the phone call is to make certain that the prospect understands the information conveyed through mail, has his or her questions answered, and is then solicited.

As in face-to-face fund raising, the process of solicitation often involves more than one call. And, it should be remembered, the process of negotiation over size and timing of the gift is key.

Because many mass donor bases contain no more information about donors than the size and frequency of their previous contributions, the role of the phone solicitor becomes paramount. It is the job of the solicitor to identify interests, aim high enough when it comes to the amount of the suggested gift, and carefully keep the prospect interested while the size of the gift is discussed or negotiated.

Once the solicitation is over, follow-up mailings come into play to confirm and collect the telephone commitment.

As in all telephone/mail campaigns the audience being addressed has a direct bearing on the efficiency of this process. One generally can expect the "best" part of a mass donor base to perform best by mail/phone. Those parts of a donor base which are marginal by mail generally will be marginal by mail/phone as well.

In all fund raising—and telephone fund raising is no exception—it's critically important that the fund-raising manager understand the efficiencies of the technique being used. Telephone has the capacity to take the best part of a donor file and upgrade it substantially. It also has the inherent weakness of being over-used as in the case where the telephone is applied indiscriminately across a file when mail or other techniques may be more efficient for some portions of that file.

If the telephone is employed properly in conjunction with mail, substantial upgrading of small gift donors is possible to a degree unimagined by mail alone. The trick is not to go overboard and use the telephone where mail could be used just as effectively in generating the same *net income*.

The successful campaign based on telephone and mail should make it possible for you to upgrade a small donor base substantially. It is not unusual to find that somewhere between 5 and 10 percent of a mass base which normally contributes $25 to $50 can be upgraded to gifts ranging from $300 to $1,000 and even more.

By way of example, a donor base of 100,000 donors might see an increase in giving of between $1 million and $2 million over and above conventional direct mail through the use of a successful telephone/mail campaign.

TELEPHONE TESTING AND DONOR INFORMATION

Until now we have addressed the use of the telephone to solicit gifts or renew contributions. But for the direct mail practitioner there are other applications.

Testing Copy Approaches

As market researchers and political pollsters long ago learned, the telephone is a remarkable research tool. Consider testing your copy approaches through telephone interviews before committing to mail. This is particularly true whenever your own donor file is concerned. A few hundred telephone calls randomly selected from your active donor files often can guide you to the most effective and efficient house appeals.

The same holds true where prospecting is concerned. However, it is critical that the samples for the telephone interviews be drawn carefully when copy testing cold lists.

Membership Alerts and Donor Information

Many organizations have members and donors who do more than give money; they are active participants in the work of the organization. This is particularly true for those groups which engage in lobbying.

The use of an incoming 800 number can be used to provide information and request timely action. The pre-recorded message delivered by a computer-driven dialing mechanism can be used to reach thousands quickly and inexpensively. Generally, these techniques are not techniques of fund raising, but ones of urgently imparting information and initiating action.

REACH OUT AND TOUCH SOMEONE?

Is telephone fund raising for you? Probably. Like all direct response media, the telephone can be tested and the benefits and problems as they directly relate to you can be discovered readily.

With the competition in mail increasing, with the public's growing acceptance of telemarketing, you owe it to yourself and your organization to find out what hundreds of successful fund raisers have already discovered—the telephone can add an exciting and enriching dimension to your program.

CHAPTER **12**

Direct Mail and Institutional Development

From the perspective of an organization's overall fund-raising efforts, direct mail has five fundamental objectives:

1. To raise money cost-effectively.
2. To broaden the donor (or member) base.
3. To enhance visibility.
4. To identify potential workers or volunteers for your cause, up to and including board members.
5. To identify prospects for other (non-direct mail) fund raising.

This chapter examines the role of direct mail in helping your organization achieve the last two results—identifying potential volunteers and prospective major donors.

A nonprofit's operating income is derived in basically two ways: through fees for service (i.e., tuition, admission fees, product sales, dues, and other earned income) and through philanthropic support. A third source for many nonprofits is income from endowment or other reserves.

Direct mail accounts for most of the *donors* to many organizations, although those donors don't necessarily account for most of the organization's philanthropic *dollars*. Other philanthropic income supporting the operating budget may come through special events, through direct personal or telephone solicitation, or through personalized direct mail (as contrasted with mass prospecting or renewals.)

Although gifts from individuals are a major category of support for most institutions, grants from foundations or government agencies and corporate contributions may also be significant. The mix can vary considerably from place to place.

Your organization also may seek philanthropic support for non-operating purposes: to buy equipment, to renovate a building or a wing, to construct a building or retire a mortgage, to fund a special project or study, to pay for research. Indeed, you may even seek and get restricted support to fund a direct mail test. Such funding is not unheard of.

And finally, as with more and more groups we see, your organization may have come to the painful realization that no matter how fast you turn the pedals on various fund-raising efforts, the operating budget simply will not balance. Therefore, you may have begun to take steps toward building an endowment whose income will help undergird the operating budget.

Regardless of the medium by which funds are raised—mail, phone, direct personal solicitation, or special events, and regardless of the uses to which funds are put—operations, capital funding or endowment, there is one common denominator, one *sine qua non*: viable prospects.

While it is *perhaps* possible to obtain large contributions from people with no known previous link to your organization, large gifts seldom appear spontaneously—i.e., unsolicited. Major donations seldom come from strangers who suddenly discover your cause, seldom from people who are not already accustomed to giving to your cause (often in response to a mail appeal), and unfortunately are seldom the result of a skillfully executed solicitation.

YOUR OWN HOUSE FILE: THE BEST SOURCE OF MAJOR GIFTS

In short, if the best source of a gift is a giver—a corollary is that *large gifts grow from small ones*. Small gifts are (1) mostly mail-generated, (2) renewed and maintained by mail, and (3) upgraded by mail. Ultimately, the steadily increased gift is large enough to excite the attention of a staff member or volunteer, and the donor is marked for personal solicitation.

The cost to build a broad base of donors, and the cost to maintain that base, is justified by this simple truism: You catch more fish in a stocked pond.

With bequests and other deferred gifts included, individuals account for about 90 percent of all philanthropic gifts in America every year. Although no one really knows, the estimate is that some 80 percent of those gifts are originally engendered by mail: some through personalized mail (e.g., a board member or other volunteer writing to people he or she knows personally), more through renewal mailings to house lists, and a very large number through mass prospecting.

The mass of individuals who (should) comprise your house list are fertile soil because *the very largest gifts almost invariably come from individuals (or family foundations)*, not from large, staffed foundations and not from corporations. But how do we move from micro-gifts to mega-bucks? The prospecting, renewal, fulfillment, acknowledgment, accounting, and record-keeping functions—the essence of a mail operation—are inordinately detailed and time-consuming, even when computerized.

Direct mail is often the area of fund raising with the least personal contact with volunteers and some of the very best practitioners are not effective with people: their medium is the blank page and a compelling idea. These gifted professionals often work with minimal supervision and within their environment are without equal. Frequently, their boards are uninformed about direct mail, unconvinced, often highly resistant, and tend to maximize every complaint.

Thus it is no surprise that some of the largest national nonprofit agencies as well as some of the smallest grass roots groups which have employed us share one great strength and one great weakness: they have failed utterly in using the house file—developed and nurtured at great cost—as a resource for other fund raising. Somehow, the idea has developed that their best prospects are "out there" and not in-house. Not true.

SOME CASE HISTORIES

One of our clients has an operating budget of about $20 million, a house file of 50,000 active donors, a board which has been derelict in accepting its fund-raising responsibility, and a steadily mounting deficit which, in recent years, has resulted in tapping the unrestricted endowment fund—a modest treasure to begin with.

This is not a situation which inspires calm. Nonetheless, a properly constructed endowment campaign—stressing deferred gifts (bequests, trusts, and gifts of appreciated property)—is the proper professional prescription for long-range stabilization. To work, the campaign must be addressed to a carefully selected group of prospects. Some—a few—are board members and other high level volunteers about whom much is already known and who, in turn, are intimately familiar with the organization.

But the rest of the prospects for this effort are drawn from the existing donor file on the basis of historic gift size and customized research. Neither we nor the client believe that much money for the endowment will be derived from "outsiders." Though serendipity is not ruled out, it is not the basis for a disciplined effort.

Another client, internationally renowned, operates on a budget at well over $250 million a year and has about 200,000 active donors, almost 100 percent mail-generated and maintained. Without a very sophisticated, on-line computer system for processing and retrieving information, it would be humanly impossible to organize the forthcoming $300 million capital and endowment campaign using the house file as a prospect data base. Because technology is available to do the donor segmenting, the professionals are freed to do what no computer can: to make the linkages between defined institutional needs and the presumed interests of the larger (special gift) donors in the multifarious gift-making opportunities the campaign offers. Our expectation is that most of the major gifts will come from prospects already identified: board members for sure, but from smaller donors as well—people originally identified and bonded to the institution by mail. (This same institution, by the way, once received an unexpected bonanza—an $8 million + bequest—from the estate of an individual who in his lifetime had never been known to give more than $99.) (Why $99 and not $100 by the way? Because most professionals segment that way: $99 and under/$100 and over.)

A successful direct mail effort is the *beginning* involvement and is not, and should not be, the end of the development effort. Logical as this may appear, in all too many organizations, the fund-raising effort pretty much hangs on direct mail (and often only on renewal mail with insufficient prospecting to assure continued viability of the house list) and a few special events.

UPGRADING DONORS: ONE IDEAL APPROACH

Here is one logical progression in place in the development office of one of our clients:

Responsibility of Direct Mail Manager	1. Original gift (mail prospecting)	($25-49)
	2. Renewal at same or upgraded level	($50-$99)
Responsibility of Development Director	3. Identification as special gift prospect	($100 +)
	4. Special gift donor	
	5. Renewals at succeeding special gift levels	($250, $500 to $999, $1,000 +)
Responsibility of Development Director, Development Committee of Board & Nominations Committee	6. Identification for volunteer leadership role and/or	
	7. Identification as major gift prospect	($1,000 +)
	8. Identification as prospect for capital campaign or special project	
	9. Identification as prospect for deferred gift for endowment	($?)

This progression, against which the donor file is evaluated, begins through, and is sustained in, the mail to the point at which other staff, and ultimately, volunteers take over. It is based on gift size as a first determinant. But as the gifts increase, and the donor reaches higher plateaus, further research fleshes him or her out. He or she is no longer just a $50 giver but a real individual with interests and concerns of immediacy to your cause.

DIRECT MAIL: THE BACKBONE OF ENDOWMENT CAMPAIGNS

Let us return for a moment to the matter of endowments: as we said, more and more organizations are anxious to build or augment them. Though not an inviolable rule, the hard fact is that endowment rarely is created by new donors but by existing ones, often donors of small gifts—$25, $50, $100—who sometimes have been giving for ten or 20 years. Unfortunately many of the groups who come to us seeking help in endowment fund raising lack a donor base of sufficient size to justify the effort. For them, it's back to the drawing board: using direct mail to build the *current* donor file from among whom we can prospect for deferred gifts—the stuff of which endowment funds are made. (Today endowments are created from outright gifts only infrequently.)

The importance of an existing house file as one of the bases of capital and endowment fund raising cannot be stressed too often. A habit of giving to your cause—even modestly—and gift size are critical determinants.

We currently are managing a $30 million campaign: $15 million for capital needs, $15 million in endowment to undergird and expand the operating budget. In 1979, our client began mail prospecting with another excellent direct mail firm, Craver, Matthews and Smith. In five years because of the appeal's inherent emotional intensity, a house file of 225,000 active donors (with a very high renewal rate) had been built.

When Oram entered the picture, we assumed (based on experience) that the top 5 percent of the list should be isolated for the campaign. Our calculation was very close to the mark. The list run of $100+ donors (a large gift to solicit by mail) came to some 9,000 names from all over the country. These donors, now prospects for the capital campaign, are a much better bet than any 9,000 strangers we could ever find. Among them are several hundred $1,000+ donors, the best of the best.

Further refinement has resulted in:

- Assignment of specific, researched prospects to board and other volunteers.
- A pool of invitees to cultivation meetings held or scheduled around the country.
- A pool of deferred gift prospects.
- Further experimentation to isolate prospects for special mailings and telephone canvasses.

And these all began as mail prospects!

As noted in Chapter 5, we are extremely wary of "piggy-back" mailings, i.e., annual fund appeals which carry additional solicitations for other purposes. Occasionally, we will add to the response device a line which says something like:

☐ "Please send me bequest information."

or

☐ "Please send me information about deferred gifts."

260

We prefer to create a special package and we usually stress bequests. While all bequests are deferred gifts, not all deferred gifts are bequests. The distinction is useful because in our experience 90-95 percent of all deferred giving is bequest-oriented.

The reasons are (1) trusts are really for the wealthiest donors—the top 2 percent; people of quite moderate lifetime means who will not create trusts do build estates large enough to result in impressive charitable bequests; (2) trusts are complicated and, despite all the contrary propaganda, intimidating to many; and (3) normally, charitable gifts by trust are irrevocable.

On the following pages is a package created recently for the San Francisco Opera Association in which we seek endowment gifts through bequests or trusts.

PERSONAL HANDLING OF MAJOR DONORS

In the same way that we segment the house file for capital and endowment giving, we use the file to achieve other objectives, of which upgrading is usually the most important.

For one national health organization, we devised this system: as returns arrived in the national office, they were immediately segmented. All gifts of $99 and under remained with the national direct mail operation for renewal (and upgrading by mail). All new donors of $100 and up, usually 2 to 5 percent of the returns, were released immediately to the organization's local chapter apparatus for follow-up.

It should be noted that this device worked extremely well on our side because the solution was mechanistic. It worked in an extremely spotty way on the client's side because the ability of local units to follow through effectively varied widely.

Most organizations which rely on the mail have been laggard in training board members and staff to solicit effectively. The transition from an all mail fund-raising function to one which uses mail as a single, even if overriding, component of all development remains a difficult challenge. It is easier, less confrontational, less threatening to mail a letter than to ask someone for money in person.

CAN MAIL "RAISE" VOLUNTEERS?

Many years ago we sent out a direct mail appeal on behalf of a historically black college. Among the first returns was a gift for $1,250, a large sum to be raised in the mail—the equivalent of $2,500 today.

Research revealed the donor to be chairman of a Fortune 500 company, and further close attention by staff identified a linkage between the company's personnel manager and the college's president: both had played All American college football and were acquainted with one another.

To keep the story short, within six months, a $50,000 gift was obtained and the gentleman joined the campaign's national committee. He has since joined the institution's board and his giving has exceeded $500,000.

Organizations devote too little time to trying to learn who their donors are; or if they get that far, fail to consider what role they might play as volunteers.

Figure 12-1. San Francisco Opera Association
Endowment Campaign Letter

SAN FRANCISCO OPERA

WAR MEMORIAL OPERA HOUSE • SAN FRANCISCO, CALIFORNIA 94102

TERENCE A. McEWEN
    General Director

Dear Friend of the Opera:

Do you remember the first time you went to the Opera? Quite a
thrill, wasn't it? Perhaps the best thing of all was that it was just
the beginning. Just the beginning of all the glorious music, the
beautiful voices, the stirring drama, and the vivid spectacle that have
made the Opera such a joyous experience each time.

If you're like me, you have experienced some very special moments
at the Opera through the years. Maybe it was the time you discovered a
new voice so striking all you could concentrate on was that one singer.
Or maybe it was the time that you witnessed the debut of a Pavarotti or
a Price and could almost touch the electricity in the air.

We each have our own reasons for loving the Opera. But I'm sure
we can all agree on one thing. The Opera must live to be enjoyed by
future generations.

That is why Mrs. Miller and I planned ahead to make sure our
children and grandchildren can start their own collection of special
moments. We have provided for the San Francisco Opera in our wills.
I'm asking you to consider doing the same.

I know discussing wills is rarely enjoyable, but would it be
responsible of us to ignore the future of something about which we care
so deeply? To preserve the Opera, we must not only work to support
next year's performances, but those ten, twenty, and thirty years
hence. That means planning now to assure stability in the future.

If you have been enriched by the San Francisco Opera as much as I
have, I know you'll want to read the enclosed brochure. Learn how you
can help with a "Legacy of Joy."

Thanks for your time and consideration in giving others the
special feeling only the Opera can give...the first time and every time
after!

                                    Sincerely,

                                    Richard K. Miller
                                    Chairman

P.S. While you have your mind on your first opera experience, I'm sure
you will enjoy reading what some youngsters wrote to the cast of 'The
Marriage of Figaro' when the San Francisco Opera Guild invited them to
a special performance. Their letters are included in the brochure.

TELEPHONE: (415) 861 4008   TELEX: 3 4459   CABLE ADDRESS: SANOPERA, SAN FRANCISCO

262

Figure 12-2. Excerpts from San Francisco Opera
Association Endowment Campaign Brochure

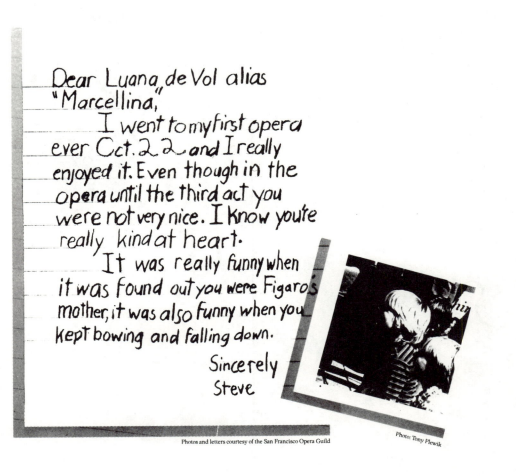

Dear Luana de Vol alias
"Marcellina,"
    I went to my first opera
ever Oct. 22 and I really
enjoyed it. Even though in the
opera until the third act you
were not very nice. I know you're
really kind at heart.
    It was really funny when
it was found out you were Figaro's
mother, it was also funny when you
kept bowing and falling down.
            Sincerely
            Steve

Photos and letters courtesy of the San Francisco Opera Guild

Photo: Tony Plewik

A Legacy of Joy

A will is a document which passes on a part of your life for others to enjoy. That is why you may want *your* will to help others come to appreciate the special joys that only the opera lover can know. By making a bequest to the San Francisco Opera, you help create a joyous legacy others will experience each time the curtain rises on another performance.

In the years ahead, it will cost us even more to produce masterful performances, sponsor telecasts across the country, provide scholarships and hold open auditions to develop the Opera's stars of tomorrow.

You may be surprised at some of the ways you can benefit when giving to the Opera. Of course, the greatest benefit is the legacy of joy you have provided in helping to preserve the great tradition of our Opera for generations to come.

2

Photo: Dennis Hudson

TRACK V
Getting on the Inside Track

CHAPTER 13

How to Hire and Work with a Consultant

Only once, as far as we know, has the Oram firm actually been hired as the result of an advertisement in the Yellow Pages. This is not to say that we don't receive *inquiries* from clients who let their fingers do the walking. But virtually all of our clients who sign contracts do so as a result of references from other clients (often their board members), professional fund-raising and public relations firms, business associates, and friends.

Those with whom we are *most* likely to develop a lasting relationship are those who come via another client. Why? Because many people do not trust their own intuition or judgment. Thus, the client who found us in the telephone book (although the campaign was a huge success) eventually went to another firm—one which had been personally recommended.

Begin your search for a consulting firm by asking your counterparts in other nonprofit organizations whom they use or know. That is the unquestioned best way. Far less reliable, but still useful if you're really in a quandary, we suggest a call to professional associations such as the National Society of Fund Raising Executives (Washington, D.C.). The American Association of Fund Raising Counsel (New York City), the Council for Advancement and Support of Education (CASE) (Washington, D.C.), the Direct Mail Fundraisers Association (New York City), or the Direct Marketing Association (New York City). Once you have a list of four to five firms, telephone for an appointment with a senior officer of each. Try to arrange all appointments within a three-week time span so that your impressions don't fade. The consultant will be more than happy to come to you unless you are very remotely or inconveniently located, but it's probably a good idea to have at least one meeting at their offices.

If you already are conducting a direct mail campaign in-house, or through another consultant, the meeting will be somewhat different than if you are attempting this for the first time. Should you have a current campaign, it is important to share confidences with the consultant. There is no need to denigrate your current consultant or in-house person. The fact that you are considering a change says all that need be said.

On the other hand, you will have to share results of past campaigns (list reports, package samples, final reports, costs) to enable the consultant to judge whether he or she might do better for you.

Sometimes we have to tell prospective clients that what they thought to be poor results were, in fact, quite good. We may not have gained a new client, but it would have been dishonest of us to have said otherwise.

To help you interview consultants, we have prepared a short list of questions below. But even before you hold your first meeting, make sure you know precisely what it is you need from a consultant. Don't waste your time and the consultant's by meeting to have a general discussion in the hope that your needs will be miraculously crystallized. Do your homework in advance and be precise about what you want the consultant to do for you. If during the course of the meeting the consultant suggests other ways that he or she might be of help—fine. But to begin, be specific.

QUESTIONS TO ASK THE CONSULTANT

1. *Does our cause philosophically mesh with your firm?* This can be important if your appeal is issue-oriented. Some firms generally are regarded as having a definite conservative bent, others a liberal one. For a "motherhood" cause—scouting, 4-H, most health causes—a consultant's political orientation is irrelevant.

2. *How do you charge?* Most firms charge a flat monthly consulting fee, and add a volume production fee per thousand units mailed. Some perfectly ethical firms charge on the basis of a percentage of the monies raised. A few even will advance all the costs of the mailing.

While the second and third arrangements appear enticing at first glance, it is important to understand what they mean to your organization. Members of the National Society of Fund Raising Executives (NSFRE) and the American Association of Fund Raising Counsel (AAFRC) abide by codes of ethics strictly prohibiting firms or individuals from charging charitable corporations on a percentage basis. There have been cases where the successful fund raiser walked away with most of the income.

Some firms will work on percentage in political campaigns (reasoning that they are not charitable in nature) but not otherwise.

For the record, Oram Group Marketing adheres to the NSFRE and AAFRC ethics codes. As for the firm that offers to cover all expenses up front, there is nothing morally wrong with such an arrangement. The consultant risks all; you risk nothing. But there are drawbacks here too. In most such arrangements, you agree to a higher fee (to be deducted from the income), leaving lower net profits for your organization. But if you still want to sign such a contract, be certain that it is written in such a manner that you are fully in charge. It has been said that the person who controls the pocketbook controls all. Many clients involved in an apparent no-risk arrangement find that they have relatively little say (never mind demands) when it comes to copy approval, campaign strategy, and income and marketing reports. After all, the consultant is taking the ride; his money, not yours, is immediately at stake.

In our opinion, in most circumstances, the best arrangement with a consultant is to begin the campaign with your own money. Have the consultant report to you regularly on how that money is being used. This way, you are definitely in charge.

If you still insist on a firm that will take the up-front risk and advance the money, make sure that the contract you sign puts you in the driver's seat as to how much fee shall be spent on all aspects of production and fulfillment and printing, and your part in the entire process.

3. *Who are your clients?* Don't be afraid to ask. Most firms proffer this information in any case. Many rosters show not only current clients, but immediate past clients as well. Ask the consultant to suggest which clients you should call for references. Call them—and then call a few he didn't suggest. The good consultant won't mind, because he knows that the firm doesn't exist that hasn't lost clients for a variety of reasons. Later, if you get a particularly bad report, you might wish to discuss the case with the consultant. There are always two sides to every story. (Of course, if all the reports you get are less than enthusiastic, you'll want to look elsewhere immediately.)

4. *How long have you been in business? How large is your staff?* The answers to these two questions may be misleading, as some of the newer, smaller firms have been started by people with great talent. If the firm is new or small or both, you will want to know more about what the senior people did prior to starting the firm. Then you will want to check with their previous employers or with people whose judgment you trust who know or have worked with them.

5. *Who will work on my campaign?* The answer to this one largely depends on the size of your campaign (and, frankly, it will depend to some extent on how busy the consulting firm is at the moment). If yours is a major direct mail campaign with the potential of mailing several million pieces annually and a complicated renewal series, it probably will be assigned to a senior account executive who will devote between one-third and one-half of his or her time to it. If it is a small to medium campaign, you can expect that your account executive also will be handling three other clients. But in either case, the senior account executive has production and clerical backing, and the less senior executive is supervised by a top senior in the firm.

You will know almost instinctively whether you are getting the attention you need and deserve. As a rule of thumb, though, you should expect your account executive to be in regular touch with you by telephone and to schedule meetings as necessary. In the beginning of a campaign, you will be seeing a lot of the account executive as you plan the first mailing. After a short hiatus, you'll start receiving reports on the results of the mailing, and finally you will receive a written report. But between mailings there is a lag time, often as long as two months, during which you are paying the consultant but not hearing from him or her as often. This lag is not only typical; it is an important breathing spell for both client and consultant. It doesn't mean that you have been forgotten. In all probability, your consultant is at work evaluating the results of the mailing and planning the second or third stage. During a non-intense period, you should hear from your consultant (perhaps his other assistant will be in touch with your assistant) every two to three weeks.

6. *May I see samples of your work?* If you are not well versed in the direct mail field, you may not know how to judge whether a package is good, mediocre or bad. Something you like may not have been a success and vice versa. Nonetheless, it is important that you like the *overall* appearance, approach, and style represented in the sample work done for other clients. You can rest assured that the consultant will show you samples that performed well. That's fair, and it would be insulting to ask to see samples that bombed. (You can rest assured that they have learned from those particular mistakes.)

After interviewing each consultant, jot down your reactions to the meeting. Did you feel positive about their attitude? Did *they* seem to want your business? It's important they do. Earlier we suggested that you call two or three current clients suggested by the consultant as references. In addition, we suggested that you call at least two current or past clients not suggested. And here's an especially important tip: the more you know about the people or institutions you are calling, the better off you will be. We know of cases where the consultant should have been shot for the poor job they did, but the client could not bring himself to say anything negative about anyone.

We saw another case where the reports on the firm were pretty bad, but according to people acquainted with the executive director of this particular agency, his good opinion could never be obtained for any job by anyone. He was reputed to be an obstreperous, difficult person who handicapped the consultant at every turn.

So, as your mother always said, in evaluating criticism, "Consider the source."

QUESTIONS TO ASK THE CONSULTANT'S CURRENT CLIENTS

1. Does the firm have a strong understanding of your organization's issues?
2. Does the firm meet deadlines, and even more important, do they allow the organization time to review copy and art in the early draft stage? (Note: five days is usually considered to be sufficient for a client to review new copy and art.)
3. Is the firm accommodating when necessary legitimate changes are required?
4. Are the firm's reports, correspondence, bills, and campaign analyses neat, comprehensive, and easy for the lay person to understand?
5. Has the campaign lived up to projections made by the firm (not the client) and, if not, was the firm (not the client) the first to suggest a new or revised strategy?
6. Do you enjoy your association with the people in the firm?

As for past clients, ask questions 2, 4 and 6 above. And instead of asking question 5, ask why the contract was terminated. There may be very good reasons. We often have received glowing recommendations from clients with whom we parted ways. Both of us agreed that we each did our best, and that the situation was just not viable.

Now that you have checked the references to your satisfaction, let us tell you how the firms you are considering will be evaluating you.

1. Did the client approach the hiring of a firm in a professional, courteous manner?
2. Did the client give us a clear understanding as to its needs?
3. Did the client *haggle* unduly about the fee or try to get the "best price" on the basis that they are nonprofit? (Remember, all of the firm's clients are nonprofit. If they weren't, fees would be at least double what they are.)
4. Does the client have a good credit record? Do they pay their bills on time? (Why should they change their bad habits just for you?)
5. Does the client appear difficult to deal with? Unless the firm is very hungry, it may refuse to deal with certain personalities at the outset.
6. Is this a client we really want? Despite any obvious inherent problems, is it an organization we genuinely believe we can help?

GET A WRITTEN PROPOSAL

Once you have interviewed two or three firms (more will only be confusing) and checked references, ask for a written proposal. Do not expect the proposal to be tailored to your needs and goals *unless* you have been willing to spend sufficient time with the consultant to educate him. And even then, do not expect it to cover every nuance of your fund-raising needs. The first three to six months you will be working together, the consultant will spend a great deal of time getting to know you.

What you can expect from a proposal, however, is a very clear and comprehensive plan detailing at least a one-year campaign. Direct mail consulting firms sometimes will provide three-year projections. The proposals you receive will probably vary in format and style. It then will be up to you to extract from each the following information and any additional information you have requested. Incidentally, if it is difficult to extract this information, be wary of accepting the proposal.

1. The projected number of mailings to be made.
2. The timing and scheduling of the mailings.
3. The direct costs of each mailing.
4. The estimated percent return and average gift from each mailing.
5. The estimated (not guaranteed) proceeds of each mailing.
6. The consultant's management and production fees.
7. The length of the contract period and cancellation clause.
8. The philosophy behind the package that will be produced.
9. The basis of the marketing plan.

Don't expect the proposal to completely detail all the lists that will be selected for the mailing or include a comprehensive idea of the package design and copy. After all, you haven't signed a contract yet. Firms recognize the danger of giving away the store on "spec." Proposals are not protected material.

On the other hand, the proposal should be specific about the following:

1. The number of prospect packages the firm will design in the course of a year.
2. If applicable, the number of renewal packages and mailings.
3. The frequency of reports.
4. How the firm will handle your fulfillment and computer needs, if applicable, and at what additional cost.
5. Whether the firm will have joint ownership of your list, and, if so, under what specific conditions.

Remember, if it is difficult to extract and understand the answers to these questions, be wary. Seemingly innocent contracts can lock you into agreements that you do not understand, and that are disadvantageous.

HOW TO DECIDE AMONG CONSULTANTS

Once you have interviewed the firms, checked references, have reviewed proposals, you will have to select one firm and one firm only.

But what if you personally like the account executive who Firm B will assign, yet believe that Firm A has written a snazzier proposal? Or what if you like the work that Firm C has produced better than Firm A's work, but don't like the firm's president?

It's a dilemma to be sure. However, assuming that all three firms are reputable and competent—personality is the key. We have seen more consultant/client relationships come to an unhappy end because of a mismatch of personalities than we have ever seen because a poor campaign was produced. Remember, you are going to have to work with representatives of the fund-raising firm every week of the year, so it's best to hire someone you like. And when you make a decision, please let the other contenders know promptly.

SIGNING THE CONTRACT

Most firms will ask that you sign a minimum one-year contract with a 30- to 60-day cancellation clause. The contract will specify, in less detail than the proposal, the work to be performed and will stipulate that the budget not be exceeded by a certain modest percentage without permission from the client. It may also stipulate that income from the mailings be obligated as follows:

First:	to pay the fund-raising firm's fees.

Second:	to pay the printers and suppliers contracted for by the firm. (Firms generally operate, by the way, as "disclosed agents"—i.e., they assume no responsibility, legal or financial, for funds owed to suppliers. The buck literally stops with verification of vendors' invoices.)

Third:	all other funds can be used as the organization sees fit, although it will probably be recommended that in the early stages, a large part of the funds be used to generate roll-outs if the test mailing is successful.

A word of caution: do not be tempted to spend the earliest income from a prospect mailing on anything other than the above, no matter how tempting. In fact, don't even begin a direct mail program if you can't afford to wait at least a year to realize spendable net income from your renewal mailings.

We have had more than one unfortunate experience where a client who was in worse financial shape than we realized, spent every nickel of income from the pilot mailing as it arrived. When it came time to pay the bills, including ours, there was no money. Naturally, the organization had to pay eventually. They did, a year later, but they had already wrecked their relationship with us, with various list brokers and owners, the lettershop, and other suppliers. We would be surprised if another consultant takes them on.

HOW CONSULTING FIRMS CHARGE

Most agencies charge a management fee payable monthly, in advance, and an additional production fee of X dollars per thousand packages mailed, billed in arrears, together with any out of pocket expenses.

The management fee generally includes:

- Planning the campaign.
- Research of the client's organization and services.
- List selection, or determining the market.
- Writing the package(s).
- Designing the package(s) with an artist.
- Revising the package(s) according to the client's legitimate needs. By this we mean that clients should review copy to make sure that it is clear, factual, and conveys an image in keeping with their own. Clients should not alter a package for style.
- Tracking, monitoring, and analyzing the campaign.
- The consultant's overhead and profit.

The production fee generally includes:

- Working with artists.
- Proofreading.
- Supervision of the printer.
- Supervision of the merge/purge operation.
- Supervision of the mailing house.
- Checking, approving, and forwarding all bills incurred for payment.

IT COSTS MORE—OR DOES IT?

Does it cost more to hire a fund-raising agency to manage your campaign than to do the work in-house? You've already seen how even a successful prospect campaign is one that breaks even, so how can you afford to add an agency fee on top of that?

Look at it this way. Assume you decide to do a mail campaign. First, you would have to hire a direct mail professional for a salary of, say, between $20,000 and $30,000. Then you would have to provide that person with a half-time secretary at $8,000. To that you add fringe benefits, and you are up to an investment of $30,000 to $40,000 a year.

Now compare this potential outlay to management fees charged by most good direct mail consulting firms. It may be a little more—but it comes with experience and without overhead.

This is not to say that many organizations cannot conduct a successful in-house campaign. Many can and do. And, after all, this is a book on how to do it yourself. But if you *are* going to do it yourself, don't delude yourself into believing that it is a lot cheaper. It's cheaper, yes. But unless you employ a talented direct mail professional, it also can be a lot more expensive in the long run.

The foregoing is addressed to those contemplating a first direct mail effort. But what of organizations that have been conducting fairly successful campaigns in-house for a number of years. Should they continue as before or should they engage outside professional counsel?

Any direct mail campaign can grow stale over time. To maximize the ongoing effectiveness of a long-range mail program, an organization must keep its approach fresh and its donors inspired—and that takes imagination! (And let's face it, sometimes the best direct mail practitioners working on the same campaign year after year simply burn out.)

In such a case, your organization might consider engaging a consulting firm to undertake a comprehensive study of your direct mail program. Some firms, ours included, will analyze your campaign and make recommendations to make a good effort even better. You can implement their recommendations yourself or you can retain the consultant for a brief period to get you started. Either way, this is less costly than engaging a firm to manage your entire campaign.

Should the consultant find creativity to be your main problem, he or she can recommend a freelance copywriter specializing in direct mail. In fact, some consultants themselves will create a complete package for you to test against your control package. Fees for packages range between $1,500 and $5,000 depending on the writer and on the complexity of the job.

MAKING THE CONSULTANT/CLIENT RELATIONSHIP WORK

One of the most rewarding things about being a consultant is that it's a continual education. In the morning we're learning about health care. At noon we're memorizing a list of endangered species. In the afternoon we're helping to pass a bill in Congress.

Still, there is no question that the consultant knows less than you about medicine or civil rights or the local zoo. *You know more* about your field. That's why it is your job to educate your consultant about your cause from the very beginning. The more he knows at the outset, the happier you are going to be with the first draft package we present to you after you sign the contract.

If the president of your organization hates the color blue or never permits the use of the word "urgent" or detests four-page letters, tell the consultant in the beginning. She can then present a very handsome artist's rendering in burgundy, use substitute words and phrases to convey urgency. As for the four-page letter, if the consultant truly feels one is needed, he can explain to the president that of course not *everyone* can send a successful long letter. However, a letter from *him*—the president of ABC institution—will be read from cover to cover.

275

You can discharge a lot of your responsibility to your consultant by providing printed literature—the more, the better. But you must also spend some of your valuable time answering his uninformed questions in as much detail as he wants. Explain why one flavor of Girl Scout cookies sells better than another, or why the white tiger and not the golden is the most popular animal at the zoo, or why the children's ward in your hospital isn't full. You never know how the creative fund-raising mind is going to turn some seemingly minor point into a major theme that will make your campaign a great success.

When you have hired a good consultant, don't try to do his job. The client who always second guesses the consultant—who even rewrites his copy and redesigns the art—is not only throwing good money away. . . not only demoralizing the consultant. . . but is actually helping to insure that either the campaign or the client/counsel relationship (or both) will fail.

This is not to say that as the client, you should never *question* strategy or marketing plans or even a certain phrase here and there in the letter. If a consultant presents you with a fund-raising letter that conveys an image totally at odds with the image your institution is working to project, you can—and should—have a serious discussion that may result in starting from scratch. But if the consultant strongly believes that the image you are trying to present won't even raise the cost of the postage—you'd do well to listen. Because the consultant has been down this road before and has given in to the client. . . has actually produced the package in the image the client wants. . . and has seen the campaign fail miserably.

So we urge you not to rewrite our copy. By all means, ask us to get our facts right. Ask us to strengthen a particular message you need to get out to the public. This direct mail campaign is also part of your public relations campaign. Ask us even to include some of your favorite phrases and photographs.

But please don't ask us not to begin an occasional sentence with the words "but," "and," and the like, and not use contractions. Don't ask us to keep the letter short because a member of your board says he never reads long letters. And, above all, don't ask us to submit a copy to a committee. Absolutely no more than three people in an organization should pass judgment on a fund-raising letter, and that includes the letter signer.

As we were in the process of writing this chapter, a client called to say that the president of his board almost had a heart attack when presented with our draft letter for his possible signature.

"He hated it so much," said the client, "that he said had one of his students turned it in as a paper, he would have given it a D minus."

"Well, that's too bad," we replied. "The copywriter who produced that letter recently wrote a letter for an organization that received a 1.6 percent return and a $35 average gift. And their president wasn't crazy about that letter either—until the money started rolling in."

Moral of the story: you're not ready to try direct mail until you have come to terms with the *direct mail style*. If you aren't there yet, save yourself and your consultant a lot of heartaches.

Our final request is that you treat your consultant with professional courtesy. Like your employees, your consultants will move heaven and earth to please you if you treat them well. This means meeting their deadlines, just as you expect them to meet yours.

We have a client who rants and raves if we are so much as one day late in presenting draft copy or art, and who claims that it is the end of the world if something goes wrong in the merge/purge process delaying a mailing by a week. But this same client takes three to four days just to return our phone calls, habitually breaks appointments, holds onto the draft copy and art for twice as long as was agreed because he is busy, and then insists that we still get the mail out on time.

We don't expect to be loved every moment. We do our best for every client, including those who are difficult. But you know who gets our very best efforts, don't you? You do! Because you help educate us in the beginning. You warn us of potential pitfalls, listen to our advice, and help us conceive the package. You compliment us when we've done a good job. You require that we meet our deadlines, but you also meet yours. Most important of all, you keep us informed of new happenings in your institution because you realize that the more we know, the more likely we are to come up with really good ideas to help you raise even more money.

You are a real pleasure to work with!

CHAPTER **14**

Careers in Direct Mail Fund Raising

As a result of reading this book, you may find yourself interested in direct mail fund raising as a career. Direct mail is diversified, challenging, and among one of the most creative areas in all of fund raising or marketing.

WHAT DIRECT MAIL FUND RAISING OFFERS

- Day-to-day variety—from working with designers and artists to planning marketing strategy to working with creative writers (or, better still, doing the creative writing yourself).
- Immediate feedback as to success or failure.
- The fun of receiving and opening stacks of mail, most containing contributions, as a result of your efforts. (Similarly, the rewards of reading the donor correspondence that accompanies the contributions.)
- The challenge of enhancing a donor's commitment to your organization.
- The rewards of building a constituency of supporters for a cause you believe in.

HOW TO GET A JOB

If you are interested in direct mail fund raising as a career, and you have little or no previous experience, make a plan that includes:

- Talking to friends and associates in the profession. (Ask them to share their professional newsletters.)
- Doing volunteer work for a nonprofit organization (be sure to ask for a fund-raising assignment).
- Taking one or more courses in fund raising at your local university. (Make friends with the instructor and other students.) Such courses generally are found in the continuing education division.
- Joining a reputable direct mail association and attending meetings regularly. If none exists in your area, join the local advertising club. In New York City you will want to join the Direct Mail Fund Raisers Association (DMFA).

- Once you are working in the profession, we recommend that you join the National Society of Fund Raising Executives (NSFRE). While NSFRE does not focus on direct mail per se, membership in this prestigious professional association will be invaluable in your development as a professional. To find the NSFRE chapter nearest you, contact the national headquarters of NSFRE in Washington, D.C. Fifty-five chapters exist today and their number is growing rapidly, so you should have little difficulty finding one.

When you are generally familiar with the profession and have made contacts, you will want to seek interviews with prospective employers.

Unless you already have some direct mail or marketing experience, it is unlikely that you will be hired by a consulting firm. (However, there are exceptions to this. Kay Lautman got her original job with Oram, without experience, through answering an ad in *The New York Times*.) Still, your best bet is to apply for a job in the membership or fund-raising department of a nonprofit organization in a field that interests you. (Don't apply for a job at a health care facility if you can't stand the sight of blood or a museum if you don't appreciate art.)

If you are a novice, you must start at or close to the bottom and work your way up. However, if you come from a background in advertising, public relations, or marketing, if you have been an active volunteer fund raiser for a not-for-profit organization, or if you are a talented writer, you will be able to get a job at the middle level and—if luck is with you—possibly somewhere near the top.

TYPES OF JOBS AVAILABLE IN NOT-FOR-PROFIT ORGANIZATIONS

Following are the opportunities available in most large nonprofit organizations. However, as nonprofits come in all sizes, shapes, and forms, you will find that many have only one executive and a secretary handling all aspects of the campaign. Work in such an agency will give you experience, but as there is little chance of moving up the ladder, you will soon have to move on to another organization. (Nothing wrong with this.)

SKILLS REQUIRED

1. Records Clerk
   - Willingness to work in the most unattractive part of the office
   - Ability to turn a routine job into something challenging (it will help to keep reminding yourself that this is a temporary step up the ladder)
   - Good organization and fast work

2. Assistant Membership Director
   - Knowledge of printing production (cost savings as well as techniques)
   - Good typing skills
   - Some training or experience in graphic design
   - Good with details
   - Ability to meet deadlines (which means ability to get others to meet deadlines, such as printers and lettershops, etc.)
   - Knowledge of mailing lists, postage regulations, etc.

3. Director of Membership
   All of #2, plus:
   - Ability to manage people
   - Good working relationships with your peers in the Public Relations Department, the Development Department, etc.

- Good idea person
- Unafraid to take chances
- Ability to read and prepare budgets, campaign analyses, and clear, comprehensive reports
- Good copywriter or good judge of copy done by freelancers you hire

4. Copywriter

Few nonprofit organizations employ a direct mail copywriter. Due to financial constraints, that job usually is done by the Director of Membership, the Director of Development, or a freelance writer. However, if you have landed any of the other jobs listed here (including the clerk job) and are a good writer, don't hide your light under a bushel. Writing skills help you move up the ladder.

It could easily happen that you will become devoted to a particular cause or organization and have no interest in working for a consulting firm. However if such is your ambition, read on.

After you have worked for at least two to three years for a nonprofit organization (and assuming that you have been promoted at least once during that time), you may be ready to apply to a consulting firm.

TYPES OF JOBS AVAILABLE IN CONSULTING FIRMS

While consulting firms are structured differently, almost all have the following job opportunities:

- Chief Executive Officer
- Account Executives (from one to many)
- Marketing Director (and often an assistant)
- Production Director (and often an assistant)
- Copywriter (or writers)
- Computer/word processing staff
- Secretarial staff

The Chief Executive Officer supervises the entire staff, and his or her particular skills (in addition to administration) demand the ability to sell, organize campaigns, motivate and manage employees, and inspire clients' confidence.

The second most prestigious job in the consulting firm is that of Account Executive. It is the Account Executive's job to keep the clients happy. And to achieve this, the A.E. must produce (with the help of the staff) successful campaigns—on time and within budget.

The Account Executive may or may not be a great direct mail copywriter. He or she may not know as much about lists as a list broker or the firm's own Marketing Director. An Account Executive is probably not a graphic designer or a computer expert or a statistician. But a really good Account Executive will be more than marginally proficient in all these specialties. If not, he will not be able to elicit the best work from the staff and, perhaps more important, will not be able to instill a sense of confidence in the client.

As for the rest of the jobs in the above list, at first glance they seem readily identifiable. But look again.

281

One staff writer does not produce the package for all clients. Account executives also write copy. The Production Director handles most production, but as all account executives occasionally find themselves in a position where they must handle production personally, it is critical that they have those skills. Similarly, the Marketing Director must understand how the Account Executive's campaign is strategized to choose the best lists for a campaign. And so on.

And because today's assistants and secretaries are often tomorrow's Marketing or Production Directors and Account Executives, they are busy learning everything their bosses know.

In our firm, it is common for people to come up through the ranks. If employees are interested in direct mail fund raising as a career, they are not only encouraged but helped to attend school (seminars, conferences, etc.) to study computers, graphics, copywriting, and marketing.

And as for the ubiquitous Account Executive, he or she not only must be able to do the job well, but also—after a suitable period with the company—be able to bring in new clients.

The primary difference in working for a consulting firm as opposed to working for a nonprofit organization is that in a firm the pressure is greater, the pace faster, the hours longer, and the quality of work judged much more severely.

On the other hand, it is unlikely that you will burn out working for a firm because your energies are divided among a variety of causes.

As far as money goes, it is commonly believed that staff members in a professional consulting firm make far larger salaries than their contemporaries in nonprofit organizations. The truth is that they may make a little more, but not the riches you may imagine. (In fact, we know of some instances where nonprofits pay better than consulting firms.)

We have worked for many wonderful causes and organizations both as consultants and as employees of nonprofits. Working directly for an organization served us well as consultants later. We are able to understand not only the clients' needs, but also the dedication of the men and women who attach their lives to a particular cause with which they identify intensely.

Which is better: being a consultant or working for a nonprofit? Both have their distinct advantages, but the better consultants have at one time worked for a nonprofit.

THE REWARDS OF THE PROFESSION

We have thus far described the nuts and bolts of the profession. Let us conclude by relating several personal experiences which may help explain what motivates us.

Hank Goldstein:

I showed up for work at the Oram firm on April 10, 1964, and was immediately turned loose on an $18 million capital campaign for Hampton Institute, a predominantly black college in Virginia. It was on this rock that I built my place in the firm.

Harold Oram was my boss, and his management style was somewhat chaotic. He went by his hunches and bet on a person's ability to pull the sword out of the rock. He was always around to offer advice and encouragement, or discouragement—depending. I had never run a capital campaign, of course. But he laid the bet because he knew I was passionately interested in the area of civil rights and equal opportunity.

My good friend and colleague, the late Paul Frillmann, and I went to work and in four years helped Hampton raise $21 million, more than anyone had ever before collected for a single black institution in a single campaign. This was a very important accomplishment for the firm and me.

Several years after the campaign ended, I found myself in Norfolk on a client assignment. It was late in the day. I had a brand new rental car. I drove to Hampton and arrived on the college campus around sunset. Without announcing myself, I drove around the new campus.

Where in 1964 had been nothing, now stood half-a-dozen major academic buildings, new dorms—an entire new area in which aspiring young men and women would at last have their opportunity to learn and grow and eventually to assume important leadership roles in our society.

The reality of what I had helped bring about hit me for the first time and it was very moving. I drove to a favorite fish place with a lovely view of Chesapeake Bay and had a good dinner; I felt I had earned it.

Kay Lautman:

Of the many wonderful moments in my long career, two experiences—ten years apart—represent the zenith.

In the early 1970s, as Associate Director of the World Wildlife Fund, I organized a national direct mail fund-raising and public relations campaign to persuade women to renounce the wearing of the furs of endangered species. This was not a PR whim, but a reaction to a crisis situation in which leopards, cheetahs, tigers, and other spotted and striped cats were on the verge of extinction due to fashion demands.

I brought WWF's cause home to family and friends. My mother-in-law willingly put her much-loved leopard hat in permanent storage, and a good friend decided against buying a cheetah rug. But the campaign reached a far broader market. Not only did WWF cause a major stir in the media, we were able to persuade leading furriers, high fashion magazine celebrities and everyday people to stand alongside us, pledging not to make or advertise or wear the products of any endangered species.

Within a very short time, spotted and striped furs became conspicuously absent on New York's Fifth Avenue and in other fashionable cities. Occasionally, when a woman dared to wear her "investment" (as many who didn't want to give them up called them)—people on the street would make negative comments. And after awhile, these furs simply were not fashionable any more. (At least not the real thing.) Fashion has a way of compensating—and today, the "jungle look" in fashion is created by stenciling the beautiful stripes and spots of endangered species on leather, fabric, synthetics, and on the skins and furs of non-endangered species.

Several years later it became illegal to import the furs of endangered species to America, but in the time it took to get legislation enacted, we had already won half the battle!

A decade later, on a biting cold day in 1983, I joined a crowd of thousands on the Mall in Washington, D.C. We had come to participate in the dedication of a memorial to the veterans who had fought and died in the most unpopular war this country has ever known—the Vietnam War.

The important moment in the ceremony came when the ribbons were cut and the crowd surged forward to touch the black granite wall on which the names of the dead soldiers are inscribed. As parents and widows and children and friends found the names of the loved ones for whom they searched, they reverently touched the name or kissed it . . . they taped photographs of the deceased beside the name or laid a flower on the ground beneath. And then they stood back from the wall to look at it and were moved to find their own images reflected in the elegant, polished black walls.

It was an especially moving moment for me because not only had I demonstrated against the war in Vietnam on that very site just ten years earlier, but because I had been instrumental (through a highly successful direct mail campaign) in helping the Vietnam Veterans Memorial Fund raise the first half-million dollars to get the project under way. And that initial sum (like so much of the money that eventually financed the project), was made up primarily of small gifts ranging from $5 to $100.

nd now it was completed—a magnificent memorial that would quickly become the most visited in the nation's capital. A monument that would forever touch and inspire millions—with a little unseen part of me inside.

Fund raisers who have watched a sick child regain his health . . . a poor family have a real Christmas . . . a juvenile delinquent return from summer camp with a new attitude . . . a hard-fought environmental law passed to protect the health of the people . . . all of these people understand the deep satisfaction I felt that day. We are not just fund raisers. We are an important part of the American process that improves the quality of life.

It is our optimistic belief that one day there will be many people, fund raisers included, who will experience those same jubilant feelings when a sane nuclear policy is implemented . . . when minorities no longer struggle for their place in the sun . . . or when a cure for cancer is discovered.

We hope that our colleagues will experience "high returns" also. And if even for a moment it concerns you that direct mail brings in the smaller gifts, remember that most charitable organizations operating today have built their own solid donor bases largely through direct mail.

Thank you for reading our book.

Afterword

When *Dear Friend* was finally completed, 14 months after we began writing it, the manuscript was sent to David Ogilvy who, after reviewing several sample chapters, had generously agreed to write the foreword. We asked for his critiques, among which was the following:

"The only thing I miss is a refutation of the criticism that, while direct mail can raise money, the cost as a percentage of money raised is too high to be acceptable for most charities. Some numbers would help this."

We agreed. To be completely fair in presenting such statistics, we put the names of all of our present and recent past clients into three hats (small mailers, medium-size mailers, and large mailers) and drew blindfolded. The following information based on each organization's most recent fiscal year speaks for itself. To maintain confidentiality we have represented each organization generically.

The number of pieces mailed includes acquisition (prospect) mailings as well as renewals and special appeals. All numbers are rounded off to the nearest thousand.

LARGE MAILERS: 900,000 to 1,000,000 plus

Political Organization

No. Pieces Mailed:	934,000
Direct Costs:	$234,000
Gross Income:	$5,866,000
Net Income:	$5,632,000
Percent Cost of Money Raised:	4%
Size of House File:	50,000

Conservation Organization

No. Pieces Mailed:	1,215,000
Direct Costs:	$270,000
Gross Income:	$1,070,000
Net Income:	$800,000
Percent Cost of Money Raised:	25%
Size of House File:	85,000

MEDIUM-SIZED MAILERS: 500,000 to 750,000

Youth Organization

No. Pieces Mailed:	617,000
Direct Costs:	$105,000
Gross Income:	$285,000
Net Income:	$180,000
Percent Cost of Money Raised:	37%
Size of House File:	24,500

Conservation Organization

No. Pieces Mailed:	504,000
Direct Costs:	$116,000
Gross Income:	$760,000
Net Income:	$644,000
Percent Cost of Money Raised:	15%
Size of House File:	36,000

SMALL MAILERS: fewer than 500,000

Health Organization

No. Pieces Mailed:	205,000
Direct Costs:	$41,000
Gross Income:	$650,000
Net Income	$609,000
Percent Cost of Money Raised:	6%
Size of House File:	6,000

Educational Organization

No Pieces Mailed:	279,000
Direct Costs:	$69,000
Gross Income:	$113,000
Net Income	$44,000
Percent Cost of Money Raised:	61%
Size of House File:	3,000

Of the six organizations represented, the cost to raise money (for all but one) ranges from an extraordinary low of 4 percent to a respectable 37 percent. The organization that spent 61 percent has been in the mail for just two years, and thus is an important case in point.

As you have learned, getting started in the mail is costly. In most instances you do not earn a net profit until the start of the second year. This particular organization earned a healthy net the first year. However, the cost to raise net money is always higher at the beginning. As their list grows, and increasing numbers of donors renew their gifts, the ratio of cost to income will greatly diminish.

Bear in mind, however, that it is not only the size of your house file that keeps the percentage of costs down. Note the organization that spends 15 percent of income on direct mail. Its house file numbers only 36,000. But its average gift is high and its donors are asked to contribute as many as five times a year.

Moral: Work hard to bring your first-time donors in at the highest possible gift level and work even harder to upgrade their contributions and to find compelling reasons for some to give more than once a year.

If you work at it, the ratio of cost to income will soon diminish to 40 percent or less, an acceptable ratio by almost anyone's standards.

KPL
HG

Glossary of Direct Mail Fund-Raising Terms*

ADD-ON GIFT. A symbolic gift, modest in size, in addition to the main gift (e.g., one anti-smoking organization requested an additional dollar—the cost of a package of cigarettes).

ACQUISITION MAILING. A mailing to prospects to acquire new members or donors (also called PROSPECT MAILING).

BANG-TAIL. Envelope with a large flap that can be used as an order form (also called WALLET FLAP).

BLEED. Term used by artists and printers for art, photographs, or other design elements that run off the edge of the paper leaving no border.

BLOW IN. Reply card that is blown (inserted) by machine into a magazine, newsletter, etc., and is therefore loose.

BLUELINE. A specially processed photograph of an artist's mechanical reproduced on blueprint paper and cut and folded to resemble the final product. A *blueline* is the final proof before printing.

BOARDS. *See* CAMERA-READY ART.

BULK RATE MAIL. Non-first class (second, third, or fourth class) mail which qualifies for special postage rates lower than first class postage.

BUSINESS REPLY ACCOUNT. An account with the post office in which funds are deposited to pay for receipt of postage due first class mail.

BUSINESS REPLY ENVELOPE (BRE). A self-addressed envelope that does not require postage; the receiving organization guarantees payment of postage on receipt (also called POSTAGE PAID ENVELOPE).

CALLOUT. Excerpt from the text (usually a letter or brochure), set apart graphically from body copy to highlight important points.

CAMERA-READY ART. A perfectly positioned artist's mechanical containing the copy set in type, the placement of correctly sized HALFTONES, screens, and any other artwork, as well as COLOR BREAKS indicated for the printer.

CARRIER ENVELOPE. The outside envelope that contains the appeal letter and other components of the direct mail PACKAGE.

CARRIER ROUTE PRESORT. Sorting mail before delivery to the post office (according to U.S. Postal Service regulations) so that it is bundled into individual carrier routes in order to qualify for discounted postage rates (abbreviated as Car-rt-sort).

CHESHIRE LABEL. The most common type of label to which names and addresses are transferred by means of a heat process. Most *Cheshire labels* are printed four across.

CLOSED FACE ENVELOPE. A plain envelope that, regardless of size, does not have a window. *See also* WINDOW ENVELOPE.

CODE. The numbers, letters, or a combination of the two (generally up to five digits) affixed to the mail label or RESPONSE DEVICE to indicate the list from which the donor resulted (also called KEY).

COLD LIST. A prospect list that has not been tested previously by your organization. *See also* COLD PROSPECT.

COLD PROSPECT. A name from a COLD LIST; a potential donor who has never contributed to your organization.

COLOR BREAK. Indications on a BLUELINE or a color key that show where each of the colors used in the printed piece appears.

COMPUTER FILL-IN. The personalized elements of a pre-printed letter, RESPONSE DEVICE, etc., included by using a computer process (e.g., the recipient's name, amount of previous gift, etc.).

---

*Words set in SMALL CAPS are defined elsewhere in the Glossary.

CONTINUATION MAILING. A second, third, fourth (and so on) mailing to larger quantities of lists that have been tested first in modest quantities (also called a ROLL-OUT).

CONTROL PACKAGE. A PACKAGE that has performed successfully against which a new PACKAGE is tested.

DECOY. A bogus name and address placed in an organization's HOUSE FILE and sometimes in prospect files (*see also* SALTING LISTS).

DEMOGRAPHICS. The study and application of social and economic characteristics and/or data; those characteristics of a population which are measured by variables such as age, sex, marital status, family size, education, geographic location, and occupation.

DISCLOSED AGENTS. Third parties such as consultants and LIST BROKERS who place orders for printing, lists, or other services on behalf of an organization which is legally obligated to pay.

DONOR UPGRADE REPORT. A computer report showing the number of donors who have increased the size of their donations as a result of a particular appeal.

DUMP AND LAYOUT. Printed information showing contents and format of a magnetic tape.

EBCDIC. Expanded Binary Coded Decimal Interchange Code, the IBM (and therefore industry standard) code for storing information on magnetic tape.

ELECTRONIC FUNDS TRANSFER (EFT). A method whereby a donor instructs his bank to make an automatic monthly deduction from his account, earmarked for the charitable organization of his choice.

FAN-FOLD. A piece of paper that has been folded back and forth like a fan leaving no double edge for the inserting machine to grip.

FIVE DIGIT PRESORT. Sorting mail before delivery to the post office (according to U.S. Postal regulations) so that it is bundled into individual five digit zip codes in order to qualify for discounted postage rates.

GALLEY. A computer printout listing donor information such as names, addresses, and any other information that is stored on the computer (e.g., date of first donation, largest donation, most recent donation, etc.).

GEOGRAPHICS. The study of markets by using geographic analysis, principally regions, states, counties, and localities. Specifically, *geographics* entails the study of markets by SMSA (standard metropolitan statistical area), zip code SECTIONAL CENTER, or other territorial designation.

HALFTONES. Printer's term for photographs.

HAND-MATCH INSERT. The process of hand-inserting personalized PACKAGE elements (e.g., inserting a personalized RESPONSE DEVICE or certificate of appreciation into a CLOSED FACE addressed envelope).

HAND-TAMPING. The process of tamping (or gently striking) the end of a batch of stuffed, sealed PACKAGES to be certain that the name and address are lined up with the envelope's window.

HANGER. An additional appeal, usually smaller in size than the main letter and usually signed by someone other than the signer of the main letter, which is enclosed in the direct mail PACKAGE (also called a LIFT NOTE or endorsement letter).

HOUSE FILE. The names and addresses of active and recently lapsed donors and members of an organization.

HICKEY. Accidental spot or marking that mars the appearance of a BLUELINE.

IMPACT PRINTING. Printing done by a computer (*impact*) printer similar to an extremely high speed typewriter.

INDICIA. A permit to mail that has been printed at the same time as the envelope. The *indicia* appears in the upper right hand corner of the outside envelope, which otherwise would be stamped or metered.

INK JET PRINTING. Printing done by a high speed printer which produces an image by spraying ink through small jets to imitate typewriter type.

KEY. *See* CODE.

LASER LETTER. A letter that has been personalized through a process where laser beam, toner, and fuser lay images on continuous computer forms.

LAYOUT. The hand-drawn composition of copy, art, and photographs which indicates how the finished product will look.

LETTERSHOP. The service bureau that addresses, inserts, sorts, bags, ties, and delivers your mailing to the post office. *Lettershops* often have printing capabilities, unlike mailing houses, which receive materials from the printer and take the mailing process from there.

LIFT NOTE. *See* HANGER.

LIST BROKER. An agent who brings the seller (list owner) together with the buyer (mailer) to arrange the sale or exchange of a mailing list (or part of a list).

LIST EXCHANGE. The exchange of donor lists between two organizations on a name-for-name basis to enable each organization to mail to the other's constituency.

LIVE SAMPLE. A sample PACKAGE that comes off the inserting machine with all components inside, sealed, and stamped.

LIVE STAMP. A postage stamp affixed by hand or machine to a CARRIER ENVELOPE.

MACHINE-INSERTING. The mechanical process of inserting the letter, brochure, RESPONSE DEVICE, and other enclosures into the CARRIER ENVELOPE.

MAIL DROP. The delivery of bundled, bagged, and postage-affixed mail to the post office.

MAIL HOUSE. *See* LETTERSHOP.

MAILING CLUSTERS. Groups or *clusters* of zip codes which are grouped together by DEMOGRAPHIC or PSYCHOGRAPHIC similarities.

MERGE/PURGE. A computer operation that merges two or more files of names in a matching process to produce one file free of duplicates.

MONARCH SIZE STATIONERY. Stationery that measures 7¼″ × 10½″.

MONITOR SERVICE. A service company that maintains a network of DECOY or bogus names by which mailers can track use and/or theft of their mailing lists.

MULTI-DONORS. Commercially called multi-buyers, these are donors or buyers found on more than one list. A donor who appears on a large number of lists is considered a better prospect than one who appears on only one list.

NIXIE. An undeliverable piece of mail returned to the sender by the post office.

NTH SELECT. A process used to select a smaller number of names from a larger file to get a total random sampling of the entire file.

NONPROFIT POSTAGE. A special reduced postage rate accorded to qualifying nonprofit, tax-exempt organizations.

OUTPUT. The final results after the information or data has been processed by a computer.

OVER-PRINTED ENVELOPE. An envelope that already has been printed with the name and address of the mailer, and then is reprinted with an additional message or art.

OVERS. Overruns of printed materials, generally 10 percent according to industry standard.

PACKAGE. The total direct mail appeal; all components of the mailing.

PARTIAL DROP. The mailing of part of the planned total drop, often caused by late delivery of a mailing list or lists.

PIGGY-BACK MAILING. The inclusion of one organization's appeal in the PACKAGE (or invoice) of another organization's to reduce costs.

PILOT MAILING. A first-time mailing by an organization to determine whether a direct mail campaign will be successful.

PLANNED GIVING. The application of sound personal financial and estate planning concepts to the individual donor's plans for lifetime and testamentary giving.

POSTAGE PAID ENVELOPE. *See* BUSINESS REPLY ENVELOPE.

POST-CALLING. Calling a potential donor after he has received your direct mail appeal.

POSTING. Recording direct mail gifts by date, mail code, and amount.

PRE-CALLING. Calling a potential donor before he has received your direct mail appeal.

PREMIUM. An incentive to give in the form of a gift offer.

PRESSURE-SENSITIVE LABELS. Mail labels which are hand-applied and do not require water or machinery for affixing.

PRINTOUT. A printed copy of any information or data from a computer.

PROSPECT MAILING. *See* ACQUISITION MAILING.

PROFITABILITY FACTOR. A factor by which costs are multiplied to determine the gross income necessary to produce the required net profit.

PROFITABILITY RATIO. The ratio of net profit to gross income which is determined by dividing the gross income into the net profit (the amount remaining after all costs have been deducted).

PSEUDO-TELEGRAM. A mailing PACKAGE designed to resemble a telegram and thus convey a sense of urgency.

PSYCHOGRAPHICS. The means of classifying consumers based on their activities and interests—specifically deals with the study of lifestyle, behavioral, and personal traits as they apply to consumers and within an identified market.

RECAPTURE MAILING. A mailing designed to re-enlist the interest and support of lapsed donors or members.

RENEWAL MAILING. A mailing to donors or members requesting renewed support.

RESPONSE DEVICE. A form bearing the name and address of the prospective donor (coded by list), on which the recipient indicates the size of his gift (and any other information requested) and returns it with his check in the reply envelope provided. The best *response devices* also restate the theme, offer, or appeal as a final sell.

REVERSE-FLAP ENVELOPE. A CARRIER ENVELOPE, the enclosure flap of which comes over from back to front instead of front to back.

REVERSE OUT TYPE. Type that is dropped out of a solid area so that the background appears dark and the type light.

ROBOTYPED LETTER. A letter that is personalized by automatic typewriter.

ROLL-OUT. *See* CONTINUATION MAILING.

SALTING LISTS. The insertion of real or fictitious names and addresses on a list to protect it from misuse or theft.

SECTIONAL CENTER. A geographic area defined by the first three digits of the zip code (e.g., 100-119 for New York City, 600-606 for Chicago).

SEEDING LISTS. *See* SALTING LISTS.

SELF-MAILER. A PACKAGE that requires no separate CARRIER ENVELOPE or REPLY ENVELOPE.

SERVICE BUREAU. Usually refers to a computer SERVICE BUREAU that offers a full range of computer services.

SINGLE/DOUBLE/TRIPLE RESPONSE DEVICE. Single: one panel, 8½" × 3½" total size; double: two panels, 8½" × 7" total size; triple: three panels, 8½" × 11" total size.

SOURCE CODE. A code or key in the form of numbers and/or letters that specifies the list from which a contribution was generated.

SPLIT TEST. The testing of a variable in the mailing by splitting the list to learn whether one approach works better than another.

SOURCE KEY REPORT. An analysis of *source keys* (or CODES) which indicates the profitability of each list used in a mailing.

TEASER COPY. A brief message, usually a sentence or phrase, used as a lead-in designed to pique the interest of the reader.

TELEMARKETING. Raising funds or selling products or services by telephone.

TEST MAILING. A mailing in which a test of any nature is conducted. *See also* PILOT MAILING.

TEST PANEL. Each component of a split test.

TURN-AROUND TIME. The time elapsed between the beginning of a job and its completion.

TYPEFACE. A style of lettering.

TYPESET. To set in type. Today most type is set photographically with the aid of computers.

UNIQUE NAMES. Net names generated after a MERGE/PURGE has identified and deleted duplicate names.

UNIVERSE. The total number of names of a particular list; also the total number of names in a particular list market.

UPDATING. Adding, changing, or deleting information on a master file of donor records to bring it up to date.

UPGRADING. A special appeal requesting a larger contribution than the donor's previous one.

WALLET FLAP ENVELOPE. *See* BANG-TAIL.

WINDOW (between mailings). The period (usually one week) between use of list by two different mailers.

WINDOW ENVELOPE. An envelope that shows the name and address through a cutout, or window, in the envelope.

ZIP STRING. A run (or *string*) of mail labels in ascending zip code order (beginning with east coast addresses and ending with west coast addresses).

INDEX

OTHER VALUABLE FUND-RAISING RESOURCES FROM TAFT...

TAFT BASIC II SYSTEM
The ultimate fund-raising resource covering the charitable giving of America's largest foundations and corporations. Consists of a one-year subscription to the Taft Corporate Information System and the Taft Foundation Information System.

TAFT CORPORATE INFORMATION SYSTEM
Detailed coverage of America's major corporate giving programs—both corporate foundations and direct giving programs. Includes annual 700-page hardbound Taft Corporate Directory—biographical data on trustees and officers and current, comprehensive analyses of contributions programs. Exhaustively indexed. Supplemented with monthly newsletters, Corporate Giving Watch/Corporate Giving Profiles.

TAFT FOUNDATION INFORMATION SYSTEM
Detailed coverage of America's major private foundation giving programs. Includes Taft Foundation Reporter—annual 700-page hardbound directory with biographical data on foundation trustees and comprehensive reports and analyses of foundation giving programs. Exhaustively indexed. Supplemented with monthly newsletters, Foundation Giving Watch/Foundation Giving Profiles.

PEOPLE IN PHILANTHROPY: A Guide to Nonprofit Leadership and Funding Connections—
Formerly titled, *Trustees of Wealth*, this unique directory contains biographical data on the thousands of individuals who control philanthropy in the corporate and foundation world, as well as profiles of many of America's wealthiest individual givers.

HOW TO RATE YOUR DEVELOPMENT OFFICE: A Fund-Raising Primer for the Chief Executive
Outstanding guide covering every detail needed to clarify and assess the success of your development office. Superb manual for every chief executive—whether you're planning to institute a new development program or looking to make your current fund-raising office more productive.

CORPORATE GIVING YELLOW PAGES: Philanthropic Contact Persons for 1,100 of America's Leading Public and Privately Owned Corporations
Here are hundreds of corporate direct giving programs and corporate foundations *not covered in any other resource!* Lists sponsoring company, contact person, address, and phone number. Indexed by location and type of industry.

AMERICA'S WEALTHIEST PEOPLE: Their Philanthropic and Nonprofit Affiliations
An invaluable complement to *People In Philanthropy*, this directory focuses in even greater detail on the charitable habits of America's rich. Over 500 in-depth profiles couple biographical data with their philanthropic nonprofit, and corporate affiliations

THE 13 MOST COMMON FUND-RAISING MISTAKES AND HOW TO AVOID THEM
This down-to-earth, witty, cartoon-illustrated book shows how adherence to a few basic principles can yield more grants, more gifts, more wills and bequests. Written by Paul H. Schneiter and Donald T. Nelson, it draws on exceptional experience in legendary Mormon fund-raising circles.

EFFECTIVE LEADERSHIP: A Guide to Better Board Performance
For every board member or nonprofit executive interacting with trustees, this succinct booklet will help you gain maximum board effectiveness through understanding the roles and expectations of each and every board member.

THE PROPOSAL WRITER'S SWIPE FILE: 15 Winning Fund-Raising Proposals
The grants-oriented fund raiser's "best friend" in helping design successful applications. Pattern your proposals on these examples of actual winning proposals.

PROSPECTING: Searching out the Philanthropic Dollar
The most comprehensive functional manual on donor research available today, covering every major aspect of prospect research. Includes valuable Forms Kit enabling you to conveniently record your prospecting research.

FUND RAISING FOR PHILANTHROPY
Not just another good book on fund-raising techniques, but straight talk about the fund-raising process in one complete overview. Written by renowned veteran fund raiser Gerald Soroker.

DO OR DIE: Survival for Nonprofits
For the nonprofit executive who recognizes the advantage of "profit thinking for nonprofit organizations." Insightful exploration of nonprofit management approaches—separates myth from fact.

UP YOUR ACCOUNTABILITY:
How to Up Your Funding Credibility By Upping Your Accounting Ability
The first nontechnical accounting "textbook" ever written specifically to meet the needs of the nonprofit manager or student. Gives you the basic information you need to understand the financial workings of a nonprofit group and to do realistic financial planning.

For more information call TOLL FREE 800-424-3761.